THE REAL-LIFE APTITUDE TEST

THE DIAGRAM GROUP

Editor	Denis Kennedy
Indexer	David Harding
Art director	Richard Czapnik
Artists	Joe Bonello
	Shelley Davies
	Brian Hewson
	Richard Hummerstone
	Kathleen McDougall
	Philip Patenall
	Graham Rosewarne
Picture research	Annabel Else

Copyright © 1987 by Diagram Visual Information Limited

All rights reserved. No part of this publication may be reproduced, stored in a retrieval system, or transmitted, in any form or by any means, electronic, mechanical, photocopying, recording or otherwise, without the prior permission of the copyright owner.

A Diagram Book first created by Diagram Visual Information Limited of 195 Kentish Town Road, London NW5 8SY, England.

First published in 1987 in Great Britain by Weidenfeld & Nicholson Limited.

First published in paperback in 1988.

Library of Congress Cataloging-in-Publication Data

Pilkington, J. Maya.
   [How to be a success]
   The real-life aptitude test/by J. Maya Pilkington and
the Diagram Group.
     p. cm.
   Reprint. Originally published: How to be a success.
London: Weidenfeld & Nicholson, 1987.
    Includes index.
    ISBN 0-88687-411-4 (pbk.): $10.95
    1. Success. 2. Success—Problems, exercises, etc. I.
Diagram Group. II. Title.
BF637.S8P55 1988
158'.1'076—dc19   88-28822
                                                        CIP

Typeset by Bournetype, Bournemouth, England.
Cover design by ICON Design, NYC

Pharos Books
A Scripps Howard Company
200 Park Avenue
New York, New York 10166

10 9 8 7 6 5 4 3 2 1

THE REAL-LIFE APTITUDE TEST

Maya
Pilkington
and The
Diagram
Group

PHAROS BOOKS
A SCRIPPS HOWARD COMPANY
NEW YORK

Contents

SECTION ONE
SELECTION

- 8 Introduction
- 10 What do you want out of life?
- 12 Choosing your areas of endeavor
- 14 Wealth: areas of endeavor
- 16 Wealth: areas of endeavor (cont.)
- 18 Wealth: the advantages and pitfalls
- 20 What is your wealth-potential?
- 22 Which kind of wealth do you want?
- 24 Power: areas of endeavor
- 26 Power: areas of endeavor (cont.)
- 28 Power: the advantages and pitfalls
- 30 Do you want to be more powerful?
- 32 Which kind of power do you want?
- 34 Status: areas of endeavor
- 36 Status: areas of endeavor (cont.)
- 38 Status: the advantages and pitfalls
- 40 Are you a social climber?
- 42 Which status do you want?
- 44 Challenge: areas of endeavor
- 46 Challenge: areas of endeavor (cont.)
- 48 Challenge: the advantages and pitfalls
- 50 Are you a challenge-seeker?
- 52 Which kind of challenge do you want?
- 54 Well-being: areas of endeavor
- 56 Well-being: areas of endeavor (cont.)
- 58 Well-being: the advantages and pitfalls
- 60 Are you well?
- 62 Which kind of well-being do you want?
- 64 Love: areas of endeavor
- 66 Love: areas of endeavor (cont.)
- 68 Love: the advantages and pitfalls
- 70 How loving are you?
- 72 Which kind of love do you want?
- 74 Does age make any difference?
- 76 Lifestage achievements
- 78 Reviewing your choices

SECTION TWO
PLANNING

- 80 Introduction
- 82 What does it take to succeed?
- 84 Generating ideas
- 86 Basic planning
- 88 Appreciating yourself
- 90 What are you good at?
- 92 What are your limitations?
- 94 What advantages do you have?
- 96 Making a time-scale
- 98 Setting standards
- 100 Enlisting help
- 102 Finding an outlet

SECTION THREE
ACTION

104 Introduction
Strategies
106 Four ways to change a situation
108 Courting failure
110 Negotiating for what you want
112 On being assertive
114 Persuading others
116 Getting feedback
118 Acquiring a positive attitude
120 A happier home life
122 Intimate relationships
Skills
124 Making decisions
126 Analyzing situations
128 Understanding finance
130 Time on your side
132 Developing a network
134 Learning and researching
136 Getting yourself trained
138 Presenting yourself
140 Knowing your environment
142 Knowing what they want
144 Displacing your hang-ups
146 Managing others
148 Resolving conflicts
150 Checking your progress

152 Rating your progress
154 A little applause
156 Guide to terms
158 Index

Foreword

The Real-Life Aptitude Test offers a stimulating approach to self-development that challenges you to discover your hidden potential and gives you the confidence to achieve your maximum capabilities. Illustrations are drawn from a comprehensive range of human endeavors to start you thinking, and to unearth your dormant talents while stirring your imagination. From the beginning you can use the practical exercises to assess yourself, to discover new directions and to learn the strategies and skills you will need to achieve what you want in life with success.

Once more the author, Maya Pilkington, and the artists and editors of the Diagram Group have added another new facet to the familiar Diagram Group style. **Who are you?** was the manual designed for you to explore yourself as you are now. **The Real-Life Aptitude Test** takes you far beyond the present into the bright lights of your future, no matter what your age or your current circumstances. **The Real-Life Aptitude Test** is not a book about impossible dreams; it is a practical guide to realizing your ambitions and the untapped potential within yourself.

The Real-Life Aptitude Test can guide you step-by-step through a process that could transform your way of life. From the generation of new ideas, through the planning and action stages, to the final review of your venture, the final choices will always be yours. Section One is for inspiration and to help you assess your current situation. Section Two shows you how to make realistic choices that are appropriate to your needs during the planning stage. Finally, Section Three offers you practical help as you actively embark upon your new project.

Throughout **The Real-Life Aptitude Test** you will find new ideas, alternative viewpoints and modern, well-tested approaches to refresh your enthusiasm and improve your skills. No matter where you choose to begin reading, you will find references to guide you. Because success results from active, personal involvement, this book will not tell you what you should be but it will show you how to set about achieving the aims you choose for yourself. With this book you are already on your way to becoming a success.

Section One

SELECTION

What are your options? In order to make a change, to improve your situation or to alter your lifestyle you need to look at the whole spectrum of human endeavors. There are thousands of possibilities but random searching can be frustrating and you could miss looking in the direction that is just right for you.

In this section, you are guided through the six main areas of human endeavor, shown their advantages and pitfalls and offered exercises to enable you to assess your own position. Your personal lifestage can be taken into account and there is ample opportunity for you to review the choices you make as you proceed.

What do you want out of life?

If you have thought about it at all, the short answer to the above question might be happiness, health, wealth, love, long life or freedom, etc. Perhaps you don't know what you want. A good way to begin is by considering your position in life at the moment. Here are some thoughts, common to people at different stages in life. Check those you recognize as being similar to your own thoughts. You may like to add any others in the spaces provided.

When you have made your selection
You may like to move directly to the suggested references or you may prefer to ponder further on which specific ventures, projects or activities might help you to fulfill your needs by turning to the pages overleaf. There you will find 72 areas of endeavor from which to make a selection.
REFER TO: SECTION ONE **Choosing your areas of endeavor** (pp. 12-3)

DO YOU NEED NEW IDEAS AND DIRECTION?

☐ 1 What prospects are there for me? I don't know what I want, nor do I know who I am or who I could be.

☐ 2 I have youth, health and enthusiasm on my side, but I just don't know how to make the best choice regarding my future.

☐ 3 There's something missing from my life. I'm doing very well at work so what else is there?

☐ 4 I didn't think I could ever lose my job. What else can I possibly do at my age? I need some ideas.

☐ 5 I am widowed, life is very lonely and my friends are all couples. What am I going to do?

☐ 6 I can't run about as much as I used to. But even in my situation there must be something else I can do.

☐ 7 I feel torn in several directions. I'd like to find out which way I really want to go.

☐ 8 What's happened to us? We used to be so happy together? Perhaps we need a new direction.

....
....
....

REFERENCES
SECTION ONE   Does age make any difference? (pp. 74-5)
SECTION TWO   Generating ideas (pp. 84-5)
              What are you good at? (pp. 90-1)
              What advantages do you have? (pp. 94-5)
SECTION THREE Getting feedback (pp. 116-7)
              A happier home life (pp. 120-1)
              Knowing your environment (pp. 140-1)

DO YOU KNOW WHAT YOU WANT BUT HAVE RESERVATIONS?

☐ 1 I've been at this job for years. I need the change but can I afford it?

☐ 2 I'm sure I have as many skills as my boss, but you don't see people like me taking charge.

☐ 3 It will take me five years to train. Will the effort and the social sacrifices be worth it?

☐ 4 I feel bad about failing...does this mean I can't start my new project?

☐ 5 I'm really enthusiastic about my new prospects, but I know my family will be upset if I make the move.

☐ 6 I'd like more recognition and appreciation, but I'm not sure how to set about achieving it.

☐ 7 I know exactly what I want to do, but have no idea how to set about it.

☐ 8 I know what I'd like to do, but I don't know if I could manage the training. I'm not good at learning.

....
....
....

REFERENCES
SECTION TWO   What does it take to succeed? (pp. 82-3)
              Basic planning (pp. 86-7)
SECTION THREE Courting failure (pp. 108-9)
              Negotiating for what you want (pp. 110-1)
              Intimate relationships (pp. 122-3)
              Making decisions (pp. 124-5)
              Understanding finance (pp. 128-9)
              Knowing what they want (pp. 142-3)

What do you want to put into life?
We humans may sometimes need to take a rest or to indulge in luxurious laziness, but passivity is not part of our nature. WANTING is an active process, so the most likely way of getting what you want out of life is to consider what you want to put into it. What effort do you want to make on behalf of yourself?
REFER TO: SECTION TWO **What does it take to succeed?** (pp. 82-3)

What is success?
Success implies not only achieving something you set out to do but also enjoying a glow of satisfaction in the process. One satisfying success then leads to another and achievement becomes a way of traveling rather than a single destination, which involves risks and the possibility of failure.
REFER TO: SECTION THREE **Courting failure** (pp. 108-9)

DO YOU HAVE IDEAS BUT NEED STRATEGIES AND SKILLS

☐ 1 I've heard about self-development, but how do I make a start? I know there are lots of things I could do.

☐ 2 I'm really quite happy, but there are some things that would make life more comfortable if I had money.

☐ 3 I have already enjoyed three occupations and I see a new opening ahead, but have I the confidence for it?

☐ 4 I am quite skilled in one or two things, but I want to broaden my prospects.

☐ 5 I've done quite well so far. I think it is time to make some plans for the next five years.

☐ 6 I don't feel I've made a success of anything yet. Why am I always the loser? I want to be a winner.

☐ 7 There's never enough time to do the things I'd really like to do. How can I reorganize my time?

☐ 8 I am in charge of my life, so if I want to improve it I can, but I'm not sure where to start.

....
....
....

REFERENCES
SECTION TWO **What does it take to succeed?** (pp. 82-3)
　　　　　　　Basic planning (pp. 86-7)
　　　　　　　Making a time-scale (pp. 96-7)
SECTION THREE **On being assertive** (pp. 112-3)
　　　　　　　Analyzing situations (pp. 126-7)
　　　　　　　Time on your side (pp. 130-1)
　　　　　　　Developing a network (pp. 132-3)
　　　　　　　Getting yourself trained (pp. 136-7)

DO YOU FEEL TRAPPED AND WANT TO MAKE A CHANGE?

☐ 1 Why am I still in this rut? I'm never given anything challenging to do at work these days.

☐ 2 I just didn't realize I got married for the wrong reasons, but I don't want to leave. What can I do?

☐ 3 Is this all there is to life? Why am I not happy when I've got everything and I'm envied by others?

☐ 4 Since the children grew up there's nothing to do and my spouse doesn't want me to go out to work.

☐ 5 How on earth did I get into this mess? Was it really bad luck or did I just drift? How can I make a change?

☐ 6 Life is such a battle. If only I could find some peace...are there any alternatives?

☐ 7 What do I have to do to get promotion? I'm always being passed over. I'm getting very depressed.

☐ 8 I know I can't make a move yet, but I can start thinking about the future and make some plans.

....
....
....

REFERENCES
SECTION TWO **What are your limitations?** (pp. 92-3)
　　　　　　　What advantages do you have? (pp. 94-5)
　　　　　　　Enlisting help (pp. 100-1)
SECTION THREE **Four ways to change a situation** (pp. 106-7)
　　　　　　　Getting feedback (pp. 116-7)
　　　　　　　Acquiring a positive attitude (pp. 118-9)
　　　　　　　A happier home life (pp. 120-1)
　　　　　　　Resolving conflicts (pp. 148-9)

Choosing your areas of endeavor

Here are 72 areas of human endeavor. Twelve examples have been given in each of the six main categories of Wealth, Power, Status, Challenge, Well-being and Love. From these you can make your choice by following the instructions in the next column.

How to make your choice
1. Read the questions at the head of each column. Check the one to which you would reply with the most unqualified and enthusiastic **Yes**.

WEALTH

☐ Do you want to be rich beyond your wildest dreams?

- ☐ A PERSONAL FORTUNE
- ☐ A DYNASTY
- ☐ PROMISSORY WEALTH
- ☐ BUSINESS
- ☐ TERRITORY
- ☐ MARRIAGE
- ☐ ARBITRAGE
- ☐ CHANCE
- ☐ ENTITLEMENT
- ☐ PROPERTY
- ☐ EQUITY
- ☐ PATRONAGE

REFERENCES
SECTION ONE **Wealth:** (pp. 14-23)

POWER

☐ Do you have an urge to express yourself effectively?

- ☐ ASSERTIVE POWER
- ☐ PHYSICAL POWER
- ☐ INTELLECTUAL POWER
- ☐ EMOTIONAL POWER
- ☐ EXECUTIVE POWER
- ☐ INFLUENTIAL POWER
- ☐ POLITICAL POWER
- ☐ SEXUAL POWER
- ☐ EVANGELICAL POWER
- ☐ REFORMATIVE POWER
- ☐ CONGRUENT POWER
- ☐ IMAGINATIVE POWER

REFERENCES
SECTION ONE **Power:** (pp. 24-33)

STATUS

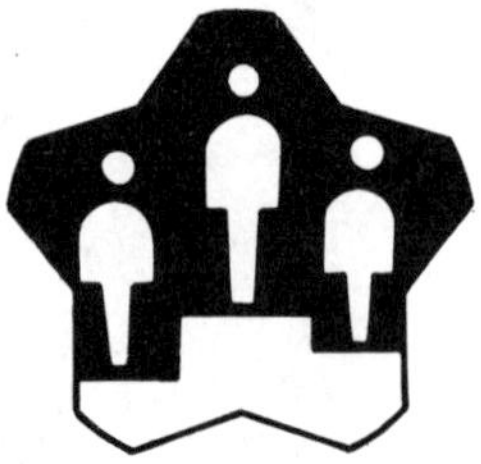

☐ Do you want a clearly recognized position in society?

- ☐ FIRST POSITION
- ☐ LEGENDARY STATUS
- ☐ UNCONVENTIONAL STATUS
- ☐ THE BOSS
- ☐ STARDOM
- ☐ THE REPRESENTATIVE
- ☐ THE MEDIATOR
- ☐ THE WINNER
- ☐ THE GURU
- ☐ THE CONTROLLER
- ☐ THE SPECIALIST
- ☐ SAINTHOOD

REFERENCES
SECTION ONE **Status:** (pp. 34-43)

2. Next read down the column of your choice, checking the areas of endeavor within that category that you find yourself focusing upon more than once. You may like to choose two or three.

3. Finally, turn to the page reference given at the bottom of the column, where you will find detailed descriptions, with examples, of each area of endeavor, together with some information about potential pitfalls and questions to help you to make a more informed choice.

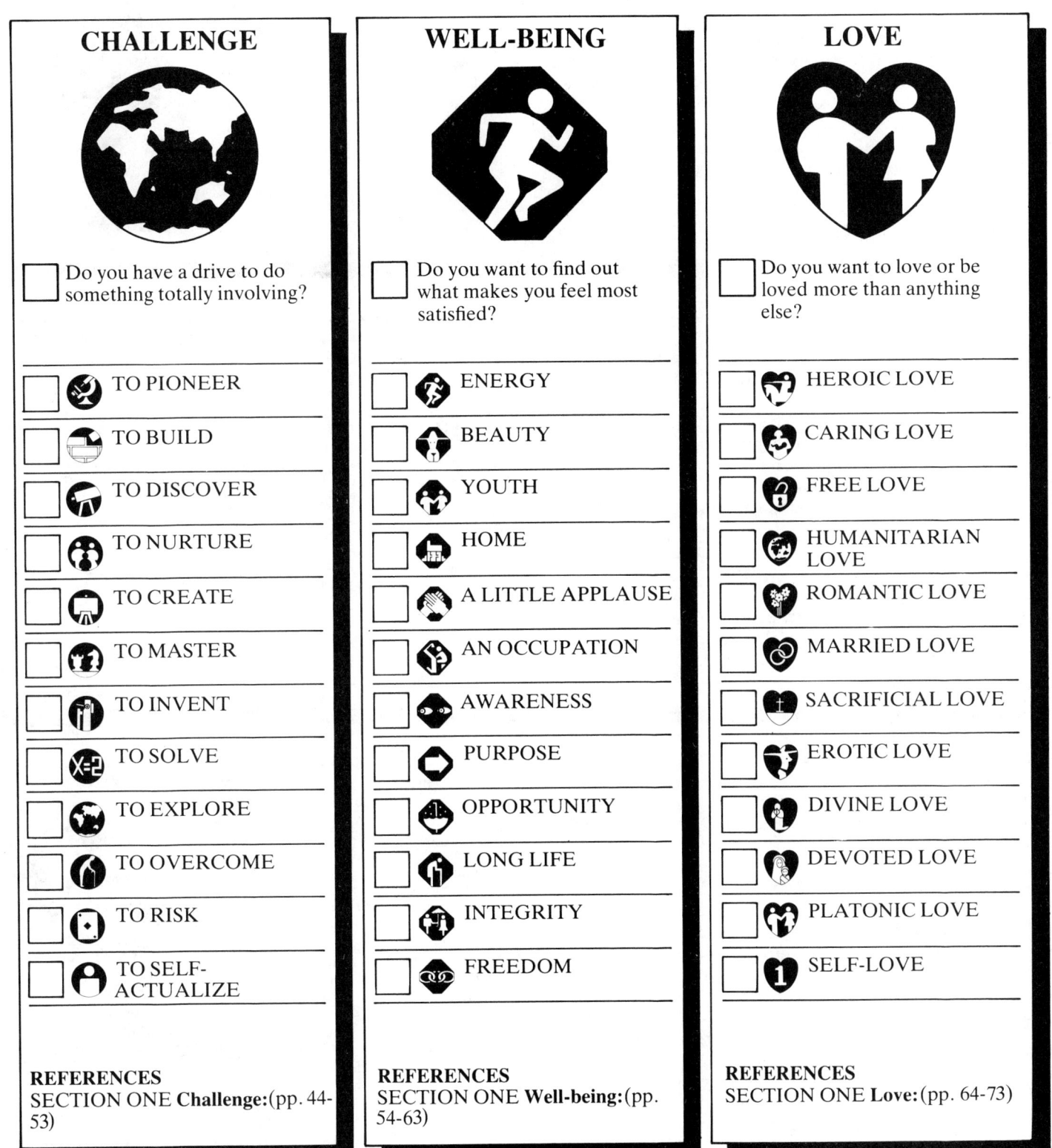

CHALLENGE

☐ Do you have a drive to do something totally involving?

- ☐ TO PIONEER
- ☐ TO BUILD
- ☐ TO DISCOVER
- ☐ TO NURTURE
- ☐ TO CREATE
- ☐ TO MASTER
- ☐ TO INVENT
- ☐ TO SOLVE
- ☐ TO EXPLORE
- ☐ TO OVERCOME
- ☐ TO RISK
- ☐ TO SELF-ACTUALIZE

REFERENCES
SECTION ONE **Challenge:** (pp. 44-53)

WELL-BEING

☐ Do you want to find out what makes you feel most satisfied?

- ☐ ENERGY
- ☐ BEAUTY
- ☐ YOUTH
- ☐ HOME
- ☐ A LITTLE APPLAUSE
- ☐ AN OCCUPATION
- ☐ AWARENESS
- ☐ PURPOSE
- ☐ OPPORTUNITY
- ☐ LONG LIFE
- ☐ INTEGRITY
- ☐ FREEDOM

REFERENCES
SECTION ONE **Well-being:** (pp. 54-63)

LOVE

☐ Do you want to love or be loved more than anything else?

- ☐ HEROIC LOVE
- ☐ CARING LOVE
- ☐ FREE LOVE
- ☐ HUMANITARIAN LOVE
- ☐ ROMANTIC LOVE
- ☐ MARRIED LOVE
- ☐ SACRIFICIAL LOVE
- ☐ EROTIC LOVE
- ☐ DIVINE LOVE
- ☐ DEVOTED LOVE
- ☐ PLATONIC LOVE
- ☐ SELF-LOVE

REFERENCES
SECTION ONE **Love:** (pp. 64-73)

Wealth: areas of endeavor

A PERSONAL FORTUNE
"Her face is her fortune" is an old saying that illustrates the connection between a talent and the money a person acquires because thousands of others are willing to pay to enjoy it.

Talented, professional, actors and actresses, entertainers, writers, designers, artists, musicians and television presenters all have to sell themselves on a freelance basis; after many years of hard work, often on a small income, some make a personal fortune. Those who do usually like to keep control over their wealth themselves.

If you have a talent to sell then you should be aware that fashion, the fickle moods of the general public, meeting the right people and being in the right place at the right time are factors that will affect your chances of making a personal fortune.

CHARLES SPENCER CHAPLIN
In 1899, at the age of ten, he was a penniless waif on the streets of his native London. By 1939, he had made a personal fortune as the pathetic and lovable tramp in the silent movies.

Chaplin had many personal talents as actor, director and writer. He also wrote and composed much of the music for his films, taking personal control of everything, including his wealth.

What many consider his greatest film, *City Lights*, was a box office sellout despite competition from the new "talking films."

A DYNASTY
Families by birth and marriage create a dynasty by concentrating their collective energy to make wealth through one main activity.

The family business may be in oil, food, transport, politics, the law or in any other profitable venture, but all members generally contribute to it and are brought up from early childhood to continue the endeavor. Many marry into other wealthy families to create larger dynasties. In a dynasty, wealth creates wealth very quickly, since everyone concerned puts the family business first.

If a dynasty for your grandchildren is your aim, you and your family will already be hard at work making money, strengthening family bonds and training your several offspring to carry on the good work!

THE KENNEDY FAMILY
Rich and glamorous, the Kennedy family are one of America's famous dynasties. They are a family held together by inheritance, occupation, religion, politics and tragedy, both public and personal.

Normally it is the male line that carries the traditions through to the next generation and adds to the wealth of the dynasty. However, both Kathleen Kennedy Townsend and her brother Joseph (Robert Kennedy's children) seem politically set to carry on the dynasty. It is said there are also some 30 other Kennedys likely to enter the political scene!

PROMISSORY WEALTH
Actions that seem to have a promising financial future sometimes result in great wealth after a period of time has elapsed.

Sponsorship is a form of promissory wealth as are royalties paid on registered or patented inventions, novels, plays, films, music, designs, techniques, formulas and recipes. For example, a writer who has barely made a living is suddenly a best-seller or an invention that took years to develop becomes an everyday object bought by millions.

People who accumulate collections of coins, stamps, medals, paintings, furniture, machinery, books and other items that they forecast will increase in value may have to wait for several years before they can sell their possessions for a much higher price.

LÁZLO BIRÓ
In 1938, this Hungarian inventor patented his prototype of the world famous biro, which combined quick-drying ink with a crude pen.

Continuing his work after emigration to Argentina, the US armed forces were among the first to buy his invention. In 1944 he was wise enough not only to patent his perfected, capillary action biro, but also to set up his own company to manufacture them; subsequently his invention fulfilled its promise of wealth. Although it is a trade name, most people call a ballpoint pen a biro.

BUSINESS

Selling goods and services at a profit is the essence of any business, whether it is a partnership, a private company, a public corporate body or a cooperative. A profit has to be made in order to service the capital invested, even if you begin a small, one-person business. It must also make you a living if you work in it yourself:

The most successful business people have a flair for marketing and selling. Manufacturers, road builders, farmers, advertising agents, car rental firms, chain stores, fast-food bars, banks, publishers, private colleges and hospitals and entertainment complexes are all businesses. The choice is endless, but it is usually wise to enter a business you know.

Running one or more businesses involves taking financial risks and carrying heavy responsibilities.

ALAN MICHAEL SUGAR

Chairman of Amstrad Electronics plc, Alan Sugar was already using his flair for responding to market demands when he was selling aerials from a car in London in 1965.

He started Amstrad in 1968, selling value-for-money hi-fi equipment and went public in 1980. Using his business flair for packaging and promoting a quality product for less than half the price his competitors charged, his personal computer, with business capacity, captured the UK and European market in 1985, increasing the value of the company shares sixfold.

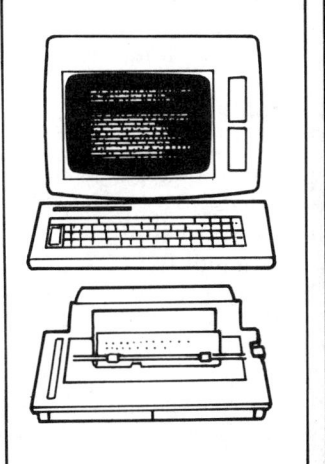

TERRITORY

The ownership of land and its resources is a major source of wealth. Rents and tariffs from people who want the use of land (e.g. buildings, bridges, ports, meeting places and other facilities) is one way of making money from territory. Other ways include buying and selling land, and the buildings that may be on it, as a commodity in itself or leasing rights to extract water, minerals, gas, oil and to erect masts and aerials.

People who make wealth from territory do not usually use the land themselves for farming or construction purposes unless in doing so they gain further territorial control.

Other ways of gaining wealth from territorial ownership is by finding and claiming wrecks at sea or by first building a business with a strong, clear image which you then franchise to others.

JOHN DAVISON ROCKEFELLER

One of the richest oilmen in history, J.D. Rockefeller was not an oil producer. He ruthlessly crushed competition and reaped huge wealth by controlling the territory and facilities that lie between the oilwell and the consumer. He bought refineries, railroads and pipelines, operating across all state boundaries and forcing many to sell out to him.

He started the Standard Oil Company in 1879, the foundation for the modern multi-nationals Esso (Exxon in USA), Mobil and Chevron.

MARRIAGE

Anyone seriously interested in acquiring wealth should never underestimate the potential available from making what is still regarded by many as a "good marriage." Marriage is a legal and financial arrangement not unlike a business partnership; indeed, marriage settlements or dowries are still customary, and "bed and bank" are often quoted as the two most common causes of a marriage break-up.

While it is true that the vast majority of wealthy people also marry into wealth, the right marriage can add to your financial assets. For many women, the route to even a modicum of financial advantage is still via marriage and it is not unknown for a penniless young man to marry a wealthy widow!

GRACE PATRICIA KELLY

Of Irish ancestry, Grace Kelly was not poor, but nor was she wealthy while earning a living as a photographer's model.

When she became a Hollywood film star, remembered for such films as *High Society* and *Rear Window*, naturally her own wealth increased, but even that was small compared with the riches she attained through marriage.

In 1954, at the age of 24, she met Prince Rainier III of Monaco at the Cannes Film Festival. Two years later she married him, acquiring not only wealth but also the title of Princess.

Wealth: areas of endeavor (cont.)

ARBITRAGE
Of French derivation, arbitrage means to estimate and settle the difference between things. People who become wealthy by arbitrage are generally doing so by profiting from the fact that the same thing is a slightly different price in different places.

Great wealth is made by some people on the stock exchanges by buying and selling huge numbers of shares quickly and making a small profit on each one. Good timing and an ability to anticipate events are important. Wheeler-dealers buy cheap in one place and often quickly sell the same articles at a slightly higher price in another.

In general, arbitrage is gaining wealth to use it over and over again to take timely advantage of the small differences between two or more economic situations.

ANDREW CARNEGIE
Although some people use illegal methods to gain from wheeler-dealing, the real skill of arbitrage relies on an instinct for good timing.

Andrew Carnegie, the steel tycoon, had this instinct. He bought plant and stock cheaply during the Depression in the 1920s, when everyone else was glad to get rid of it. When the demand for steel rose again, Carnegie was ready to go into production, thus providing the foundations for his well-known industrial empire.

CHANCE
Wealth by chance is money that comes your way without you making very much, if any, direct or intentional effort at all.

Inherited wealth comes by chance of birth and death while big winnings from gambling come by chance of circumstance or guesswork. People place bets on almost anything in the hope of winning a fortune.

The chance purchase of an object that turns out to be valuable or the chance discovery in your attic of a package of letters that passed between your great grandmother and some famous person are ways in which people become wealthy by chance.

There is nothing much to be done, except keep laying your bets or poking around in attics if you want to come upon chance wealth!

IVAN SERGEVITCH TURGENEV
During his early life, this great Russian writer just about scraped a living by working long hours in a local government office. He began writing stories in his free time, a task not so easy without electric light or a typewriter.

Then, in 1850 and by chance of birth, he inherited a huge fortune from a far distant and unknown relative.

This enabled him to give up his job and write full-time in comfort, producing plays and classic novels such as *Fathers and Sons* and *Virgin Soil*.

ENTITLEMENT
Wealth acquired because the person holding a particular office is not only paid well for doing the job but is also given many gratuitous advantages is wealth from entitlement.

Important and well-paid jobs with formal titles in government, religious organizations, trusts or public bodies often entitle the holder of those offices to high allowances and many other benefits while they remain in office. In addition, the office itself may open doors to future opportunities to make money.

The mayor of a town may ride around in a Rolls Royce, the chairman of the board may travel widely in great comfort, be accompanied by his wife and put in a claim for expenses, the Prime Minister of the UK resides at 10 Downing Street and the President of the USA lives in the White House.

HIS EMINENCE THE POPE
While no part of the Vatican's huge wealth becomes the personal property of the Pope on his election as head of all the Catholic Church, whoever has held this position throughout history has also been entitled to enjoy a lifestyle supported by this great wealth.

In common with most of those who acquire wealth by title, the duties and daily routines of the Pope's life are very clearly defined and include obligatory rituals based upon the policies and beliefs of the organization of which he is the figurehead.

PROPERTY

Investing money in buying or constructing property, such as houses, hotels, offices and factories, which are then leased, rented or used for a business purpose is the way some people create wealth.

The property owner is usually involved in construction activities or refurbishment and improvements for a particular use. Anyone who lets holiday apartments or room in their house is gaining from making their property work for them.

Property magnates make money from both owning a building that is increasing in value due to inflation and from making their property work for them by charging rents, etc. They depend for their wealth both on the market demand for the use of buildings and on an economy in which the value of buildings is inflating.

CONRAD NICHOLSON HILTON
President of the Hilton Hotels International Company, Conrad Hilton's interest in the lucrative value of property began as a boy in San Antonio, New Mexico, when he helped his father turn their large family house into an inn for traveling salesmen.

After working for a bank he began buying hotels in 1918. By 1939, despite setbacks during the Depression, he was buying, building and leasing hotels. Now there are Hilton hotels in every major city in the world, some of them franchised. His son became the Hilton President in 1966.

EQUITY

Equity is money put to work as an investment in the stocks and shares of a company and is the proportion of the total value of the shares issued by a company on which an investor receives a dividend of the profits; dividends vary from year to year, and can be quite low compared with interest rates on savings accounts.

Equity usually remains invested over a long period of time in the hope that the value of the shares will increase as the business flourishes.

The net value of a mortgaged property is another form of equity; due to inflation this is a way of gaining moderate wealth for many people who bought homes on a mortgage when house prices were low.

CALOUSTE SARKIS GULBENKIAN
Nicknamed "Mr. Five Percent," this oil magnate made his fortune by retaining equity in the Middle Eastern oilfields which he was instrumental in exploiting.

Born near Istanbul, in Turkey, he went to London in 1900 as financial counselor to the Ottoman Embassy.

He had already helped to form the Turkish Petroleum Company and negotiated a deal in 1914 that split control between Anglo-Persian, Dutch and German interests, personally retaining a 5% equity for life.

PATRONAGE

Generally speaking, wealth from patronage is only available when you have already made a good reputation. Patronage is an indirect and additional income due to the fact that you or your product is already well known.

In the past, a king or duke may have patronized a promising artist or musician in exchange for ownership of all work done during the period of patronage. Today, a sportsman may be bought by a club for a period of time, or a musical festival patronized by a bank.

All of us who buy a T-shirt carrying an ad are patronizing the product we are advertising when we wear it, but well-known entertainers and others in the public eye are handsomely paid to patronize a product when they appear in advertisements.

EDSON ARANTES DO NASCIMENTO
Better known throughout the world as Pelé, the great soccer (association football) player who led his Brazilian team to three victories in the World Cup in 1958, 1962 and 1970.

In his time, he was probably the most famous and best paid athlete in the world, both receiving and giving patronage because of his skill: a combination of accuracy, power and the ability to anticipate moves. In 1969, he scored his 1000th goal in his 909th first class match. (Pelée is the name of a volcano and Pele is also the Hawaiian goddess of fire!)

Wealth: the advantages and pitfalls

COMMON ADVANTAGES
Wealth of any kind has undoubted advantages. Here are five of them.

1 Basic security
No shortage of food, warmth, shelter, now or in the future.
2 Purchasing power
Buy as much as you want, when you want it and change it as often as you want.
3 Choice
Choose where to live, how to live, when and where to go on holiday, where to work and how to have fun.
4 Quality
Have the best of everything.
5 More wealth
Make your money work for you and generate even more wealth.

COMMON PITFALLS
There are also many myths associated with wealth, usually invented by those who are not yet wealthy. Here are five myths about wealth and the pitfalls into which you may fall if you believe them.

1 When I'm wealthy I'll be safe
Rich people have to guard and insure themselves and their wealth against theft, attack, competition, etc.
2 I'll please myself when I'm rich
True, you may do that and end up friendless and hated.
3 When I'm rich I'll have no more worries
Wealth does not reduce worry but does enable you to worry about things in comfort.
4 Wealth will ensure I get priority in everything
You can buy your way to power and status but buying favors is costly and can result in obligations, mistrust and even court action.
5 With money I can give my children everything
You can also deprive them of challenge, spoil them or make them believe that money is love.

ADVANTAGES AND PITFALLS OF EACH KIND OF WEALTH
Each of the twelve types of wealth represent different ways of making or acquiring money and each has its own particular dangers and delights.

People who become very wealthy generally stick to one main way of making money, because that way matches their particular talents, situation or opportunities and they can take advantage of this match. However, being forewarned of the dangers is equally important, since if financial disaster strikes the result can be loss, debt, bankruptcy, imprisonment and even suicide.

A PERSONAL FORTUNE gained from selling yourself and your unique talents.

ADVANTAGES
You can enjoy the limelight, be yourself and assert yourself. Possibility of fame and fortune overnight. Your product is directly under your own control.
PITFALLS
Loss of talent or contracts due to stress, illness, accident, public whim, younger talent. Egomania. Loss of privacy. Vulnerability to gossip. Typecasting.

DYNASTIC WEALTH built through a large and expanding family business to which all members contribute.

ADVANTAGES
A collective commitment is always greater than the sum of individual efforts. Fame. Security. Family loyalty.
PITFALLS
Competition and jealousy. Family feuds. Family skeletons. Lack of suitable offspring. Kidnappers.

PROMISSORY WEALTH amassed from royalties, sponsorships, commissions or the sale of collected valuables.

ADVANTAGES
Future security while you develop a new idea or take a rest. Excitement, choice of occupation, variety.
PITFALLS
Lack of commercial value or ability to sell your work; piracy; failure to perfect or patent an invention. Objects collected may deflate in value.

BUSINESS WEALTH from the sale of goods or services at a profit.

ADVANTAGES
The product or service can be adjusted or changed should the market change. You are your own boss. Opportunity for constant expansion.
PITFALLS
Numerous! Changes in trends, costs, climate, markets, technology. Takeover bids, labor disputes, competitions, industrial espionage, stress.

WEALTH FROM TERRITORY such as land and its resources.
ADVANTAGES
Control of combines, facilities, commodities and buildings which other people need to rent, buy or use.
PITFALLS
The oil well may run dry, drought may ruin a crop. Competition from an alternative route or form of transport. Value of land may fall. Sanctions.

WEALTH BY ENTITLEMENT because of a position held in public life or a corporate heirarchy.
ADVANTAGES
Status, power and attention. Tax advantages. You can conserve personal income and make useful contacts.
PITFALLS
Redundancy; fall from favor. Your behavior and attitudes must at least appear to be impeccable.

WEALTH BY MARRIAGE through a dowry, settlement or a partner with high earning power or an inheritance.
ADVANTAGES
No need to earn money. Opportunity to exert influence. Clearly defined occupational role.
PITFALLS
Marriage problems, unhappiness, power struggles in the home. Financial dependence. Loss of partner.

WEALTH FROM PROPERTY that is owned and subsequently leased, franchised or used for business purposes.
ADVANTAGES
Long-term income that is largely unearned. Assets that can be used as collateral. Inflating value of property.
PITFALLS
Collapse of value due to deflation, change in market demand, deterioration or compulsory purchase.

WEALTH FROM ARBITRAGE by taking advantage of small economic differences.
ADVANTAGES
The world is your oyster. Power and political control. Non-involvement and detachment; no messy emotions.
PITFALLS
Loss of human contact. Huge losses from small mistakes. Bad timing. Other arbitreurs. Change in stock exchange procedures. Other people's revenge.

EQUITABLE WEALTH from dividends on share investments and their increase in value.
ADVANTAGES
Long-term unearned income. Control of policies. Opportunity to trade daily. Calculated risk-taking.
PITFALLS
Economic fluctuations. Bad judgement. Impatience or greed. Lack of liquid assets.

CHANCE WEALTH from making little or no effort.
ADVANTAGES
Pleasure from working out the odds and anticipating results. Few responsibilities. Lots of fun.
PITFALLS
Nothing at all may happen. Gambling debts. Lack of ability to handle money. Inclination to spend freely.

WEALTH THROUGH PATRONAGE by cashing in on an established reputation.
ADVANTAGES
Reputation creates wealth exponentially. Wide range of opportunities to sell your name to highest bidder.
PITFALLS
Limitations determined by the patron. Loss of reputation by association with wrong patron. Loss of patronage when you cease to be "flavor of the month."

What is your wealth-potential?

The joy of money!
We have heard much about the joy of sex, of every person's right to enjoy physical pleasures, regardless also of age or infirmity, so what of the joy of money? Do you feel that everyone, including you, has the right to enjoy money... the right to enjoy negotiating a bargain, making a profit, or getting a raise? The more you enjoy doing these things, the higher is your wealth-potential.

ARE YOU AIMING FOR WEALTH?
The pertinent questions to ask yourself are:
(a) How much money do I want?
(b) Do I have a positive attitude?
The more positive your attitude toward money, the greater will be your "wealth-potential," since the biggest threat to your success will be any inner feelings that conflict with your aims.

Similar attitudes to money and sex, such as fear of not having enough and guilt at wanting more, should not be overlooked by anyone who wants to achieve wealth.

Most of us want a satisfactory love life and enough money for a decent standard of living, yet both lust and lucre are surrounded by taboos and hidden conflicts.

In general, money and sex give us status and a place in the "pecking order." Consequently, instead of enjoying money and sex, it is tempting to use them as a means to an end, which leads to conflicts.

At moderate levels, both money and sex can be used as substitutes for love, but at the extremes, greed and rape are condemned while charity and faithfulness are generally encouraged.

Some people believe it is fine to want money, so long as you really need it or you are going to use it wisely. Others point out that the more money is generated the healthier is the economy. Often we have conflicting attitudes, such as resentment about being underpaid mixed with fear of asking for a raise.

HAVE YOU GOT WEALTH-POTENTIAL?
Your attitude, and therefore your wealth-potential, is reflected by the way you handle financial situations. Choose one answer to each of the following questions, look up the value given on the scorecard (*bottom right*), then calculate your total score. You have wealth-potential if your score is +20 to +50.

Having calculated your total score, read the comments column (*far right*) and note that there are no scores given for **6**, only comments.

1. You would very much like to buy a house that is advertised at a price of $80,000. Which offer would you make to the owner?

(a) $77,000
(b) $80,000
(c) $72,000
(d) $65,000
(e) $85,000 with an immediate contract.

2. You want to sell your car privately. You think it is worth $3,000 and you know its small defects. At which price would you advertise it?

(a) $3,000 or nearest offer
(b) $3,500
(c) $4,000 or nearest offer
(d) $3,000
(e) Without any price stated.

3. You have to move house to take up a new job on a five year contract at an increased rate of pay. You expect to sell you present house for $92,000 on which you still owe a mortgage of $46,000. The rate of inflation has been falling steadily over the last few years and is now 3%. You estimate the cost of making the move will be $6,000. You do not have enough cash savings available to pay for the cost of moving. Which would you do?

(a) Buy a house at $46,000 with a $8,000 mortgage.
(b) Buy a similar house at $92,000 and increase your mortgage to 60%.
(c) Sell your house and rent another near the new job.
(d) Use the opportunity to buy a better house at $115,000 on a 75% mortgage.

4. After leaving a shop, you discover you have been given short change. What do you do?

(a) Return and get the correct change.
(b) Leave and put the loss down to experience.
(c) Go home and write to the customer services.

5. Estimate the total current value of all your assets. Include your home, if you own it, possessions such as a car, jewelry, etc, and any savings or insurances. How long would it take you to double this figure?

(a) 5–10 years;
(b) 10–15 years;
(c) 15–20 years;
(d) Longer.

6. Three months ago you were fired from your job. You now have $15,000 of your severance pay remaining; you are also the outright owner of a house valued at $77,000 and a car worth $5,000. You have spent three months researching your options. Without stopping to think, choose which of these would be the most attractive to you:

(a) Accepting the offer of a permanent job you know you would enjoy, but a salary slightly lower than your previous one.
(b) Accepting a paid place on a two-year training scheme learning something new that you always wanted to do, but with no guaranteed job at the end of it.
(c) Accepting the directorship of a currently thriving business, using skills you already possess, in which you would be required to invest $46,000 and from which you would draw a personal income higher than your previous salary.
(d) Investing $46,000 in a small business of your own, which you have already investigated and from which you think you could make the most money in the long run.
(e) Reorganizing your whole outlook and lifestyle to join an expedition or undertake a venture or project that you (and perhaps your family) have always said you would do one day.
(f) Spending another $5,000 of your severance pay and three months of your time following good leads you have acquired in order to find another job better than your last one and with a higher salary than before.

ASSESSING YOUR WEALTH-POTENTIAL SCORECARD						
	a	b	c	d	e	Scores
🏠	−5	−10	+5	+10	−15	
🚗	−10	+10	−15	−5	+5	
👜	+5	−5	+10	−15		
💰	+10	−10	−10			
🔒	+10	+5	−5	−10		
					Total score	

COMMENTS

🏠 **1. (a)** You are conventional aren't you! $77,000 is so close to the asking price that the seller will expect you to pay it.
(b) You aren't even trying. If there is another buyer you could find yourself paying *more*!
(c) A tough enough start to make the seller think his price is too high.
(d) You have real wealth-potential; able to risk not getting the house you also stand to get it very cheap.
(e) You are terrified of losing and must have more money than sense.

🚗 **2. (a)** 'Or nearest offer' means you will drop your price.
(b) $3,500 is close to what you want and gives you bargaining space so you stand to get more.
(c) Unrealistic and weakened by o.n.o.
(d) You aren't trying and may have to drop lower.
(e) Good if there is a demand for your make of car.

👜 **3. (a)** If you really must buy another house during a period of deflation, then better a cheaper one on which you reduce your mortgage, releasing money to invest in other ways. People with wealth-potential never follow the herd in believing that because the value of houses rose out of all proportion for 30 years, that they will go on doing so!
(b) Read the above and you will see why increasing the money you pay out for a depreciating possession is a bad idea.
(c) By renting you pay off your mortgage debt and release at least $38,000 to invest. In five or so years time when house prices have dropped even further you can buy one with money to spare.
(d) You must be a lemming [see (a)] and deserve to drown in debts you won't be able to repay.

💰 **4. (a)** You are good at relating to people and always get mistakes corrected easily... aren't you?
(b) Money thrown away through lack of effort.
(c) You'll end up in lengthy arbitration which will cost you more in postage and telephone calls!

🔒 **5.** Anywhere between 5 and 10 years is a realistic answer. For example, if you have $31,000 invested at 12% it would double its value in 6 years. Invested at 9% it would take 8 years to double its value.

6. Your main choice of direction. There are no scores for any of these, as they are all viable choices and depend on personal priorities, (c), (d) and (f) are choices in which money has a high priority and are more likely to be chosen by people with a higher wealth-potential.

Which kind of wealth do you want?

The dream of wealth and what can be done with it is very different from the reality of deciding what kind of wealth you want, how to set about making it and how to manage it when you have got it.

If your prime ambition is to become very wealthy, then the making of money will be more important than your trade or profession, although it is always wise to work in something you have a feel for.

For example, some people go into the business of making bread because they enjoy baking. Others do it because they enjoy making money... so if bread doesn't make enough money they may produce other kinds of food instead.

Your general characteristics will largely determine which kind of wealth should be your aim, or whether you are a potential wealth-maker at all.

WHICH WEALTH-MAKING CHARACTERISTIC HAVE YOU GOT?
While money-making is always the first priority, different kinds of money-makers have different characteristics. Some of them are shown (*right*). Check the one that is definitely true of you. Check more than one if you feel it is also true.

Which kind of money-making would most suit you?
Compare the numbers of the items you have checked against the key numbers (*below*) to find out which kind of wealth-making matches with your characteristics.

If you have checked more than one, then there may be several routes you could follow, but do bear in mind that most wealthy people have stuck to one kind of wealth-making activity.

You may also like to take into account your wealth-potential score from the previous page.

Key list of wealth

1 Personal Fortune
2 Dynasty
3 Promissory wealth
4 Business
5 Territory
6 Marriage
7 Arbitrage
8 Chance
9 Entitlement
10 Property
11 Equity
12 Patronage

1 I have a strong need to demonstrate my considerable personal talents and gain public approval.

2 I am the head of a well-trained family that I have brought up to pull together.

3 I am never short of ideas and I know how to develop the ones that have commercial potential.

4 I am always in touch with the public mood and I know how to sell them what they want.

5 I thoroughly enjoy being in control and ensuring that the public has the facilities it needs.

6 I like to have someone who depends upon me because I am capable of loyalty and can give excellent support.

7 I am unemotional and cool-headed, and I have an excellent understanding of international trading.

8 I think systematically and do not waste money, although I am a gambler at heart.

9 I have already mapped my route to the very top of my chosen occupation and I know how to behave in order to reach that position.

10 I understand the value of property and how to make it pay for itself.

11 I am good with figures, follow the financial news and manage my own money carefully.

12 I am already very good at what I do and I am becoming well known in public.

Marketing and selling
The generation of any kind of wealth begins with two questions:
1 **What have you got to sell?**
2 **Is there a market for it?**
Your answers to these two questions will indicate the direction you should take if you want to make money, whether it is a modest income or a mighty fortune.

WHAT HAVE I GOT TO SELL?
In the boxes (*below*) make a note of assets, skills or advantages you have in as many categories as you can. Some examples are given to stimulate your ideas.

If you have difficulty recognizing your advantages, then turn to SECTION TWO **What advantages do you have?** (pp. 94-5)

Following-up your choices
If you have selected **2, 4, 5, 7, 10** or **11,** then you will need a sound understanding of financial affairs. If you have selected **1, 3** or **12,** you will need to present yourself well. For **6** and **9** you will need to build a good network of contacts. Whichever you have chosen, you will need to find a market for your talents, goods or services.

You will find further information about all of these things from the following:

REFERENCES
SECTION TWO   **Finding an outlet** (pp. 102-3)
SECTION THREE   **Understanding finance** (pp. 128-9)
                 Developing a network (pp. 132-3)
                 Presenting yourself (pp. 138-9)

1 **Personal Fortune** e.g. a personal talent.

2 **Dynasty** e.g. a family tradition.

3 **Promissory Wealth** e.g. antiques or an invention.

4 **Business** e.g. selling or bartering skills.

5 **Territory** e.g. knowledge of land usage.

6 **Marriage** e.g. social skills; sophistication.

7 **Arbitrage** e.g. knowledge of corporate business.

8 **Chance** e.g. good at working out odds.

9 **Entitlement** e.g. diplomacy or good contacts.

10 **Property** e.g. an instinct for long-term profit.

11 **Equity** e.g. good memory for figures.

12 **Patronage** e.g. ability to predict fashion.

Power: areas of endeavor

ASSERTIVE POWER

When we assert ourselves we express in words or actions our personal convictions in such a way that others take notice and are aware that we mean what we say or do.

Assertive power can be felt very strongly; some people quietly insist while others make themselves known more actively. Either way, those who are on the receiving end of assertive power are stimulated to respond and often comply or cooperate. Sometimes there is an opposite reaction; assertive people tend to be disliked by those who themselves are rarely assertive or feel afraid to risk standing their ground alone; assertive people often have to stand alone.

Assertion is a personal, self-expressive power; it is not aggression, which is a form of attack. Unfortunately the two are often confused.

NAPOLEON BONAPARTE

Born in Corsica, Napoleon was a powerfully assertive Emperor of France for eleven years until 1815, during which time members of the government were afraid of him. An outstanding military man and tough disciplinarian, he strongly believed in the idea of a united Europe.

Even from his exile on the island of Elba, he returned to regain support in France. Later, after his defeat at Waterloo, he was banished to St. Helena where it is said he proceeded to rule his captors with the same iron-willed assertive power.

PHYSICAL POWER

When we use our bodies for action we are exercising our physical powers in order to go somewhere, do something or communicate something. Physical power is also linked with both ugliness and attractiveness; the noisy growls associated with some of the martial arts appear threatening, while a gentle sway of the hips while walking across the beach is a very seductive power.

Strength, flexibility, grace, accuracy and speed are all expressions of physical power which are developed in everyday life, in sport, dance and drama. Some people acquire specialized physical power in particular parts of the body; for example, surgeons use their hand and eye powers, musicians use their hand and ear powers and disabled people may use their foot power to write and paint.

DALEY THOMPSON

Combining every expression of physical power, Daley Thompson, the British athlete, has proven himself to be the world's greatest decathelete.

Selected for the 1976 Olympic Games at the age of 18, he subsequently won the gold medal for the decathalon in both 1980 and 1984. He gave a stunning performance of all-round physical ability and endurance in all ten events, gaining 8,797 points, just one point short of breaking the world record held by Jürgen Hingsen of West Germany.

INTELLECTUAL POWER

We exercise our intellectual powers when we are using our minds. We may be thinking about something that is happening to us here and now, about things we are observing at a distance or about what has happened in the past. We also use our intellectual powers to speculate about the future or to plan ahead.

Collecting information and ideas, reasoning, discussing, understanding situations and proposing theories are all part of the power of the intellect. Equally our intellects can misunderstand!

Some people develop specialist skills using their intellectual powers; for example, memorizing, speed reading, adding up numbers or estimating sizes. Others can visualize colors and designs in their mind's eye or hear sounds in their mind's ear.

ALBERT EINSTEIN

This happy-go-lucky, kindhearted Bohemian Jew, who went to a Catholic school and studied physics in Zurich, spent more than twenty years forming his theory of relativity using his intellectual powers of reasoning and mathematics.

His famous equation $E = mc^2$ has affected the development of physics, nuclear power and space travel. Einstein, the greatest scientist of this century, worked by thinking. He once showed a friend a well-chewed pencil saying, "Here is my laboratory."

EMOTIONAL POWER

Although the power of emotions that stir us are largely invisible, they are certainly felt within our bodies. We exercise our emotional powers when we give expression to feelings from within ourselves.

Finding a way to identify or express those feelings may be a problem to some people who keep their emotional power tied up, often causing stress.

There are many ways of expressing emotional power; direct, immediate expression through sound and movement is common to all of us, for example when angry we may raise our voices and thump the table or when in love we may touch, kiss and speak softly.

Some people develop skills to give form to their emotional power through poetry, music, dress, sculpture, cooking, dance and lovemaking, etc.

KERI HULME

Few writers throughout history have given expression to common, powerful human emotions through myth and story combined with an original way of using language. Keri Hulme, who lives at Okarito on the west coast of New Zealand, took twelve years to achieve this in her first novel, *The Bone People*, which was awarded the Booker McConnell Prize for the most outstanding novel of 1985.

The story is of a man, a woman and an autistic child. A critic said of the book, "...makes you feel you are discovering what an aspect of real life is like."

EXECUTIVE POWER

The power to take charge, make things happen and get things done is a way of defining executive power. Executive power is used by all of us when we complete a task or organize others to do something.

In more formal terms, executive power infers being in a recognized position, at a particular rate of pay, such as that of captain, foreman, chairperson, principal, manager or leader.

Strictly speaking, in industry, for example, executive positions are generally held by those who also own a share of the business, which enhances their executive powers.

It is often said that possession is nine tenths of the law. Parents sometimes use this aspect of executive power in family affairs and children, too, quickly learn the executive power of ownership!

RUPERT MURDOCH

From the time of his inheritance, in 1954, of the failing *Adelaide News* from his father, this Australian newspaper executive made things happen, turning almost every paper, magazine and TV station he touched into a runaway success.

Splashy headlines about sex, crime and sport, hard-driving promotion, cost-cutting and uncompromizing calculated risk-taking are the methods he has used to build his publishing empire throughout Australia, the UK and the USA...a pyramid of executive power.

INFLUENTIAL POWER

Influence is a subtle and often covert form of power that, over a period of time, affects the attitude of another person, or of a small group of people, who themselves make major decisions and take effective actions. Influence is the power *behind* the throne.

Rarely are people who exercise influence to be found in the highest office, although in some instances they may hold positions of importance and come under public scrutiny. Quite often their names are unknown and their influence unrecognized by many.

Advisers, civil servants, consultants, lawyers, brokers, personal assistants, secretaries, butlers, mistresses, wives, husbands and parents are all in positions to exert influence directly or indirectly.

Even when you are asked to give a reference for someone, you are using your influential power.

HENRY ALFRED KISSINGER

A political scientist, adviser and former Secretary of State, Henry Kissinger was influential in shaping the foreign affairs of the United States from 1969 to 1976. He initiated the strategic arms limitation talks (SALT), and influenced agreements made between the US and Pakistan, the USSR and the People's Republic of China.

In 1973 he shared the Nobel Peace Prize with Le Duc Tho, the N. Vietnamese representative, for negotiating the agreement by which the war in Vietnam was ended.

Power: areas of endeavor (cont.)

POLITICAL POWER

The power to determine policies in government, unions, associations, organizations, alliances, campaigns and splinter groups has two sources which are only fully effective in combination.

The first source is from within individuals: personal convictions, willingness to express and work towards those convictions, knowledge of the constitution, the law and the viewpoints of opponents... all these, and more, contribute to political power.

The second source comes from a consensus of opinion, from the votes of an electorate or from the loyalty of a military force.

One without the other will not work. You cannot exercise your political power without the support of others; nor can a body of political opinion find expression without a channel.

MARGARET HILDA THATCHER

A chemist, lawyer and politician of strong conviction, Margaret Thatcher was first elected a Member of the British Parliament in 1959, later becoming the Secretary of State for Education.

In 1975 she made history by winning the vote, by a large majority, to become the first female leader of a British political party.

Her policies brought victory in two parliamentary elections and as Prime Minister her political prowess earned her the title of the "Iron Lady."

SEXUAL POWER

Sexual power is the use of sex as a means to an end. It is not related to sexual desire, sexual potency, sexual love or sexual pleasure and satisfaction, although one or more of these may become involved.

Sexual power is used by both men and women in many situations; it is simply a way of getting what you want by using sex as barter.

Classic stories of military or industrial espionage often include a scene in bed where all secrets are revealed! Sex in return for money, sex in return for a favor (or undying loyalty), sex for control and for blackmail... all of these illustrate the use of sexual power. Deliberate flirting and the calculated withholding of sex are also expressions of sexual power. Sometimes this power is used with malice and sometimes everyone involved simply enjoys the game.

JEANNE ANTOINETTE POISSON

Better known as Madame de Pompadour, she first met King Louis XV of France in 1744. The following year, Louis installed her in the Palace of Versailles.

As his mistress she used her sexual power over Louis to gain what she wanted: wealth, status and political influence.

During the remaining nineteen years of her life, the policies of Louis were her policies and they were not always in the best interests of France. Her insistence on an alliance with Austria led eventually to the disastrous Seven Years War.

EVANGELICAL POWER

The modern meaning of evangelism is using the power of words to stimulate awareness and rouse large numbers of people to believe in themselves or in their cause because it is their right.

A strong sense of justice and fair play is usually the driving force of evangelical power, often associated with christian principles but not always. The involvement of all who attend evangelical meetings is achieved through singing, dancing or the taking of vows as hundreds are moved to respond to the message.

Evangelists generally conduct crusades rather than campaigns, appealing to people through their emotions. Hence evangelists may be deeply loved and respected by millions who recognize them as inspiring and caring leaders and hated by some who feel a strong resistance to their message.

MARTIN LUTHER KING

This patient, wise and kindly man was the founder of the Southern Christian Leadership Conference in the United States.

His aim was to awaken all the population to the cause of black people and achieve civil rights for American Negroes.

His ministry was one of firmness without violence and he became admired and respected throughout the world for his evangelical powers and personal example.

Awarded the Nobel Peace Prize in 1964, he was assassinated in 1968 by a white fanatic at a public meeting in Memphis.

REFORMATIVE POWER
This is the power to progressively reorganize human affairs for the better.

Reforms may affect only one person, such as when you progressively stop doing things that cause you stress or when a young vandal is induced to redirect his energies into community work.

Reformations that affect large numbers of people are similarly expected to improve the situation, as is the case during educational or religious reforms.

In order to exercise your reformative power, the present situation and its history must first be understood; reform is not concerned with doing something in an entirely new and different way, but with an evolutionary process such as the removal from an existing system of faults, imperfections or abuses as they become evident.

SIDNEY HILLMAN
Imprisoned in his native country at the turn of the century for advocating labor reforms, this Jewish Lithuanian became Vice-President of the World Federation of Trade Unions shortly before he died in 1946.

In 1909 he emigrated to America and began work in a Chicago clothing factory. As President of the Amalgamated Clothing Workers of America during the 1920s and 1930s, he reformed union functions to include social services such as unemployment insurance, housing and banking.

CONGRUENT POWER
When what we think, feel, say and do are the same, we are behaving in a congruent way. Unfortunately, for much of the time, many of us demonstrate our incongruency, for example by smiling when we feel aggressive, by teaching our children to be honest while we steal the odd tool from work or by making a promise to be faithful while carrying on an affair!

When we use congruent power we feel whole and strong because all our parts are working together with the same intention.

When we are consistently incongruent, we tend to lose our sense of identity, feel isolated or afraid and behave defensively. Consequently we lose trust in ourselves and we may lose interest in life itself.

Congruent power is greater than the sum of our parts.

PLACIDO DOMINGO
This great Spanish tenor has brought the magic of his music to millions through live opera and films such as *La Traviata* and *Carmen*.

His popularity is largely due to his power of congruency...he both sings and acts his parts with total conviction, unerring musicality and with the feelings and optimism that are natural to him in his life off-stage.

True to himself, he acted upon his beliefs after the Mexican earthquake in 1985 and arranged a series of charity performances to raise cash for his adopted country.

IMAGINATIVE POWER
Imagination is the power to conceive images in the form of shapes, colors, sounds or movements which may be composed into poetry, stories, plays, pictures, music, songs and dances.

This power can also be used to present new ideas or a new angle on an old idea in the form of metaphors which stimulate thought, pleasure and even shock.

Imagination draws upon unconscious memories, images, ideas and mixed-up thoughts and feelings, juxtaposing and freely associating them in a variety of ways with objects and events happening in the present.

Imaginative powers often cross cultural and national barriers, touching the collective unconscious we all have in common.

HANS CHRISTIAN ANDERSEN
Born in Denmark and orphaned at an early age, Hans Andersen wrote fairy stories that have touched the souls of people throughout the world. He used his imaginative power to reveal the depths of human longings and sadness.

From his childhood unconscious came the story of the ugly duckling, which, almost a century later, inspired the imaginative powers of Walt Disney, who brought that same ugly duckling to life on the cinema screen.

Power: the advantages and pitfalls

Power has four features, each of which can be positive or negative; there are no neutral positions, so either you take advantage of your power or it will cause your downfall.

1 Power has an energy source
POSITIVE
Life processes are the energy source of all human powers, so take advantage of the fact that you are alive!
NEGATIVE
Your human potential is a vast reservoir of energy, and reservoirs that aren't flowing put pressure on the retaining dam wall and stagnate, resulting in stress or depression.

2 Power has quantity
POSITIVE
All power needs to be regulated. Self-regulating people can tick over when they need a rest and draw upon huge reserves of power when appropriate.
NEGATIVE
You can use your power or let it use you. It all depends if you are in charge of your life. Are you being driven by pressures of your unused power or do you feel under pressure because you are having to resist power from outside yourself?

3 Power has quality
POSITIVE
Power that matches the thoughts and feelings you have when you go into action will have the right quality. Rather like a thermostat, you can regulate the temperature of your power output.
NEGATIVE
Without an inner thermostat you lose the power of expressive action. For example, as when shouting "Help" in a loud but flat voice.

4 Power has an effect
POSITIVE
Your own power can affect you and others. Either way you can get things done, achieve results and enjoy life.
NEGATIVE
If you aren't aware of your own powers, the effect you have may not be what you hoped for. Fear of your own power or misuse of it can also lead to a downfall.

ADVANTAGES AND PITFALLS OF THE TWELVE POWERS
Each of the twelve ways of using your life energy has its own particular advantages and pitfalls. All powers have the same energy source and consequently tend to spill over and easily become mixed-up.

You can take advantage of this characteristic but you should also be aware of the pitfalls, because each kind of power can be used to express different parts of yourself and to achieve different ends.

ASSERTIVE POWER is used to express yourself and your personal convictions.

ADVANTAGES
You can put your point of view clearly, gaining confidence, direction and self worth, and avoid becoming submissive or downtrodden.
PITFALLS
Losing your sense of humor; become dominating, self-opinionated, oppressive or aggressive; forcing issues so that others react negatively.

PHYSICAL POWER is used for movement and action with flexibility and grace.

ADVANTAGES
Health, strength, beauty, attractiveness and the ability to enjoy movement and work effectively.
PITFALLS
Use of strength to control or abuse others; use of beauty to deceive. Danger of becoming an object to be admired or worshipped for physical appearance only.

INTELLECTUAL POWER is used for thinking, working out problems and reasoning.

ADVANTAGES
The ability to reflect on a situation, collect information and come to a conclusion without becoming too involved in what is happening.
PITFALLS
Believing that a theory is a fact because it seems rational or ought to make sense. Loss of contact with reality due to detachment. Being ruled by intellect.

EMOTIONAL POWER is used to express inner feelings.

ADVANTAGES
Good contact with other people; trust, understanding, the ability to learn new skills; imagination, intuition and compassion.
PITFALLS
Believing that a feeling is a fact; projecting your own unacceptable feelings onto other people; failing to recognize or use facts. Being ruled by emotion.

 **EXECUTIVE POWER is used to get things done by organization, leadership and direct action.**

ADVANTAGES
Can make and implement decisions on behalf of small or large groups of people, taking all opinions and needs into account.
PITFALLS
Become the scapegoat if things go wrong. Personal motives may replace collective intentions. Loss of contact with people and issues at ground level.

 **EVANGELICAL POWER is used to rouse people to believe in themselves and their rights on religious grounds.**

ADVANTAGES
Become the adored figurehead of a large organization. Feel good at achieving something seen as worthwhile.
PITFALLS
Resistance and threats from people or organizations who disagree or are frightened. Enormous drains on your energy by the people you have roused.

 **INFLUENTIAL POWER is generally used behind the scenes to change the opinions and actions of others.**

ADVANTAGES
Having an effect on human affairs without necessarily being the one who takes ultimate responsibility.
PITFALLS
Being blamed for failures by both the person you have influenced and others who think you have been the root cause of upsets.

 **REFORMATIVE POWER is used to bring about improvements in human affairs over a period of time.**

ADVANTAGES
Long-term satisfaction. Pleasure of solving a series of problems in a way that is demonstrably effective.
PITFALLS
Getting worn out from abortive efforts. Resistance from others. Wandering off your original track.

 **POLITICAL POWER is used to determine and implement policies for which you were voted into power.**

ADVANTAGES
Whatever you do, you always have a body of electorate behind you. Opportunity to control and direct affairs and reach a position of high status too.
PITFALLS
If you fail to please enough of the people you will be voted out or thrown out. Vulnerable to loss of image and assassination.

 **CONGRUENT POWER is the use of all our powers combined in such a way that they balance.**

ADVANTAGES
Versatility and satisfaction as you are able to express yourself fully. Enormous energy resources.
PITFALLS
Dissipation of energy into too many different directions at once. Trying to be perfect.

 **SEXUAL POWER is used as a means to an end.**

ADVANTAGES
Achieve your ends and satisfy yourself in the process. Gain control over someone who becomes emotionally involved with you. Build yourself an image of potency.
PITFALLS
Lack of contact with others. Abject loneliness. Disease. Revenge on the part of others. Problems if you get emotionally involved yourself.

 **IMAGINATIVE POWER is used to create images and ideas that can be applied at work, in the arts and in love.**

ADVANTAGES
Ability to resolve problems easily and to satisfy unconscious drives. Acquire understanding and joy.
PITFALLS
Get stuck in a rut or held back by fantasies that you allow to take control over your life.

Do you want to be more powerful?

If you would like to be more powerful than you are already, where would you expect your increased power to come from? From yourself or from someone else?

Power is not a magic potion that can be bestowed upon you by a greater authority or a guardian angel. Power comes only from within.

Even if you do have a powerful position bestowed upon you, it means very little if you lack the inner power to use it effectively.

Are you really powerless?
Everyone has inner energy resources which can be converted into power... power to influence those "in power," power to communicate effectively and power to get you what you want. So if you often feel powerless, is it a reality or is it just that your energy is held back or being drained down unsatisfying channels?

There are a few situations in life in which we are totally powerless. For example, if someone points a loaded gun at you, then you are in a physically powerless position. However, in many other kinds of situations you may feel powerless only because you believe you are and you haven't yet learned how to use your power or it is being drained during unproductive activities. In SECTION THREE there are some exercises to help you to learn how to use your power, such as: **On being assertive** (pp. 112-3).

Is your power being drained?
Early in life we internalize some fixed ideas about how we should behave in order to survive and get what we want; these ideas become fixed beliefs and subconsciously we tend to obey them.

There are five main beliefs (or injunctions, as they are called in transactional analysis) that most children seem to learn from their parents and other adults. In adulthood, if you act according to these beliefs without question, they become a heavy drain on your energy.

The five common beliefs (injunctions)
1 BE STRONG Never, never must you be weak or fail. Nor must you ever waver from what is morally right.

This belief stems from injunctions such as: "Be a man!... and don't cry like the weaker sex!" or "Never, never show him you are hurt, because a man does not like a wailing woman!"

2 BE PERFECT In everything you do, you must aim for impeccable perfection. You must never be disorderly, untidy or messy... and certainly you must never be vulgar! How could anyone respect you otherwise? In marriage you must also be the perfect wife and mother, or the perfect husband.

This belief stems from injunctions such as: "Practice makes perfect." or "Buy Goofy Gurgle to keep your house clean and bright!"

3 TRY HARD Never boast about your achievements because it's the amount of effort that is put into something that really counts. You should never give up or stop trying. How else can you prove yourself?

This belief stems from injunctions such as: "If at first you don't succeed, try, try and try again." or "Pride goes before a fall."

4 BE GOOD In all things and at all times you must be pleasing and please others. You are such a good person when you do what pleases others. Nobody could possibly love a bad person who displeases.

This belief stems from injunctions such as: "Be a good girl and daddy will buy you a new doll." or "Be a good boy and mummy will love you."

5 HURRY UP There really isn't any time to be wasted, life is too short. If you don't hurry, you'll get left behind... and then you'll get left out, or you'll have to put up with second best. People who are slow are not very bright anyway and who would want an idiot.

This belief stems from injunctions such as: "Not now, dear, I haven't time." or "Don't be long, or I'll get impatient."

ARE YOUR BELIEFS A DRAIN ON YOUR ENERGY?
To find out if you are draining off your energy, check as many of the statements given in the five sections **A–E** (*below*) that are true of you.

Section A
1 I put up with a lot more than anyone would guess.
2 I think reason is better than being emotional.
3 I rarely feel hurt by anyone.
4 I always stay outwardly cool, even if I feel angry.
5 I don't usually let people help me very much.
6 I can't stand people who make a fuss.
7 I am usually the last person to complain.
8 I am not a soft person.

Section B
1 Carelessness does tend to irritate me.
2 I do like to see people get things right.
3 If I want a thing done properly I'll do it myself.
4 I don't like people who make excuses for poor work.
5 I like to tell people when they are making mistakes.
6 I can always find where improvements can be made.
7 I like things done properly even if it takes longer.
8 I like to get things right first time.

Section C
1 I ought to get more done as I put in a lot of time.
2 Things are more complicated than you imagine.
3 I don't like things coming to an end.
4 I put a lot of effort into anything I do.
5 Nothing's easy in this world.
6 My enthusiasm drops off once I've begun something.
7 To make sure, I tend to repeat things I say.
8 I explore all alternatives before starting anything.

Section D
1 I adapt easily to other people's ideas.
2 I can usually guess what others need.
3 I usually smile or nod during conversation.
4 I take others' wishes into account before deciding.
5 I find it hard to ask a favor.
6 I don't like to feel I've upset someone.
7 I would call myself a very considerate person.
8 It is hard for me to refuse a request.

Section E
1 If I had more time I'd be able to relax.
2 I want to interrupt people who talk slowly.
3 I use the minimum time necessary to get anywhere.
4 I'd rather get on with things than plan them.
5 I often talk too quickly and can't stop.
6 I often do things at the last minute.
7 I am at my best when there is a lot to do.
8 I'm always thinking ahead of what I'm doing.

Interpreting your choices
The five sections list characteristics of the beliefs:

Section A	Section B	Section C	Section D	Section E
BE STRONG	**BE PERFECT**	**TRY HARD**	**BE GOOD**	**HURRY UP**

The more checks you have in a section, the more you are likely to unconsciously hold that particular belief... and the more your energy will be drained away trying to live up to it.

The more you become aware of energy-draining beliefs, the easier it becomes to change your attitude and release the power they divert.

General characteristics
BE STRONG and BE PERFECT people find failure a terrifying prospect. They project a tough, calm, controlled exterior and are not at ease with irrational things like playing for fun or using intuition. They tend to be rather dominating.

TRY HARD and BE GOOD people find success a terrifying prospect. They project a pleasant, malleable, cooperative exterior and are not at ease with rational things like logical discussion or planning processes. They tend to be rather submissive.

HURRY UP people find commitment a terrifying prospect. They project a busy, energetic and eager exterior and are not at ease when they have nothing to do. They tend to be either isolated or hard to pin down.

Which kind of power do you want?

Power is the application of your energy in particular situations, so it is useful to try and identify which power you want to develop in which kind of situation.

TABLE OF POWERS
In the table (*below*) first identify the areas of your life into which you would like to put more energy by placing a check in the white triangles corresponding to the Life Areas. Three spaces are left vacant for you to add further areas of your own which may not have been listed. You may like to add the name/s of particular people or activities under the life areas listed.

When you have identified the areas, put one or more checks on the chart, indicating which kind of power you would like to develop in that area. Always remember that powers are the different ways of using your energy. For example, under **Occupation** you might want to write the name of your boss and check the column headed **Influential power**, or under **Intimate relationships** you might write "marriage" and check the columns headed **Reformative power** and **Emotional power**.

When you have completed the table you will be able to see at a glance which powers you want to develop in which areas of your life.

REFERENCES
If you want to develop your powers, you will find the following helpful:
SECTION TWO   **Appreciating yourself** (pp. 88-9)
SECTION THREE **Four ways to change a situation** (pp. 106-7)
               Negotiating for what you want (pp. 110-1)
               On being assertive (pp. 112-3)
               Persuading others (pp. 114-5)
               A happier home life (pp. 120-1)

KEY FOR TABLE

▶ THE TWELVE POWERS
▷ LIFE AREAS

Life Areas: Home life, Intimate relationships, Occupation, Financial affairs, Social life, Hobbies, Political, Sexual, Evangelical, Reformative, Congruent, Imaginative

The Twelve Powers: Assertive, Physical, Intellectual, Emotional, Executive, Influential, Learning, Personal development, Community affairs, Other, Other, Other

32

THE POWER BALANCE IN A MARRIAGE

You may like to examine the power balance in your marriage by scoring who you think is the more powerful in the expression of each of the twelve powers within the marriage. Give a score of 3 for **Very powerful**, 2 for **Sometimes powerful**, 1 for **Rarely powerful** and 0 for **Never powerful**. You may find it interesting to ask your partner to do this exercise independently, and then discuss your different ratings.

Status: areas of endeavor

FIRST POSITION
To achieve something ahead of anyone else is to take first position. Direct competition is not usually involved, although a winner, for example, may achieve a first in addition to winning.

Record-breakers are always in first position until someone else runs a mile faster, jumps higher or talks non-stop for a longer period.

Unique firsts are unrepeatable and normally result from teamwork. However, one name is remembered because he or she was either the leader of the team or the first to take the actual step as did John Glenn, the first man on the Moon. Occasionally a temporary, record-breaking first is accorded the status of being unique, such as when a mile was first run in less than four minutes by Roger Bannister.

To be given priority is to be attended to first.

ROALD AMUNDSEN
First to reach the South Pole in 1911, this Norwegian and his team achieved a unique first. Although they will always remain the first to do it, their achievement remained unique for only a short time. Another team, led by Captain Scott for Great Britain, also reached the Pole only a month later.

Amundsen lost his life in 1928 searching for General Nobile, an Italian who had crashed during an attempt to be first to cross the North Pole in an airship.

LEGENDARY STATUS
When stories circulate about people they may be achieving legendary status, even during their own lifetimes. Quite often the legend accelerates after death, especially if their demise was sudden or at a young age.

Legends may be true or complete fabrications; like gossip, legends change in the telling.

An outstanding personality, an unforgettable event or simply a small circumstance create legends. Thousands of people identify with, admire, criticize or are envious of someone and a legend is born. Many pop stars, statesmen, sports people and others in the public eye each build a unique image, but it is public mood and media coverage that in the end turns that image into a legend.

LUCREZIA BORGIA
The beautiful, clever and lively daughter of Pope Alexander VI was a legend in Italy even before she died in 1519.

As a result of her father marrying her off three times for political reasons and also because she established a brilliant court entertaining nobility and artists, such as Titian, gossips accused her of murder and interference in state affairs.

Recent research has proved that this childless but rich and powerful woman devoted much of her time to charitable work among children.

UNCONVENTIONAL STATUS
Someone who behaves differently from the expectations of social convention is being unconventional. For example, the woman of eighty who is successfully studying for a degree would be regarded as unconventional; so would be the man who, by choice, stays at home to rear young children.

Although unconventional status is becoming more commonplace, unconventionality is usually an important personal decision. We are all brought up with beliefs about how we should be. As teenagers we may react against those assumptions for the sake of reaction; in adulthood we can choose to take an unconventional position. We may have to face some opposition or ridicule; being unconventional is regarded by some people as threatening.

LEE MILLER
American photojournalist Lee Miller was a woman who fought convention all her life.

Lee did not want the status of appendage to any man, possessed as she had been by her first husband, Man Ray, a surrealist artist; yet nor did she reject men.

She achieved unconventional status as a World War II photographer and later built upon this reputation in Europe, reporting on what had happened to people after the war for *Vogue* magazine. During all this work she always wanted to go where it was hard to get.

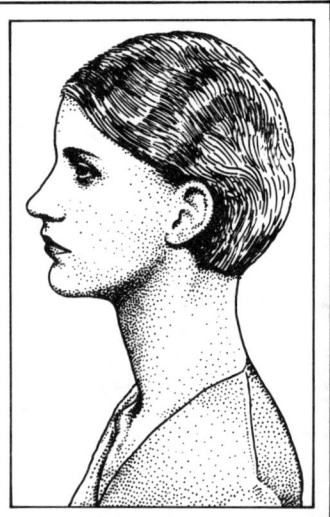

THE BOSS

Recognized by all around as the one in charge, the boss is also expected to take final responsibility. Consequently, being the boss means being at the top of a hierarchy, which itself may be part of a system or of another hierarchy. It can be an isolated position, so bosses often tend to mix socially with people of similar status.

Bosses may be foremen, managers, heads of department, the leader of a team or the owner of a business. Whatever their personal style, there is often something parental about the status of boss and the more parental a boss becomes, the more childish can become those who work for him or her. It is not uncommon for those roles to be reversed when "us and them" attitudes persist between bosses and workers.

HELENA RUBENSTEIN

A self-confessed matriarch, this Polish lady lived to the age of 87 as President of her world famous cosmetic empire.

Her first salon and success came when she emigrated to Australia, and later she opened salons in Paris, London and New York. Eventually her companies appeared in over 100 major cities as she pioneered mass production and marketing methods.

The empire she built is a family heirarchy. She put family members in charge of each new company. Even today the bosses are her nephew and neice.

STARDOM

The outstanding shining light who is also the biggest box office draw is the star of any show. The ability to project personality, capture the sympathy or imagination of millions and keep the cash registers ringing are essential if you want to become a star.

Stars are highly paid because they generate income for the film company, the TV network, the sports club, the sponsors, the promoters and others in the business of selling entertainment. Talent alone will not bring stardom.

To become a star you have to get noticed and be prepared to lose your privacy; stars belong to their fans who love them for what they are. Children and animals are notorious for stealing the limelight and even governments and royal families produce a star turn from time to time.

MARILYN MONROE

From the back streets of Los Angeles, Norma Jean Mortenson (Baker) first gained acclaim as a model and an actress.

By 1953 she had become Marilyn Monroe, the last studio-launched Hollywood star and one of the greatest.

Her extraordinary charisma and physical appeal made her a box office star as the sex-goddess of the 50s, and she was also an outstanding comedienne and dramatic actress.

She died at the age of 38 in 1962 but remains a star in every sense of the word.

THE REPRESENTATIVE

Representation is a position gained because a number of other people have given their support and consent directly. Their decision may have been made by consensus, by vote or by other constitutional processes.

As a representative you may be given some freedom of action within the political parameters of the body you represent, but all representatives are under a certain amount of constraint.

Committees, boards, councils, senates, unions and governments may consist of representatives elected to carry out tasks on behalf of large numbers of people. Similarly, attorneys, lawyers, brokers, assessors and investigators may be retained to do a specific job of representation for one person.

DAG HAMMARSKJOLD

Elected Secretary-General of the United Nations in 1953, this gallant and unselfish Swede was once described by the President of the Assembly as "our supreme international civil servant."

Dag Hammarskjold actively represented the hopes and aspirations of many nations as he set about the task not only of building the authority of the U.N. but of making personal representations.

Notably he negotiated with Chairman Chou En-Lai for the release of eleven American airmen captured during the Korean War.

Status: areas of endeavor (cont.)

THE MEDIATOR
The status of mediator is that of a third party who directly, or by invitation, enables two other parties to settle a dispute between them. The most successful mediators are those who have no vested interest in the issues at stake.

Arbitration is a difficult process, since the situation has usually reached a bitter impasse before the mediator is called in to help.

Mediators are expected to understand the issues at stake and the differing points of view of the protagonists and yet remain objectively fair and just. The mediator has to find a way in which a balance can be achieved between myriad opposing details; it is the mediator's job to reveal an acceptable link, to take a previously unseen viewpoint that satisfactorily accommodates differences and to resist taking sides!

MAIREAD CORRIGAN and BETTY WILLIAMS
Mairead, a secretary, and Betty, a wife and mother, were awarded the 1976 Nobel Peace Prize for initiating the Peace People Movement in Northern Ireland that raised hopes for peace all over the world.

They were true mediators who attempted to bridge the enormous and bitter divisions between religious, national and political groups in Northern Ireland, and to find ways that would resolve and heal the hatred that has been present for so many generations.

THE WINNER
To become a winner generally means competing successfully against others. A more subtle meaning is to succeed against all odds, for example, as meant when people say "He won through a terrible illness."

The desire to win socially, sexually, educationally and at work seems to be a national characteristic in many societies. If you want to be a winner in an activity of your choice, you need to disregard all else and keep your sights on that spot just past the winning post.

Aggression, determination and much hard work goes into any form of competition in order to get the highest score, wipe out opponents, make your way to the top of the ladder or attract the biggest contract.

Potential winners should be aware that this status is only recognized so long as a large number of people accept the rules, which may be bent but never broken!

HAROLD ABRAHAMS
The competitive athletics of this British sportsman have been dramatized in the award-winning film *Chariots of Fire*, made in 1982 just four years after his death.

Harold Abrahams set out to win. He did not take part in races for the joy of it, nor did he run because running was the most important aspect of his life. Becoming the winner was his aim, which he did in Paris at the 1924 Olympic Games, taking a gold medal for the 100 meters.

THE GURU
Guru status is attained by those who are or appear to be knowledgeable in a particular area. Enlightenment is a common characteristic and genuine gurus may be contradictory and even mischievous, taking what we consider serious rather lightly and trivialities very seriously. True compassion, self-esteem and great vulnerability are common among gurus. A guru's role is to prod others into realizing that they, too, are gurus in their own right!

Gurudom is, alas, frequently abused, both by the false guru who manipulates his or her followers, and by followers who either only hear the message they want to hear or who expect their guru to take total responsibility for them.

It has often been said that wanting to be a guru makes it unlikely that it will ever happen!

MAHARISHI MAHESH YOGI
When his own guru died in 1952, the Maharishi took over the work of keeping the tradition of transcendental meditation alive in the Hindu religion in India. Later he traveled to Los Angeles where he founded the Spiritual Regeneration Movement. He has been described as youthful, mischievous and gentle, urging everyone to "Enjoy who you are."

His followers have included the Beatles and many other well-known people, but he urges rich and poor alike to meditate in order to end suffering and realize their full potential.

THE CONTROLER

Controlers hold positions in which they exercise a greater or lesser degree of control over events, other people or themselves.

There are two kinds of control: delegated and manipulated. Controlers by delegation are those in whom we have agreed to put our trust to some extent, for example, drivers, pilots, conductors, dentists and people at the controls of a nuclear power station.

Politicians, personnel selectors, garage mechanics and those who design and construct bridges are also in positions to control events.

Manipulation is a form of competitive control in which it is the order and timing of play rather than the move itself that is important as in selling, advertising and negotiating. Some human relationships are based on covert manipulative controls.

THOMAS EDWARD LAWRENCE

Known as Lawrence of Arabia, he was sent to Cairo at the outbreak of World War I as an intelligence officer attached to the Arab leader Feisal to help in a campaign against the Turks. He learned that to lead his Arab troops he had to live at the same level as them but appear to be better than they were.

He took manipulative control of the campaign, leading the Arabs to triumph. Later he was dismayed at the failure of the Allies to fulfill promises to the newly independent Arab states, for which he felt responsible.

THE SPECIALIST

When others regard you as having exceptional skills and knowledge you may then become known as an expert. A specialist is usually an expert who has narrowed but deepened an interest in a particular aspect of their occupation.

Surgeons, gardeners, computer programmers, cooks, dressmakers, writers, lawyers and almost anyone else in any kind of occupation can become a specialist, usually through long experience.

Being a specialist does not make you "special," i.e. fundamentally different from others; it means you have specific knowledge and skills.

Being regarded as "special" by someone else is quite a different matter. For example, parents may think of their children as special, but this isn't because they are fundamentally different from other human beings.

JONATHAN LIVINGSTONE SEAGULL

The fictional, seagull hero of a story by Richard Bach, Jonathan Livingstone took to learning how to fly with greater expertise than other seagulls.

Soon he became a specialist in flying at speed and could execute streamlined high-speed dives. The more of a specialist he became, the more the rest of the flock turned their backs on him.

Perhaps because he was made an outcast he got the idea that he was not just a specialist, but also special... "an unlimited idea of freedom," not a common gull like the rest of the flock.

SAINTHOOD

To be acknowledged a saint, you have to be canonized by an official religious body, which only occurs long after death.

The implication of sainthood is exceptional holiness which deserves veneration, although many of the saints also achieved something of immediate benefit to many other people, performed miracles or suffered martyrdom in the name of their religious beliefs.

The urge to live in peace and harmony, to follow a code of morality, to give care and consideration to others, and to respect human rights is the desire of many people. This kind of saintliness is a quality of personality much admired by many of us who are all too aware of human frailties.

ST. JOAN OF ARC

A peasant girl from a small French village, Jeanne d'Arc believed she had been called by God to deliver her country from the invading English.

In 1429 the Dauphin let her lead the army against the English at Orleans. After that she is said to have inspired the French and led them to success.

Captured in 1430, she was burnt at the stake after a trial that was rigged in order to "prove" that this nineteen year old woman was a witch! Five centuries later, in 1920, she was canonized and made a saint.

Status: the advantages and pitfalls

Over the years, "rules" emerge in every society that define the status of the people who live in it. In organized competitions, sports, elections and some bureaucracies, the rules may be clear. In other situations, the rules evolve from historical roots, social convenience and struggles for dominance.

There are many ways of changing your status; here are eight of them.

1. Playing the game according to the rules, but doing it better than others. For example, running faster and winning the gold medal.
PITFALL when the rules become more important than the game.

2. Keeping to the rules but bending them. For example, using barter, pressure, flattery, or the "old boy network" to get promotion or a leading role.
PITFALL when you don't return the favors given.

3. Following the rules for a change of status. For example, making promises before witnesses and signing a contract of marriage.
PITFALL when you can't keep your promises.

4. Changing the rules. For example, a couple agreeing to change their roles as child-rearer and salary-earner.
PITFALL when either party cannot accept the reversed dependency relationship or maintain the roles.

5. Dropping out and creating a new set of rules. For example, building a totally new community on a remote island.
PITFALL when human nature takes over the community and re-establishes a conventional dependency structure.

6. Interpreting the rules differently. For example, assuming your equal rights, developing your skills and working your way to become the first female president of the USA!
PITFALL when you begin to behave like a male president!

7. Opting to ignore certain rules while keeping others. For example, employing a clairvoyant to advise you on fiscal policies and ignoring your economic advisers.
PITFALL when the new rule, i.e. the clairvoyancy, begins to look as if it might just be a better tool for making financial decisions.

8. Breaking the rules. For example, operating outside the law to finance a business venture.
PITFALL when you get caught.

Involuntary changes of status
Sometimes natural and sometimes by chance, these are changes in status due to age, bereavement, accident, inheritance and events such as weather, technical developments and political changes.

ADVANTAGES AND PITFALLS OF THE TWELVE KINDS OF STATUS
Each position has its own advantages and pitfalls. If you want to change your present status, you will need to be aware of the risks involved.

FIRST POSITION: achieving something ahead of others.

ADVANTAGES
Immense personal satisfaction; probably public acclaim and recognition; being remembered in history.
PITFALLS
Failure or inability to produce proof that you were the first; lack of public interest; being overtaken by someone who breaks the record again very soon after you established it.

LEGENDARY STATUS: doing something that captures the public imagination.

ADVANTAGES
Easy to expand your reputation or find outlets for new projects.
PITFALLS
Being typecast; losing your personal identity; vulnerability to gossip; one mistake could destroy your status.

UNCONVENTIONAL STATUS: behaving differently from the expectations of social conventions.

ADVANTAGES
Personal fulfillment; freedom from pressures that were unproductive or unpleasant.
PITFALLS
Being laughed at; being regarded as a danger to the status quo or a freak.

THE BOSS: taking charge of a situation and the responsibilities entailed.

ADVANTAGES
Doing things the way you think is best; being regarded as the leader or figurehead; being respected.
PITFALLS
Being used as the scapegoat for all failures; being expected to solve all problems and be all things to all men (and women).

STARDOM: drawing a large box office turnover due to energy and a greater or lesser amount of talent.

ADVANTAGES
Admiration; a position in the limelight; wealth; excitement, travel and many opportunities.
PITFALLS
Loss of privacy; intimate details of your life revealed in public; isolation; a lot of criticism; abuse from cranks.

THE GURU: stimulating others into realizing their full potential.

ADVANTAGES
Affection and adoration; fun, creativity and lack of restrictions; pleasure in the development of others.
PITFALLS
Egomania; opposition from authority and cranks; being regarded as all powerful; energy drain.

A REPRESENTATIVE: acting on behalf of those who have given their proxy.

ADVANTAGES
A clear definition of your purpose; appreciation of the people who elected you; opportunity to work in an area you believe is important.
PITFALLS
Clashes between your personal beliefs and the beliefs of those you represent; limitations to your freedom of action.

THE CONTROLLER: controlling events or situations by delegation or manipulation.

ADVANTAGES
A sense of power or importance; self-reliance; opportunity to make significant decisions.
PITFALLS
Dictatorship; loss of confidence; being assigned powers beyond your capabilities.

THE MEDIATOR: arbitrating in a dispute between two parties.

ADVANTAGES
Non-involvement in the issues at stake; opportunity to hear detailed information about opposing points of view and make a judgement; power to create a new viewpoint and negotiate its acceptance.
PITFALLS
Fatigue through pressure; loss of impartiality; reactions from either party; stalemate.

THE SPECIALIST: deepening knowledge and skills in a selected area of expertise.

ADVANTAGES
International contacts and respect; opportunity to follow an interest to ultimate ends.
PITFALLS
Narrowmindedness; failure to relate knowledge to developments in other areas; getting out of touch.

THE WINNER: competing successfully according to clearly defined rules.

ADVANTAGES
Acclaim, rewards, medals, honors; personal satisfaction; if amateur, the opportunity to turn professional.
PITFALLS
Defending your title; expectations that your performance will always be as good; loss of goals to aim for in future.

SAINTHOOD: being canonized and venerated for exceptional holiness.

ADVANTAGES
Remembered in history; affirmation of your life work and character by a widely recognized body.
PITFALLS
No longer being regarded or remembered as a human being with whom others can easily identify.

Are you a social climber?

Do you want to go up in the world or are you trapped in a rat race? Are you on your way to the top of the ladder of success or have you not yet found the bottom rung?

Finding your position on the SOCIAL STATUS LADDER
Several factors determine the position you attain, ranging from the kind of education and training, income or occupation you have, to the more general aspects of your life. These factors have been categorized to create **Ladders 1-4** (*far right*); the information given (*below*) should enable you to discover your position on each of them. Finally, the scores on **Ladders 1-4** can be added together and the result marked on the **Social Status Ladder** (*far right*).

LADDER 1. (Education & training)
If you left school at the statutory leaving age and have not done any further training or education, mark the first rung.
For every six months of full-time, part-time or in-service education or training you have completed since the statutory leaving age, add another rung.
Then add a rung for every recognized certificate, diploma or degree you have received as a result of this training. Mark the rung you have reached so far. Odd scores should be increased to the next even number (i.e. for a score of 11, assume 12 rungs).

LADDER 2. (Occupation.)
When marking this ladder, do remember that this is NOT an indication of the intrinsic value of your occupation but of the status it gives you in the social pecking order.
If you are retired, unemployed, a student, or do entirely voluntary work, mark the fourth rung up.
If you have paid work of any kind, select which of the descriptions (*right*) best describe your job (whether you are an employee or self-employed) and mark the rung on the ladder corresponding to the figures given in brackets.

Director or principal (**20**)   Junior professional (**12**)
Senior executive (**18**)   Skilled trade (**10**)
Senior professional (**16**)   Semi-skilled (**8**)
Middle professional (**14**)   Unskilled (**6**)

LADDER 3. (Income.)
Include all your personal income, salary, wages, benefits, pensions, dividends, rents, etc. Mark the rung appropriate to your total annual income.
If you are a person wholly or partly dependent upon someone else's income, for example a married person, then you may like to mark two rungs; one for the joint income and one for the income you would have if you were suddenly left on your own.

LADDER 4. (General aspects.)
Start counting from the ground upwards. Add the number of rungs indicated for each item (*below* and *right*) that is true of you.
Add up your total score then half the score to ascertain which rung you have reached on **Ladder 4** (*far right*). Odd scores should be increased to the next even number (ie for a score of 23, assume 12 rungs).
The scores given indicate the difference in status generally accorded to these aspects in Western countries. If you feel some of the scores are inappropriate in your locality, then amend them accordingly, but be consistent.
These scores are not a judgement of you.
+**5** if you are of statutory voting age.
+**4** if you are married and your spouse is living.
+**1** if you have at least one child.
+**5** if you are a member of a titled or nationally famous family.
+**3** if you have no criminal record.
+**4** if you hold an official public position.
+**2** if you are a member of a club or association for which you had to be nominated for membership.
+**3** if you have been awarded an official title, cup or prize for any kind of activity.
+**3** if you have had positive publicity in the national media on more than two occasions.
+**2** if you have been asked to officiate in any capacity at a public function.
+**1** for each friend you have who is a well-known or influential personality. (Maximum score +**5**.)
+**3** if you run your own business.

The SOCIAL STATUS LADDER
Add up the scores achieved on each of **Ladders 1-4**, count the same number of rungs from ground level, and then mark the highest rung you reach. This position indicates your present social status.
Now repeat the whole exercise to find your position ten years ago. Has your social status risen since then? If you are more than 20 rungs farther up the ladder, you are a social climber.
You may like to estimate where you would like to be in ten years' time.

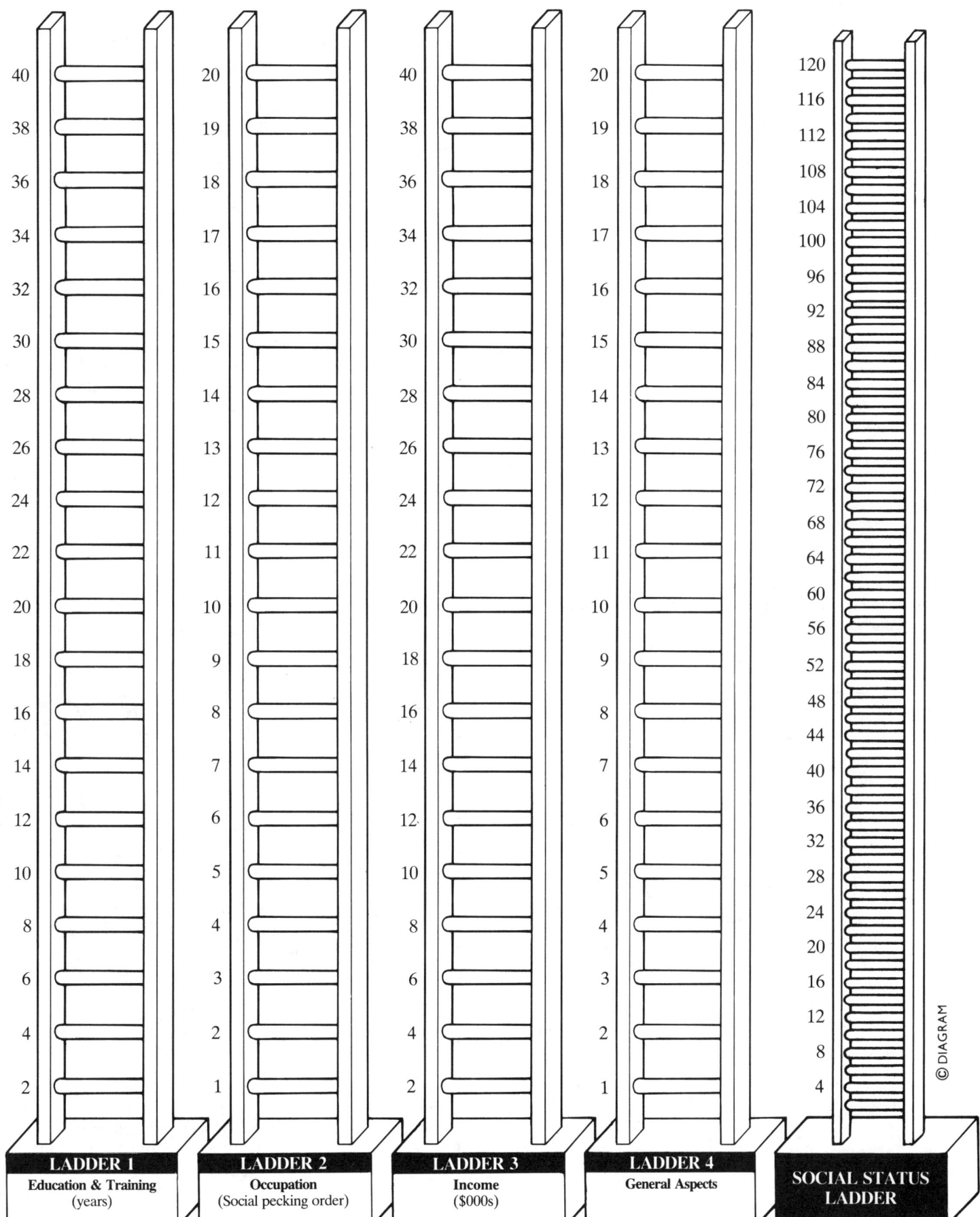

Which status do you want?

Your status is your position in relationship to a group of other people according to rules defined by a consensus of opinion.

For example, Jim, aged 35, is a childless married man, and is a high school teacher.

On the other hand, Laura, aged 35, is a widow with two children, and is a high school teacher.

Although both Laura and Jim hold the same kind of job-status, their actual position in society is affected by their sex, color, age, religion and their marital and parental status. It is interesting that the terms in which we describe people are those from which we form an opinion about their status.

Don't break the rules
If you want to retain your status, whatever it is, you should not break the rules. So long as you don't step over the boundary of opinion that defines your status, then your position should be stable.

CHANGING YOUR STATUS
It is clear that your status is fixed in some respects by the consensus of opinion of millions of people which changes slowly. However, you have the freedom to choose how you relate to others within your own smaller circle of contacts, by choosing which form of dependency you prefer, and is best for you, in each type of relationship. In this way you can decide which position to take and determine your status.

THREE STATES OF DEPENDENCY
You depend on others for your status and they depend on you to keep to the rules governing your status. To take the best advantage of your position, you need to understand the nature of the dependency relationship and use it.

In choosing which positions you would like to occupy in different areas of your life, you will also be choosing which kind of dependency states best suit you.

There are three ways in which dependency relationships are organized: by hierarchy, by network, and by differences.

The dependency of each kind of status
Above the descriptive text of each of the three dependencies (*below* and *right*) are seven kinds of status, four described earlier in this section, together with three additional examples (shown in *italic* typeface). These represent only a few of the hundreds of types of status. You may like to add any of your own to the appropriate list, for example, in which of the three types of dependency organizations do you place yourself as husband, wife, parent, worker, jogger, cook, dog-owner, committee member, motorist, lover, etc? Consider the relationship between yourself and the other in order to make your choices.

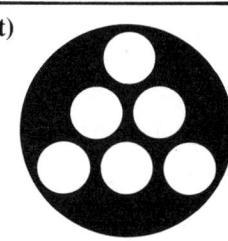

BY HIERARCHY (Order-dependent)
First Position
The Boss
Stardom
The Winner
Income-status
Gender-status
Age-status

This is the most common state of dependency, often known as the *pecking order*. In a large group there can be more than one person in each position from top to bottom, all of whom are order-dependent.

All top positions depend on there being many lower positions. In a top position, you have the advantage of a large body of support, rather like a triangle with you on the top point. Usually the one on top has something that the others want.

If you are lower down, you usually depend on the person at the top to take the responsibility and make the decisions. In return for your support you expect to bask in their reflected glory.

Two people can also form a mini-hierarchy in which one is top dog and the other the under dog; one dominant and the other submissive. While it may appear that the dominant one has the upper hand, the submissive one can control the situation too, by withdrawing the support that keeps the dominant one on top.

BY NETWORK (Inter-dependent)

The Representative
The Controler
The Mediator
The Guru
CB radio
The Red Cross
Interpol

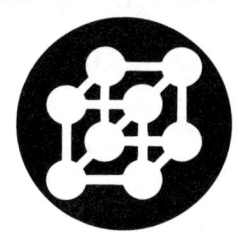

In a network there is interdependence, each person helping to hold the network together. If one person withdraws, the network is broken and everyone in it has to adjust in order to close the gap. Similarly, if everyone in a network is not pulling their weight, the whole organization has to adjust.

The power and the responsibility is generally shared out among the members of a network and changes usually occur by agreement or by natural selection.

The advantage of having a position in a network is that your skills and abilities match your status and you can freely contact the other members of the network without having to use the channels defined in a hierarchy.

A small network can exist within a larger hierarchy, and members of networks who try to build empires may turn the whole system into a hierarchy if other people support them.

BY DIFFERENCES (Independent)

Legendary status
Unconventional status
The Specialist
Sainthood
Minority groups
A football referee
Shangri-La

Independent individuals or groups of people become outsiders when they cease to depend upon each other for their social status.

To maintain this kind of status takes a lot of courage, determination or skill. Sometimes people who simply feel they have little in common with others around them find themselves in this position.

For example, stepping off a plane alone in a foreign country where the customs, the language and the climate are unfamiliar makes a person an instant outsider. The advantage to be gained from this situation is a fresh view of another culture and of oneself.

Small groups of people who identify with each other form sets for mutual support within the alien culture. Sets of people may overlap with each other and with sets of people in the culture itself.

Independent sets of people and independent individuals may form a network when they communicate with each other, or they may settle into a hierarchy of sets.

TABLE OF DEPENDENCIES

AREAS OF LIFE	In a hierarchy (Order-dependent)	In a network (Inter-dependent)	In Different sets (Independent)
Intimate relationship			
Family life			
At work			
Income			
Social life			
Hobbies			
Local community			
Health care			
Gender			
Nationality/race			
Age			
Personal talent			
Training			

In the table of dependencies (*above*), check which state of dependency you would prefer in each of the listed areas of your life, adding any other areas that are applicable to you.

Do your choices match your personality?
Order-dependent status would be chosen by people who are either competitive or use the power of compliance.
Inter-dependent status would be chosen by people who enjoy cooperation.
Independent status would be chosen by people who see themselves as outsiders.

REFERENCES
To help you achieve your preferred status, turn to:
SECTION ONE   **What is your wealth-potential?** (pp. 20-1)
              Do you want to be more powerful? (pp. 30-1)
              Are you a challenge-seeker? (pp. 50-1)
SECTION TWO   **What are you good at?** (pp. 90-1)
SECTION THREE **Developing a network** (pp. 132-3)
              Getting yourself trained (pp. 136-7)
              Knowing what they want (pp. 142-3)
              Managing others (pp. 146-7)

Challenge: areas of endeavor

TO PIONEER

Pioneers begin by doing something ordinary in an entirely new and original way, which may or may not be recognized and followed by others.

The kind of venture a pioneer undertakes may have been done many times before, such as running a business, a school or a family. It is the way in which we do many kinds of ordinary things that gives us all some pioneer potential.

A pioneer is not only a self-directed individual with strong beliefs about how a thing should or could be done but is also one who puts those beliefs into action, disregarding any personal cost. Hence, fame and fortune rarely go hand-in-hand with pioneering.

The word *pioneer* derives from an old French name given to those infantrymen who went ahead to cut a route for the main body of troops to follow later.

BRIGHAM YOUNG

When Joseph Smith, the founder of the Mormon Church, was lynched in 1844, Brigham Young took command. His belief in the Mormon way of life drove him to find a place for the Mormons to settle, once and for all.

He pioneered a route through the wilderness from Illinois to the Salt Lake area of Utah, a task that took three years.

Even as the Mormons arrived in Utah, Brigham Young, in the way of all pioneers, had already prepared to ease their arrival by organizing reception centers and irrigation schemes.

TO BUILD

The challenge that spurs a builder into action is to establish gradually something of lasting value by a process of construction.

Some builders put solid materials together to build a new town, a monument, a ship, a landscape, a model, a computer or a piece of furniture. Others prefer to combine people, money or talents to build teams, bank accounts, organizations or whole empires.

A builder is essentially a practical person with a strong set of values. What is built must be indestructible and have a purpose that is realistic. A builder wants the finished project to be greater than the sum of its parts. Empire-builders recognize the collective power of a well-constructed organization. The climax of satisfaction for a builder is reached when putting the last brick into its correct place.

ALEXANDRE-GUSTAVE EIFFEL

For the French Government's exhibition in 1889 to commemorate the French Revolution, Eiffel was commissioned to build a symbolic monument. His 984 ft (300m) wrought iron tower caused a stir; nothing like it had been built before and it was twice the height of the dome of St Peter's in Rome.

To Eiffel it was a culmination of his work as a builder of bridges; a revolution in civil engineering construction and design. He was appropriately nicknamed "the Magician of Iron."

TO DISCOVER

Many of us like to poke around, probing the secrets of the world, hoping to find something that was previously unknown or that has lain hidden for many years.

True discoverers not only have an insatiable desire to find out what's going on but they also need to make sense of it and to tell others about it.

An intense, but innocent, curiosity drives all discoverers. They will probe outer space and inner space, discovering a myriad of details that they try to make into a sensible whole. They move from the particular to the general, i.e. by a process of induction. Apparently doing things just to see what happens, they frequently reveal new worlds that bring benefit to mankind, if not always to themselves.

CHRISTOPHER COLUMBUS

In the style of all discoverers, Columbus put two and two together and made five. He hoped to find the riches of China and India when he sailed west across the Atlantic in 1492. Instead he discovered a route to the West Indies and to North & South America. Yet he hardly realized what he had discovered, for while his probing brought many benefits to others over the centuries, he himself died in poverty at the age of 47.

Like all discoverers, he boasted of his achievements, which made this courageous man rather unpopular in his time.

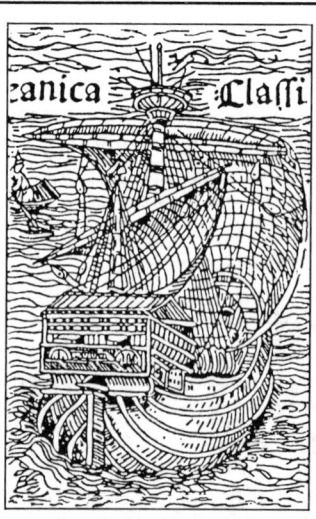

TO NURTURE

To nurture is to give help and support to another without return. While those who accept this kind of challenge are sensitive to the needs of the life they nourish, they neither sacrifice themselves nor do they take possession of the other. People who offer nurturing usually learn a great deal about themselves as they do it, so honesty and a strong grounding in reality are essential qualities.

People who nurture give long-term attention to plants, to animals, to other people or sometimes to small groups of people. They may encourage the development of a particular talent, help a person to learn or take the responsibility for an intensive training program; whatever form their nurturing takes, they encourage independence and are consequently rarely well known themselves.

ANNE MANSFIELD SULLIVAN

It is no surprise if you have never heard of Miss Sullivan, for she was the American teacher who, in 1887, began to nurture the seven-year-old Helen Keller who had been deaf, blind and mute since an early childhood illness.

Miss Sullivan taught her pupil to communicate so well that Helen Keller attained her own sense of independence and, after graduating, devoted her own life to promoting education for others who were similarly incapacitated, with the continued help of Anne Sullivan.

TO CREATE

The urge to create usually emerges unexpectedly. At a most inappropriate moment when busy doing something else, inspiration comes and will quickly drift away unless we are ready for it and know what to do with it. An idea, a design, a solution or a sudden flash of insight can occur to anyone; truly creative people are those who can grasp these fleeting ideas and give them form for others to see, hear, and enjoy.

Since creativity is 1% inspiration and 99% hard work, creators have to be thoroughly accomplished in the skills of their trade, profession or occupation.

Creative insight can reveal hidden worlds both of beauty and of horror, which are disturbing and challenging in themselves and can lead to the edge of madness. Many creators struggle to give full expression to these insights at great personal cost.

VINCENT VAN GOGH

For 37 tempestuous years, Van Gogh, the Dutch artist, was inspired to paint with strength and color the passion that he saw in people and in the landscape, which he struggled to express at the cost of his own sanity, finally shooting himself in 1890.

Named after a dead brother, he always felt unwanted. His younger brother, Theo, was his only link with security. He found inspiration in ordinary people and ordinary things; giving lasting form to the terrible power of beauty in life itself.

TO MASTER

The master is one who has learnt a skill so well that using it becomes effortless. When we are able to do something without effort, we are free to express ourselves fully. The fluent touch-typist is no longer hampered by having to look at which key to press, the racing driver and the car become one and the dance takes over the dancer.

The mastery of a skill requires dedication to the exclusion of everything else, at least while the skill is being learnt. Practice for long hours is not uncommon and many small steps are climbed toward improved performance. A master performs with such ease that we are entranced by the results and never embarrassed by the performance.

JOSEPH CONRAD

Born a Pole in 1857, Jozef Teodor Konrad Korzeniowski had a passion for everything British and was destined to become a master three times over.

First a master seaman in the British Navy, he set about learning English, mastering a language that is notorious for its illogical contrariness!

Finally he became a master novelist who has entranced thousands of readers with his powers of description, drama and characterization.

Challenge: areas of endeavor (cont.)

TO INVENT
Invention is taking delight in the practical activity of putting things together in such a way that something new happens; the challenge is to make an idea work, one way or another.

Something to improve visibility in fog, a failsafe can-opener, a cheaper form of energy, a patent baby-feeder or an indestructible car... many of us have a dream world full of marvellous inventions.

The true inventor makes these dreams a reality, often by trial and failure, and is frequently short of funds for the next trial run. Inventive people often have a passion to bring order out of chaos.

Inventors have a reputation for being clever eccentrics who *potter* about in sheds or laboratories full of strange contraptions. The ability to *play around with things* is crucial to successful invention.

PERCY SHAW
In 1933, a Yorkshire (UK) road repair man, Percy Shaw, caught the reflected eyes of a cat in his car headlights. This gave him the idea of inventing the "cat's-eye," a reflective roadstud, now used down the center of roads. He also invented a way of keeping them clear; depressed by a car wheel, the rubber mounting wipes the reflectors clean.

Months of experimenting and a trial run of 50 studs placed at a crossroads strained his finances, but dimmed headlights and the blackout during World War II finally proved their worth.

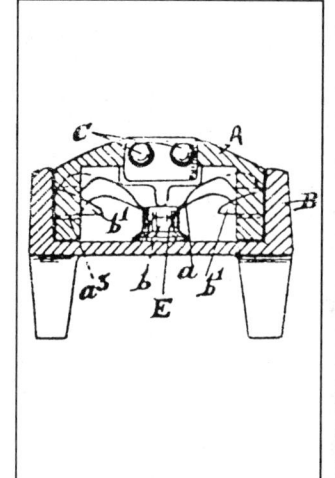

TO SOLVE
Meticulous attention given to unraveling and understanding *all* aspects of a situation leads to the solution of problems. To solve a mystery, a crossword puzzle or a murder investigation, all previous assumptions have to be challenged. To do this takes courage, patience, a cool unflustered mind and a taste for truth, even when unpalatable.

We all want problems of employment, health, finance or social justice to be solved; few of us are prepared to break through the two-dimensional barriers of conventional beliefs in order to find those solutions. The person who takes up the challenge to become a solver is neither left or right wing nor in the center; the solver is usually the one who steps, alone, into a new dimension.

GALILEO GALILEI
The Italian astronomer and physicist, Galileo, solved many scientific problems by patient observation and a cool, objective passion for truth.

A professor of mathematics at the University of Padua, he presented revolutionary solutions to many problems of speed, movement and gravity.

Early in the 17th century he collected evidence through his own astronomical telescope, to prove that the planets moved round the Sun; a theory that Polish astronomer, Copernicus, had suggested a century earlier.

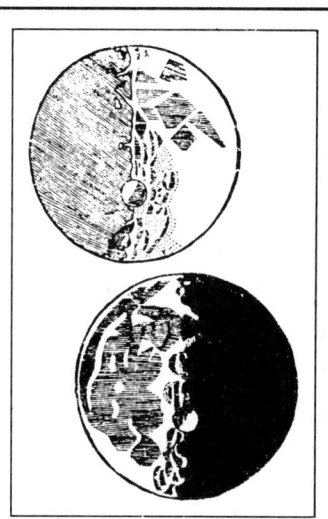

TO EXPLORE
The freedom to travel, investigate, examine, touch and enjoy a place on earth, in outer space or in the imagination would appeal to many of us. But comfort and security are an encumbrance to a born explorer to whom the act of exploration is a total way of life. Even those who explore the imagination actually *live* in it.

Shangri-la, the bottom of the ocean, the streets of San Francisco, the dark side of the moon, or the depths of a relationship... explorers take the broad view and make deductions from it. Their driving ambition is to push back barriers and expand horizons. It is of little consequence to an explorer if the ground has been covered by someone before, they will come to their own individual conclusions.

SIR HENRY MORTON STANLEY
Famous for his greeting, "Dr. Livingstone, I presume," Stanley was a Welsh orphan who ran away to New Orleans. That was only the beginning of his urge to explore the world, which he did both in the U.S. Navy and as a foreign reporter for the New York Herald.

In 1869 the Herald sent him to Africa to find the Scottish missionary and explorer, Dr. David Livingstone, who had set out to trace the source of the Nile. Their famous meeting was at Ujiji. Livingstone refused to return to Europe; exploration was also his way of life.

TO OVERCOME
To prevail, by willful effort and control, over circumstances that might otherwise be intolerable, is the challenge of overcoming adversity or opposition.

A personal disability, tragedy or piece of bad luck can be overcome by those who accept the challenge and find a way to do it. Political repression or social injustices are some of the challenges others accept.

A sense of self worth and endless energy resources are usually required to succeed. Those who set out to overcome either adversity or opposition must have determination, discipline and a long-term plan. The means they use may be active or passive... they may become irresistible forces or immovable objects; either way, they rarely stop trying.

EMMELINE PANKHURST
Emmeline fought all her life against political and social repression that had denied women the vote in Britain. The Women's Social and Political Union, which she founded in 1903 in Manchester, tried to overcome opposition by reasoned argument.

The government of the day agreed in principle, but when pressed to take action, used imprisonment to repress the women even further. However, Emmeline and the WSPU members persisted, even by chaining themselves to railings, until all women were given the vote in 1928.

TO RISK
Those who take risks are never fearless, in fact they welcome the state of readiness that is stimulated by fear and use it to accomplish something; all great actors are familiar with stage fright.

A risk may be physical, such as walking a tightrope across Niagara Falls, or driving a car, but emotion is always involved. Speculating on the stock market or being honest to a lover may be emotionally risky.

Some people risk their reputations and even put others at risk. A risk-taker is a person who is spurred by the challenge to survive against the odds. A high toleration of pre-action anxiety and an immaculate sense of timing are characteristic of genuine risk-takers. They are usually better prepared than anyone for the unexpected and even then sometimes don't survive.

PETER HABELER & RHEINHOLD MESSNER
These two Germans risked climbing to the top of Mount Everest without the use of oxygen equipment. In 1978, they joined a traditional expedition who gave them no encouragement.

They knew they were risking brain damage, burst blood vessels, lunacy and death. Even Sherpas, who are acclimatized, have died without oxygen. At 2,438m (18,000ft) they made a pact that one would carry on and not risk failure, even if the other was affected. They both survived, but only just.

TO SELF-ACTUALIZE
Self-actualization is the development of our talents to their fullest extent in ways that are uniquely individual. For many of us, the urge to become who we truly are may only be recognized intuitively after years of trying to become what we think we ought to be. For others, the way forward has always been perfectly clear, though not always easy.

Self-actualizers are familiar with change as they continue to discover new parts of themselves; they also genuinely "enjoy themselves."

The urge to escape from a particular way of life may be the first indication that we are ready for yet another change; circumstances, too, may give us a push in the right direction. To accept the challenge is to lose the self we already know!

MARK TWAIN
Self-actualization isn't something that ever has an end but Samuel Langhorne Clemens certainly had the humor and satire for it. He was willing to change his name at the request of an editor and became Mark Twain, reporter, though his occupations and places of residence continued to change frequently. He hated to be tied down, but he did stay married. His finances, too, were always changing, but the success of *Tom Sawyer* and *Huckleberry Finn* resolved his debts. As for enjoying himself, his writing is testimony to that.

Challenge: the advantages and pitfalls

The five characteristics common to all challenges each have their own advantages and pitfalls.

1 A challenge is concerned with change.
ADVANTAGES
The generation of new ideas, material improvements and advances in social conditions, knowledge and skills.
PITFALLS
A danger of throwing out what is old in favor of something new without real consideration.

2 Challenge is concerned more with process than with achieving an end-result.
ADVANTAGES
Pleasure in the "here and now," improvement of skills, satisfaction from activity and stimulation.
PITFALLS
The activity may never reach any kind of conclusion or a job may never get finished.

3 A challenge is very demanding and fully involving.
ADVANTAGES
There is always plenty to be done and little likelihood of becoming too attached to things, people or places.
PITFALLS
There may be a tendency to become a fanatic who is always short of time or to become totally isolated without family, friends, home or basic comforts.

4 To accept a challenge requires flexibility and adaptability.
ADVANTAGES
Opportunity to use a range of talents and gain a wide variety of experience.
PITFALLS
A danger of dissipating energy and of becoming unreliable, confused or lost.

5 Challenges demand originality.
ADVANTAGES
Considerable opportunity for self-expression.
PITFALLS
Becoming regarded as odd, non-conformist and eccentric or of becoming addicted to originality for its own sake and losing track of any real challenges.

ADVANTAGES AND PITFALLS OF THE TWELVE CHALLENGES.
Each type of challenge has its own joys and sorrows. It would be wise to be aware of them all, since challenge-seekers usually become involved in more than one kind of challenge.

However, most people who seek a challenge will also enjoy the added challenge of finding a way to turn pitfalls into advantages. More than anyone else, true challenge-seekers know the value of failures, losses and disappointments.

PIONEERING the way for others to follow because you believe yours is the right way.

ADVANTAGES
You can do something in your own way and don't have to compromise your beliefs.
PITFALLS
Losing faith in what you are doing or being ostracized because others try to follow your direction.

BUILDING something that is greater than the sum of its parts by a process of gradual construction.

ADVANTAGES
Opportunity to exercise a sense of priority in organization and an ability to see the composite value of small parts.
PITFALLS
The parts may be faulty or difficult to obtain; the building or organization may be weak or even collapse; popular opinion may devalue your work.

DISCOVERING by making sense of something and sharing it with others.

ADVANTAGES
You can satisfy a desire to be "in the know" and increase your understanding of the world.
PITFALLS
Getting bogged down in a mass of detail or reaching the wrong conclusion; being ignored or laughed at when you try to communicate.

NURTURING by encouraging the independent development of another.

ADVANTAGES
Using your talents of perception and empathy while gaining satisfaction from watching something grow.
PITFALLS
The one nurtured resents help or becomes totally demanding; danger of neglecting your own development.

CREATING by giving form to indefinable insights and inspirations.

ADVANTAGES
Having an outlet for a driving passion. Communicating intuitively with others directly or symbolically.
PITFALLS
Frustration through lack of skill; unhappiness, insanity, violence, suicide, poverty, etc.

EXPLORING by expanding horizons and taking a broad view.

ADVANTAGES
Total freedom of movement and independence of spirit.
PITFALLS
You may trip up over a detail you missed, get lost, belong nowhere or inadvertently wander into a swamp.

MASTERING a skill until it becomes effortless.

ADVANTAGES
Being able to do something superbly well with ease and continue learning with hardly any effort at all.
PITFALLS
Becoming so concerned with technique that depression sets in or your performance is frigid.

OVERCOMING oppression or adversity by persistence and effort.

ADVANTAGES
Opportunity to develop self worth and discipline while giving constructive expression to anger.
PITFALLS
Danger of becoming a masochist or an extremist of one kind or another; you may encounter violent resistance.

INVENTING something new that has practical application.

ADVANTAGES
Pleasure gained from playing with things and ideas. You might even get rich if you remember to patent it.
PITFALLS
Somebody steals your invention or makes it better than you do; stagnation through acquiring too much junk.

RISKING in order to survive against all odds.

ADVANTAGES
Survival, in whatever terms that are meaningful to you; beating the odds; satisfying the gambler in you.
PITFALLS
Failure to survive: death, disability, pain, loss of reputation, collapse, rejection, etc.

SOLVING a problem by unraveling every knot.

ADVANTAGES
Being able to get to the heart of a matter and manipulate from all manner of alternative viewpoints.
PITFALLS
Working in secrecy due to threats made by those who find your solutions totally unacceptable; becoming dishonest or impatient.

SELF-ACTUALIZING by developing talents to their fullest extent in a very personal way.

ADVANTAGES
Joy in living, honest communication with others, experience of a full range of emotions, skills, etc.
PITFALLS
Coming up against something in yourself that you allow to stop the process; loss of social identity.

Are you a challenge-seeker?

Do you welcome change?
All real challenges are concerned with changes, whether as variety or as a fundamental shift. Challenge-seekers often change the way they are doing something and either bring about a change or change themselves as they become involved in their particular challenge.

A challenge is an active process; all processes cause some kind of transformation or change to take place.

Those who regard any potential change with distrust or suspicion, or who prefer stability and security, should examine their motives when taking up a challenge; it may only be a pseudo-challenge.

For example, Bill feels insulted and challenges Tom to a duel with pistols at dawn. In accepting, Tom is not seeking a change; defense of honor, status or power are usually the primary motives for fighting a duel. Of

course there is a risk that Tom or Bill may end up injured or dead, but that is a secondary consideration.

Do you get bored when there's nothing to do?
Challenge-seekers like to be up and doing, forever seeking yet another route to pioneer, another skill to master, another risk to take or another problem to be solved.

Challenge-seekers are rarely content to sit back on their laurels or count their blessings. For example, when on vacation, Bob likes to get away from it all and relax in the sun with Mary, taking life easy and generally doing nothing much at all. A vacation to Bob is a time to recharge his energy, ready for his return to work as the principal of a large school.

Mary, on the other hand, misses the telephone, the newspapers and the TV. She also wants to visit places of interest and talk to the people. Lying on the beach is a waste of time to Mary, she would rather go

beachcombing or help the children to build elaborate sandcastles. Can you guess which of them is the challenge-seeker?

Do you enjoy being "different"?
An originality which can be demonstrated is common among challenge-seekers. They may like to dress differently, live differently, time their day differently or even just sign their names differently.

Strict conformity to every convention, tradition or social expectation is anathema to a challenge-seeker in at least one, if not more, aspects of daily life.

For example, George started work in a bank because he wanted to explore the world of finance, but his junior position did not offer him much challenge, so he began arriving each morning with a flower pinned to his immaculate suit. He persuaded his mother to make him a yellow velvet bowler hat and borrowed his grandfather's elaborately hand-carved umbrella. George's arrival at the bank each morning became quite an event. On the day he arrived with dollar signs painted in bright colours on his briefcase, his manager was wise enough to recognize and encourage his talents. George became a very creative investment consultant.

Is the process more important than the result?
Although a satisfactory conclusion is pleasant, does the activity of doing something interest you more than getting it finished? Do you welcome a succession of new mini-challenges as you get more deeply involved with the process of learning, building, risking, creating, etc?

Challenge-seekers don't usually have very specific aims. For example, if Jane definitely wants to become an airline pilot, her primary motive may be status, power or wealth, but not challenge, unless it is the challenge of overcoming resistance to a woman becoming an airline pilot. In that case, her suitability for the job would be questionable and it would be more appropriate if she took up the challenge using different means.

Similarly, if she feels the challenge to master flying,

then becoming an airline pilot is unlikely to satisfy her ambition. Airline pilots may spend a lot of their time in the air, but have little opportunity to enjoy the actual process of flying.

Are you flexible, adaptable, or even eccentric?
If you accept one kind of challenge, you are likely to become involved temporarily in other challenges. For example, an inventor may have to overcome the cynicism of others, the pioneer may need to invent a way of building a temporary bridge and a sideways step may have to be taken to discover new facts before a problem can be solved satisfactorily.

Challenge-seekers do not always take the logical course of action; they can adapt their point of view or flex their imagination to generate new directions.

For example, the executives of a wholesale distributing company were discussing problems of storage space; they had been offered extra ground space adjoining their warehouse, but it was too expensive. The office junior entered during the

discussion, bringing cups of tea. "What you need is a sky-hook," she commented cheekily, taking an eccentric leap typical of challenge-seekers. Eventually the flat roof was used for extra storage.

Read the questions in the table (*below*) and select one of the 4 answers: YES, SOMETIMES, VERY RARELY or DEFINITELY NOT. Enter the value of the answers in the appropriate boxes and add up your scores.

Are you a challenge-seeker?	YES Scores 3	SOMETIMES Scores 2	VERY RARELY Scores 1	DEFINITELY NOT Scores 0
1 Do you welcome change?				
2 Is the process of doing something more important than the result?				
3 Do you get bored when you have nothing to do?				
4 Are you flexible, adaptable or even a little eccentric?				
5 Do you enjoy being "different"?				
Totals				
Total Score				

If your total is 10 or more you are likely to be a challenge-seeker.
If your total is from 9 to 5 you may sometimes enjoy a challenge.
If your score is 4 or less, you probably dislike challenges.

Which kind of challenge do you want?

Finding a challenge
The quickest and most efficient way to find which kind of challenge appeals to you is to become aware of those seemingly irrational feelings that are commonly known as intuition. Intuition is a wonderful storehouse of normally unconscious ideas, ambitions, information and dormant talents.

How do you know when your intuition is working?
You feel a growing sense of excitement and your interest in someone or something gradually accelerates. You notice an idea keeps coming into your thoughts, or a particular place, a new hobby or a new group of people seem increasingly more attractive, while odd notions or strong convictions begin to demand your attention.

For example, you casually pick up a magazine and in it read a story or article that captures your imagination... but it doesn't end there. Over some weeks or months it begins to dawn on you that you would like to do something like that.

Challenge-seekers rely upon their intuition for direction
The successful ones also use their past experience to distinguish between valuable intuitive knowledge about themselves and those occasionally inappropriate or neurotic intuitive urges that would only lead to a dead end. If you are unaccustomed to using your own intuitive faculties, it will take a little practice to learn to distinguish between the two.

How to distinguish valuable from neurotic intuition
Valuable intuitive information usually emerges slowly. As it begins to demand more and more of your attention, your long-standing interest in something else will begin to wane or you may find you have to make a big effort to do something that previously was easy.

A sudden passionate interest in someone or something should be treated with a little caution and may need to be tested out with reality before proceeding further, as your commitment may vanish just as suddenly.

An example familiar to many of us is the phenomenon of intuitively "falling madly in love at first sight." While it is true that sometimes a good, long-term relationship becomes established, quite often it doesn't work out in the long run or at best is only partially satisfying. Making the same mistake several times is a painful but certain way of distinguishing between valuable and neurotic intuitive desires!

How to access your intuition
If you rarely feel excitement, if you tie yourself up in knots full of shoulds and oughts or if you control your life with a will of iron, then to access your intuition, you will have to make space for it to surface. Here is a space-making process that can be helpful.

A way to make space for your intuition
On your own and at your own pace, first do some simple, general physical activities (*not* structured exercises). Playing around in a swimming pool, digging the garden, free dancing, cleaning the car, letting the dog take you for a walk or a variety of household chores would be fine. Avoid anything that is repetitively rhythmic or that needs too much thought. Enjoy it until you feel warm and glowing all over and are tired but not totally exhausted.

Then relax in comfort where you won't be disturbed, perhaps with some light music, at low volume, or in a room perfumed by flowers. Put your attention only on where and what you are feeling inside your own body. Search casually for tickling, pulsing, throbbing or fizzing sensations. Take note of where you feel warm or a bit stiff! Enquire gently how your toes are feeling and perhaps give them a friendly wriggle. Visit all parts of yourself without expectations. You might even doze for a while. Then get up when you feel like it and do whatever pleases you.

During this process, your intuition will be stirring, all you have to do is to welcome it; all kinds of ideas and odd notions will begin to take form, though not necessarily immediately. The more you begin to enjoy this space-making process, the easier it will become to access your intuitive storehouse.

Are there limits to intuition?
The only barriers to your intuition will be in your attitude of mind... the limitations which you mentally place on yourself.

For example, if you conclude that the space-making process sounds silly or illogical, *before you have tried it*, this is your first barrier.

If you judge yourself to be a terrible failure just because nothing much happens the first time you try it, that could be another of your barriers, or you could limit yourself by wondering if a better idea that occurs to you while you are doing it is "right." Always assume it is and check it out for yourself. In the end, everyone finds their own best process.

REFERENCES
To understand your barriers more clearly turn to:
SECTION TWO **What are your limitations?** (pp. 92-3)

USING YOUR INTUITION TO FIND A CHALLENGE

Without giving each statement (*below*) too much thought, check the ones that feel familiar to you or that appeal to you in column **A**. They are all characteristics of different kinds of challenge-seekers.

Now go through the list again and mark the two or three that you feel are most true of you in column **B**. Then find out which kind of challenges you have chosen by checking the numbers on the key list of challenges (*below*).

	A	B
1 I love finding out how to make my ideas work.		
2 I like to get things organized in a practical way.		
3 I love being on the move and traveling.		
4 I like to get to the root of a matter.		
5 I really prefer doing things my own way.		
6 I can't bear not knowing what's going on.		
7 I enjoy taking calculated risks.		
8 I often feel the need to express myself.		
9 I enjoy practising things.		
10 I like being in control of a situation.		
11 I really enjoy myself most of the time.		
12 I like to see people doing well.		

Key list of challenges

1 Inventing   2 Building   3 Exploring   4 Solving

5 Pioneering   6 Discovering   7 Risk-taking   8 Creating

9 Mastering   10 Overcoming   11 Self-actualizing   12 Nurturing

Confirming your selection of challenges

By studying the pitfalls associated with the type of challenges you have selected, you can see if your selection is accurate. (Refer to **Challenge: The advantages and pitfalls** (pp. 48-9).) Pitfalls that are familiar to you will confirm your choices; every challenge has its own type of pitfalls which stimulate challenge-seekers to resolve them.

Confusion or conflict

If you are experiencing doubt, confusion or conflict about your selection of challenge, then you can get more information from the following:

REFERENCES

SECTION TWO	**What are you good at** (pp. 90-1)
SECTION THREE	**Making decisions** (pp. 124-5)
	Resolving conflicts (pp. 148-9)

Well-being: areas of endeavor

ENERGY

Energy is what we need to keep us alive and kicking.

Some people appear to languish for days on end before they spring into life and become so energetic they leave others behind.

Other people seem to be able to keep up a fairly steady pace day after day, year by year. It would appear that different people are born with different levels of energy.

The quality of a person's energy may be as important as the quantity when it is put to use. Chopping wood, having children, standing on your head, or making a decision all require different kinds of energy.

Some positive energy is also required to fight ill-health, to sustain good health and to cope with the difficulties of a permanent handicap.

QUEEN VICTORIA

Her name now synonymous with energy that is solidly enduring, Victoria became Queen of Great Britain at the age of 18 in 1837, ruled for 64 years, had nine children and increased the advisory influence of the throne in politics.

The matriarch of British history, she was a plump, inquisitive and energetic woman with quick hands, a sharp eye and a taste for domestic morality, plain clothes, hard work and correct manners. Even mourning the death of her beloved Albert, she carried out her duties fully and revived to head the expanding Empire.

BEAUTY

It has often been said that beauty is only skin deep and it is true that those who want to be beautiful spend a lot of time and effort on their appearance.

Many people would agree that when they look good, they feel good; others would argue that when you feel good, you also look good! You will have to decide for yourself what exactly it is you want if being beautiful is one of your aims.

Bone structure, body size, hair color and style, skin condition, clothes, the way you walk and talk, the condition of your teeth, the way you smell, your attitudes and general outlook are the kinds of things you will have to take into account.

HELEN OF TROY

In Greek mythology, the young shepherd, Paris, was called upon to decide which was the fairest of three goddesses, each of whom offered him an inducement to choose her. Athena promised wisdom and glory, Hera promised wealth and power but Aphrodite promised he should have the most beautiful earthly woman...Helen.

He chose Aphrodite, carrying the beautiful Helen off to Troy as his wife. As she had already been married to the King of Spartaca, so the myth grew that her beauty caused the Trojan Wars.

YOUTH

If a sense of well-being was only possible during youth, then a lot of people would have to give up hope of ever feeling content. Some people even associate certain ages with failure; perhaps this is due to physical changes. Certainly it is a mistake to believe that sexual pleasures are confined to youth.

Being youthful means always being young at heart, ready to welcome new ideas, take up new interests and see the world with fresh eyes.

Some women fear that their encroaching wrinkles will make them less attractive, while some men try to imitate youth by running themselves into an early grave! If feeling young is essential to your well-being, you would be wise to consider exactly which it is you want: to avoid growing old or to retain the qualities of youthfulness?

PETER PAN

The Oxford Dictionary defines a peter pan as a person who retains youthfulness and appears not to age. The fictional creation of author J.M. Barrie, Peter Pan was the lost boy on whom Wendy, the daughter of the Darling family, took pity and looked after like a mother throughout their adventures in Never Never Land.

While Peter Pan was for ever young, he was also the little boy who didn't want to grow up, who said in the story, "...to live would be an awfully big adventure."

HOME

For many people, a place to call "home" is essential to their well-being. It may be a mansion in a large estate, a cardboard box under a city bridge, a corner of an office, a country cottage or a tent.

Home is a place of rest, a place to collect things needed for daily living, that not only gives shelter but also feels safe. The most luxurious hotel suite is not home until some personal things are strewn around and identical apartments soon take on a different air once they are occupied.

A family, some friends, animals and plants may help to make a place homely, although some people feel more at home when alone. It is always worth considering whether or not you feel at home with yourself and your marriage.

THE THREE BEARS

An old fairy story tells of a young girl, Goldilocks, who, hungry and tired, comes across the home of the three bears while they are away.

Entering the little house she tries each of the three chairs and the three bowls of porridge before going upstairs to bed.

When the three bears return, they are dismayed and alarmed to find that someone has been in their home. "Who has been sitting in my chair?" they each ask in turn. Even to bears in fairy tales, home is a private place full of personal things.

A LITTLE APPLAUSE

Encouragement and appreciation from others brings a glow of pleasure and satisfaction. A little applause gives many people extra confidence and confirmation.

The victor carried shoulder high amid cheers from the crowd, or the friend being thanked for help, are both receiving applause for something they have done. Rewards and gifts may sometimes accompany the applause, depending on the situation: medals, financial rewards, promotion, a gift, a warm hug or a further contract for a job.

In daily life, a positive response from someone else can make even the dullest day brighter in very subtle ways: a touch, a look, a tone of voice and a smile each add their message. Knowing when to give yourself a little applause is important too.

ELVIS PRESLEY

One of the first American rock 'n' roll stars, he thrived on not just a little applause but massive world wide popularity. At the age of 21 in 1956, 'Elvis the Pelvis' became a show business phenomenon when his songs hit the top of the charts over and over again and the first of his 28 films, *Love Me Tender*, was released.

In the mid-1960s, The Beatles overtook him in popularity and Elvis began to feel the loss of some of the attention he had commanded. He died in 1977 but the applause for Elvis has never really ceased.

AN OCCUPATION

Quite often we assess people on the basis of their occupation. "What do you do?" is a common question. Frequently, the reply reveals our attitudes; for example, the woman who says, "I'm only a housewife" or an unemployed person who says, "I'm self-employed in the business of finding a job."

Having an occupation and having something to do may be equally important. Some people find it very difficult to do nothing for any length of time and need to fill every moment with some kind of activity. Others only feel content if their occupation is "respectable" or well-paid.

Doing something with interest and satisfaction is usually the aim of a person seeking an occupation, no matter what it is.

MARTIN EPP

To meet Martin Epp is to know immediately that he would want no other life than his occupation. His job would formally be listed as a mountain guide, but this enthusiastic and wiry little man with a warm handshake is more than that.

In Yosemite, in Alaska, in Lapland or in his native Swiss Alps, he encourages resilience, concentration and a harmonious understanding of nature. He is a firm believer that you reap what you sow. His occupation is his life, as those who have ventured to stretch themselves on his famous ski tours know so well.

Well-being: areas of endeavor (cont.)

AWARENESS

Ignorance can lead to problems, unhappiness and even disaster. To be aware means to be conscious of the practical realities of everyday life and of the feelings, needs and ambitions of ourselves and others.

Expatriates living in cultures very different from their own have to learn the ways of that culture, such as the traffic laws and the rules of social behavior.

Although we spend the whole of our lives living with ourselves, it is often a much more difficult task to become fully aware of our own characteristics and personal inclinations. Growing awareness can lead us in unexpected directions and bring support or opposition from others as we give expression to our expanding awareness.

JUDY CHICAGO

Born in 1939, she became aware at a young age that women artists had been ignored and devalued throughout history. At the University of California she had to take a post in sculpture because women were not allowed to hold posts in the painting department.

As an artist, she has given expression to her awareness by encouraging women and launching many feminist enterprises. In 1979 she completed a massive cooperative work of art, *The Dinner Party*; a banquet table honoring the achievements of 1,038 women in history.

PURPOSE

Are you a person who needs to have an aim, a goal or a good reason for doing something? The drive to reach an end is fairly common, but some of us prefer to have a predetermined goal in mind. Doing something for the sheer pleasure of it is also purposeful; in this case the process itself is the aim!

Having a purpose can involve both an end and a way of getting there. The outcome may actually change, but the driving force carries us along to a conclusion.

It has often been said of success itself, that once achieved there is nothing to do but to begin a new venture. Consequently some people prefer to travel well, but never arrive anywhere. This can be just as purposeful as reaching a very clearly defined destination.

MARIE CURIE

Born in Poland, Marie moved to Paris when she married Pierre, and had but one purpose in life: the isolation of a pure sample of the element which they first named radium in 1898.

Pierre joined Marie in her driving ambition, which was achieved at the turn of the century, and they won the Nobel Prize for Physics with Henri Becquerel in 1903. Marie continued in her purpose after her husband died and herself became the first known victim of death from radioactivity in 1943.

OPPORTUNITY

"If only I'd had the opportunity..." Have you ever said this kind of thing? It is quite true that unfavorable circumstances interfere with our well-being; traveling by chance on a plane that crashes in the desert or being born into a culture that denies human rights are certainly adverse circumstances.

Recognizing and taking advantage of favorable circumstances is not always so easy. While sometimes there may be a real absence of opportunity, on many occasions we either miss an opportunity when it arises or are not sufficiently well prepared to take advantage of it.

Opportunities arise for everyone; some people also learn how to create opportunities. Either way, grasping them and using them can certainly contribute to a greater sense of well-being.

SIR WINSTON LEONARD SPENCER CHURCHILL

British World War II leader, statesman, writer and painter, Churchill might have sunk into relative obscurity had it not been for the opportunity that arose in 1940, when Britain most needed the qualities for which he had already become unpopular in the English Parliament.

He was also an opportunist and took every available chance to exercise his talents: strategic planning, inspiring speeches, practical direction and his own brand of bloody-minded leadership.

He also won the Nobel Prize for Literature for his wartime memoirs.

LONG LIFE

How much time would you like to have on this earth... and for which reason: to enjoy life or to avoid dying?

In the West during the Middle Ages and in some areas of the world today, the average life expectancy is only 35 years. As improvements are made the average life span increases. Active and interested centenarians are now more common than a few years ago.

In certain areas of the world, many people have always lived to be 120 or more. The only thing they seem to have in common is regular physical activity doing the daily chores and participation in local affairs.

If you aim to live a long life, participation, with moderation, in all things should be your way of life now.

GEORGIA O'KEEFFE

Born in Wisconsin in 1887, Georgia O'Keeffe has become recognized as a major figure in art and, on the publication in 1976 of a full color book of her paintings, she was still at work, living alone in a ghost ranch in New Mexico.

Throughout her long life she believed that, "...it is what I have done with where I have been that should be of interest."

After watching a young potter, she took up working in clay and said, "I cannot yet make the clay speak – so I must keep on living until I do."

INTEGRITY

Integrity means wholeness. Well-being for some people means integrating or combining all the parts of themselves, so that inner conflicts are reduced and they can become wholeheartedly involved in whatever they are doing.

Integrity is not easy to achieve. We all have several inner voices that argue with us about what we should or should not do. The "real", complete or integrated YOU may emerge slowly or appear in a sudden flash of insight.

Following up the discovery of your integrated self may also cause problems: extricating yourself from a current situation will usually affect other people's lives and finding an outlet for your integrated inclinations may require patience.

DIAN FOSSEY

In her book *Gorillas in the Mist* American Dian Fossey described her work among the almost extinct mountain gorillas on the borders of Zaire, Rwanda and Uganda.

It was in 1963 that she first began working for their preservation. Her integrity led her to both oppose the poachers who made a living from capturing the gorillas and promote tourism that would replace their loss of income. The Mountain Gorilla Project became a model of cooperative conservation, but Dian herself was murdered in 1985, it is thought by resentful poachers.

FREEDOM

Are you looking for freedom from something or freedom for something?

Millions of people fight for freedom from poverty or oppression and those same people work for the freedom to have money, power, status and well-being in society.

A distinction needs to be made between freedom and license. Freedom, in any situation, involves taking full responsibility for the consequences of your actions. A great deal of trust is required to achieve this, in yourself and in others.

License consists of doing exactly as you please regardlessly and complaining if someone else reacts! Freedom always has a price; license is the attempt to get something for nothing!

EDITH CAVELL

When she was young, this famous English nurse did not have the freedom of choice available today, but she exercised her sense of freedom and chose to give up teaching to become a nurse. As matron of a Belgian clinic she collected an international staff to train young nurses, inspiring all and raising the status of nursing.

She freely chose to be honest at all times and, in 1915, confessed to helping young allied soldiers return home. As a result the German Military Court sentenced her to be shot.

Well-being: the advantages and pitfalls

Personal well-being grows from general, all-round satisfaction with life. In seeking to satisfy our needs, we often get rather fixed ideas about what will make us happy; sometimes those ideas are picked up from the media or from people around us.

Fixed ideas about how we should be, what we should have or what we ought to do, can lead to our downfall. For example, some of the ideas that push us in the wrong direction are wanting to be seen as correct in the eyes of our colleagues or trying hard to keep up with the latest fashion.

We may even go to endless trouble to climb a fence because the grass looks greener on the other side, only to discover when we get there that it isn't.

Three basic needs
Having, doing and being are the three fundamental needs common to most human beings. They are like the feet of a tripod: if one is missing, the tripod will fall over, regardless of the size of the other two feet.
HAVING is owning or possessing something. What is yours could be abstract, like having time, having an aim or having a feeling, or it could be concrete, like having a house, having a dog or having a present.
DOING is taking action or being involved in a process. For example, what you are doing could be running, working, deciding, laughing or leading a campaign.
BEING is how you are; the true nature of your personality. For example, one person could be an honest, happy-go-lucky man while the next person could be an intelligent, good-looking woman.

Keeping a balance
In general, advantage comes of keeping a balance between the three basic needs while pitfalls occur when too much attention is given to one need at the expense of the others.
HAVING TOO MUCH means concentrating too much on acquiring things and regarding everything and everyone as a possession.
DOING TOO MUCH means concentrating too hard on activities and finding it impossible to take a break.
BEING TOO MUCH means concentrating exclusively on becoming how you think you ought or should be.

THE ADVANTAGES AND PITFALLS OF THE TWELVE KINDS OF WELL-BEING
To be well and happy, all our basic needs must be satisfied. The twelve ways to reach this condition can each make a contribution; however, they can also trip us up if we concentrate too much on any one of them.

ENERGY is drive, ambition, life, movement, thought, feeling and health.

ADVANTAGES
Keeps your human batteries well charged and always ready for use; without it, you would die.
PITFALLS
The quantity or the quality being inappropriate; being overcharged and doing nothing with it; trying to do too much when undercharged.

BEAUTY is being attractive in appearance and in the way you move, talk, listen and think.

ADVANTAGES
Gain the attention or admiration of others; feel good inside yourself; give pleasure to others.
PITFALLS
Attracting unwanted attention: being regarded as an object of beauty to be owned; believing you would not be loved if people knew about the less beautiful parts of you.

YOUTH is being youthful at heart and ready to see the world with fresh eyes.

ADVANTAGES
Optimism; the ability to play; curiosity; constantly surprised by new angles on the world.
PITFALLS
Failure to grow up and mature; throwing out old ideas just because of a new one; fear of growing older.

HOME is having a secure base from which to move out into the world.

ADVANTAGES
A place to rest, relax and enjoy privacy; love, warmth, stimulation and loyalty with a family; a sense of identity; somewhere to potter about, lose your temper or create a nest.
PITFALLS
Cost of mortgage, rent, repairs and services; family upsets and feuds; over-attachment; exclusivity.

 **A LITTLE APPLAUSE** is having the fact that you are loved or appreciated clearly demonstrated.

ADVANTAGES
Self-confidence; confirmation of your standards; stimulation; rewards, awards or gifts; status.
PITFALLS
Trying to live up to expectations; emotional blackmail; depression when there is no applause.

 **OPPORTUNITY** is using chance circumstances to do something.

ADVANTAGES
Achieve what had appeared to be unlikely; optimism; learn how to create further opportunities.
PITFALLS
Self-recrimination; belief that you are totally reliant on outside chance; addiction to gambling.

 **AN OCCUPATION** is doing something that is interesting and satisfying.

ADVANTAGES
Outlet for energy and talents; improvement of skills; fulfillment; contact; earning potential; status.
PITFALLS
Getting stuck in a rut; being too busy to give attention to other things; stress; obsession.

 **LONG LIFE** is having time to participate fully in all stages and varieties of experience.

ADVANTAGES
Ideas can mature; activities can be fully developed; everything can be enjoyed to the full.
PITFALLS
Time on your hands; boredom; getting involved in too many things at once; procrastination.

 **AWARENESS** is being conscious of realities other than familair ones immediately in mind.

ADVANTAGES
Understanding; safety; better quality of communication with others; information on which to base decisions.
PITFALLS
Confusion; failure to organize, or to distinguish between the trivial and the important.

 **INTEGRITY** is being who you are, totally and without incongruencies.

ADVANTAGES
Trust; insight; wholeheartedness; pleasure; ability to welcome change; confidence; character; individuality.
PITFALLS
Becoming too "good" or "perfect" to be true! Opposition from others; being ostracized.

 **PURPOSE** is having a reason or desire to do something or a defined goal or aim to reach.

ADVANTAGES
Pleasure in what you are doing; satisfaction on reaching a goal; sense of success and achievement.
PITFALLS
Failure to adapt to changing circumstances; feeling bad because a goal isn't reached; trying too hard.

 **FREEDOM** is doing what is right for you and taking full responsibility for the consequences of your actions.

ADVANTAGES
Self-discovery; honesty; personal achievement; improvement of conditions for others; emancipation.
PITFALLS
The price of freedom can be high; discomfort; loss of money; status and security; pseudo-freedom, e.g. license.

Are you well?

What state of well-being are you in? To assess this yourself is not easy. Nor can just one other person assess your situation for you, although people close to you will probably give you some good feedback about yourself.

In order to get as accurate a picture as possible of your own current state of well-being, the Man from Mars approach is recommended.

The Man from Mars approach
The Man from Mars is a mythical character who is not human, but very intelligent. Consequently this person can give a reasonably objective report on your situation, combining everything everyone knows about you, including you.

Imagine that you have asked the Man from Mars to give you an unbiased report in reply to the question: How well is X? You, of course, are X.

Now, YOU are going to become the Man from Mars, and write the report (*right*) as requested, being as fair and honest about this person X as you can be, answering each question in the way you think is best in the space given underneath each question. Use note form if you wish. If you are sharing this book with someone else, then use a separate piece of paper.
When you have completed the report, you will be aware of how you feel about yourself and how satisfied you are currently.

How accurate is the report?
Have you been harsh with yourself? Perhaps you are aiming for standards that are unrealistic or letting one unsatisfactory part of your life color the rest of it.

Have you drawn a completely rosy picture in which everything in your life is perfectly satisfying? Perhaps you should get on with enjoying your good luck, rather than spending your time looking for new endeavors just now!

Are you a reasonably contented person? Count how many positive things you have written about yourself. If there are 10 or more you should be reasonably contented. If you have only 5 or less, then either you are very unhappy or you are a pessimist.

If you look at the report (*right*), you can explore which areas of well-being you want to do something about.

A REPORT BY THE MAN FROM MARS ON THE WELL-BEING OF X.

ENERGY
How much drive and ambition does X have? Is X lively and interested in life? Does X enjoy reasonably good health?

....
....
....
....

BEAUTY
Is X attractive to look at and well dressed? Does X listen well to other people, giving them proper attention? Is X fairly active? Does X speak pleasantly and communicate well? Can X think clearly when required?

....
....
....
....

YOUTH
Does X carry his age well? Is X open to fresh ideas, yet mature enough not to jump to conclusions without giving both old and new ideas a balanced consideration? Does X feel glad to be alive?

....
....
....
....

HOME
Does X have a secure base of some kind, whether a family, a friend or a place to call home? Does X feel free there to give expression to whatever X feels? Does X have an identity and a sense of belonging in the world?

....
....
....
....

A LITTLE APPLAUSE
Is X appreciated by other people both in private and in public life? Does X have self-confidence? Does X thank others and give them genuine appreciation when appropriate?

....
....
....
....

AN OCCUPATION
Does X have at least one thing to do in life that is interesting and satisfying? Does X enjoy learning and improving skills? Does X communicate enthusiasm about work, hobbies and other interests?

....
....
....
....

AWARENESS
Is X aware of X's own attitudes and beliefs and how the attitudes and beliefs of others differ? Can X understand and appreciate those differences? Is X aware of his own feelings? Is X aware of other people's feelings? Is X aware of problems that need solving at home and at work? Is X aware of the really good things in life?

....
....
....
....

PURPOSE
Does X have a sense of purpose or a reason for being in this world? Does X enjoy being who X is? Does X do things with pleasure and satisfaction? Has X got what X wants in life?

....
....
....
....

OPPORTUNITY
Does X see and take advantage of opportunities? Does X ever create opportunities? Is X willing to take an optimistic view of changes or does X avoid change?

....
....
....
....

LONG LIFE
Does X use time wisely or waste it frequently? Is X always short of time and under pressure? Does X enjoy the moment or does X tend to live in the past or spend a lot of time thinking about the future?

....
....
....
....

INTEGRITY
Does X practice what X preaches? Does X come across as genuine and not devious? Is X keeping feelings or thoughts hidden so that others don't really know how X feels and thinks? Does X have an interesting personality? Does X have insight and use it with consideration? Is X afraid to discuss certain matters?

....
....
....
....

FREEDOM
Does X say and do what X believes is right and take the full consequences? Has X a quite distinctive personality? Does X relate with all kinds of people without feeling either superior or inferior?

....
....
....
....

Which kind of well-being do you want?

First check in the squares (*below*) which of the twelve kinds of well-being you think you would like to explore further. If you have done the exercise **Are you well?** on the previous pages you will find it helpful when deciding.

THE TWELVE KINDS OF WELL-BEING
Which do you want?

 ☐
1 ENERGY
To do things with more sustained energy and drive?

 ☐
7 AWARENESS
To be more aware and less naive?

 ☐
2 BEAUTY
To be more attractive in looks and personality?

 ☐
8 PURPOSE
To have a direction in life?

 ☐
3 YOUTH
To be young at heart and see life with fresh eyes?

 ☐
9 OPPORTUNITY
To use or create opportunities?

 ☐
4 HOME
To have a place that is truly a home?

 ☐
10 LONG LIFE
To have more time or to use my time better?

 ☐
5 A LITTLE APPLAUSE
To have more appreciation from others?

 ☐
11 INTEGRITY
To be released from my inner conflicts?

 ☐
6 AN OCCUPATION
To do something interesting and involving?

 ☐
12 FREEDOM
To do what is right for me, taking responsibility?

When you have made your choice/s, refer to the appropriate number in the table (*right*). Check any of the suggestions that are true for you and add anything, in the space provided, that occurs to you from your own life. Be as specific as you can. This will help you to clarify exactly what you want. References to useful skills, to be found throughout the book, are given in brackets at the end of each list.

EXPLORING YOUR OPTIONS

1. More energy for what?
☐ To get rid of depression
☐ For life in general
☐ To start a new project
☐ To finish something
☐ In a particular situation

(**On being assertive** (pp. 112-3), **Acquiring a positive attitude** (pp. 118-9)).

....
....

2. In which way more attractive?
☐ My body or my appearance in general
☐ A particular part of my body or my appearance
☐ The way I walk, talk or listen
☐ My personality in general
☐ A particular aspect of my behavior

(**Presenting yourself** (pp. 138-9), **Enlisting help** (pp. 100-1)).

....
....

3. What kind of rejuvenation?
☐ A fresh look at life itself
☐ A new angle on an old problem
☐ A better love life
☐ A new job, house, interest, etc
☐ A new challenge

(**Acquiring a positive attitude** (pp. 118-9), **Which kind of challenge do you want?** (pp. 52-3)).

....
....

4. What kind of home?
☐ Where do I want to live
☐ Building, layout, furnishing, improvements
☐ Shared or on my own
☐ Better relationships in our existing home
☐ A private place in our current house

(**Analyzing situations** (pp. 126-7), **Intimate relationships** (pp. 122-3)).

....
....

5. What kind of appreciation?
☐ A prize, award or title that is rightfully mine
☐ Promotion or recognition at work
☐ Thanks or reciprocation from someone
☐ Love from my family
☐ A reward for effort, such as money

(**Getting feedback** (pp. 116-7), **Appreciating yourself** (pp. 88-9)).

....

....

6. What kind of interest?
☐ Something alone or with others
☐ Something outdoors or indoors
☐ Develop something I already know
☐ Take up a totally new hobby
☐ Change my career

(**Learning and researching** (pp. 134-5), **What are you good at?** (pp. 90-1)).

....

....

7. Aware of what?
☐ My inner feelings
☐ Other people's thoughts and feelings
☐ What's going on at work
☐ Local, national or international news
☐ Things I could prevent by anticipation

(**Knowing your environment** (pp. 140-1), **Negotiating for what you want** (pp. 110-1)).

....

....

8. Which direction?
☐ Away from what's happening now
☐ Back to a time when things were fine
☐ A completely new start
☐ Develop what's happening now even further
☐ The same as someone else

(**Generating ideas** (pp. 84-5), **Does age make any difference?** (pp. 74-5)).

....

....

9. Opportunity in which area of my life?
☐ To make money
☐ To improve my status
☐ To exercise my power
☐ To take up a challenge
☐ To be loved

(**Four ways to change a situation** (pp. 106-7), **Courting failure** (pp. 108-9)).

....

....

10. Time for what?
☐ To do my work properly
☐ To make plans ahead
☐ To be with my family and friends
☐ To take up a new interest
☐ To relax properly and recuperate

(**Time on your side** (pp. 130-1), **Making a time-scale** (pp. 96-7)).

....

....

11. What kind of conflicts?
☐ The need to succeed and the fear of failure
☐ The love of my spouse and a love affair
☐ Too many different demands from others
☐ What I believe and what I do
☐ What I'd like and what I ought to do

(**Resolving conflicts** (pp. 148-9), **Displacing your hang-ups** (pp. 144-5)).

....

....

12. What is right for me?
☐ Freedom from something
☐ Freedom for something
☐ A different career
☐ Emancipation from an inferior position
☐ Speaking the truth of what I know

(**Basic planning** (pp. 86-7), **Setting standards** (pp. 98-9)).

....

....

Love: areas of endeavor

HEROIC LOVE
This is the love of those who go to the rescue of others, giving them aid and protection at a time of great need.

Heroic love has an air of intrigue, excitement and danger about it, although the hero or heroine may not always risk their lives rescuing the loved one from the jaws of death, killing the monster or saving the world, like Superman.

Heroic love may involve taking some initiative for a just cause or from a desire to see fair play, as when fighting for your country or your liberty.

In fairy stories, heroic love is expected of princes who battle through thorn hedges to awaken sleeping princesses and of fairy godmothers who transform Cinderellas to give them a chance of release from their bondage in the kitchen.

FLORA MACDONALD
After his defeat, at the Battle of Culloden in Scotland in 1745, Bonnie Prince Charlie, rightful heir to the British throne, was a wanted man with a large price on his head.

His narrow escape in 1746 from imminent capture by government troops was entirely due to the heroic love of the courageous young Flora MacDonald. It was she who took the Prince, disguised as her maid, on the perilous journey by sea from Benbecula in the far north-west of the Hebridean Islands and across the wild interior of the Isle of Skye to safety.

CARING LOVE
This is the practical, sensible, down-to-earth kind of love that comes of understanding a situation and doing something about it regularly over a period of time.

Caring love gives attention to small details such as remembering how the person you care about likes their coffee, lending your skills when the car needs fixing or taking the trouble to praise something well done.

Caring love can be given to people you never meet, like leaving the bathroom clean for the next person who might use it.

People often learn to care for each other over a period of time and come to trust and rely upon each other, even if they do not see each other very often.

Nature and the physical environment in which we live also need some caring love from us all.

MARIA MONTESSORI
The first Italian woman to qualify as a doctor, Maria Montessori cared for children who had psychiatric and learning difficulties.

Her practical attention to detail and her loving care ensured their successful education and sharpened our awareness of the educability of all young children.

Her caring love is still reflected in her lasting influence on modern toys, which satisfy children's needs for fantasy and are also related to their perceptual and intellectual development.

FREE LOVE
In general, free love is the freedom to discover a million ways of loving and the desire to love all people, all things and all of nature. It is the love that, freely given, seeks truth and discovers the loveliness in all of life. Free love is never jealous and always joyous, whether physical, emotional, intellectual, or all three.

Having a series of lovers or love-affairs without too much attachment is a more specific variety of free love. Although there may be consequences, such as reactions from others who disapprove or who feel hurt, free love of this kind is not intended to do harm.

Free love is unconventional, there are no exclusive commitments, nor is loyalty expected in return. Free love is for the pleasure and fun of loving. It is not a game like husband- or wife-swapping!

GIOVANNI GIACOMO CASANOVA
Casanova, the great 18th century Venetian libertine, was a spy, writer, translator, traveler, soldier and adventurer. He mixed with high society, fought duels, gambled and spent time in jail.

The only constancy in his life were his many affairs with a series of fascinating women whom he loved affectionately, leaving them happy, in the true spirit of free love. Finally, he became infatuated with a London courtesan, who refused him her favors. This episode made him so unhappy that he retired to become a librarian in Paris.

HUMANITARIAN LOVE

This is the love of practical compassion for all of humanity, a love that respects the fundamental needs and rights of all human beings, regardless of age, race or any other conventional groupings.

Humanitarian love can be given in a small local community or felt for a whole world of people.

Humanitarian love is often expressed in song, in drama or in speeches. Sometimes this is as far as it goes, but when humanitarian beliefs are translated into realistic action, then the love comes to life.

Humanitarian love is collective... a dozen people move into action to get a new health center opened or a hundred people take other families into their homes when a disaster strikes. Sometimes one or two people take the lead, in response to a common feeling, and rouse humanitarian love among many more people.

BOB GELDOF

Do They Know Its Christmas?, recorded by Bob Geldof's Band Aid, expressed the humanitarian love of millions, which, transformed into practical help, became the first shipment of supplies for the starving people of Ethiopia in March 1985.

Other extraordinary efforts followed: USA for Africa, Sport Aid and Fashion Aid to name a few.

Interviewed on British TV, Bob Geldof insisted that artists simply respond to and give voice to the feelings of the public, which they certainly had in creating Band Aid.

ROMANTIC LOVE

Romance is often the dream of an "exclusive, perfect, pure love," unsullied by practical considerations like having to earn a living or needing to satisfy the ungainly, earthy activity of sex!

In some cultures it is the erotic anticipation of a more enduring love that combines physical love and growing respect. Whatever it is, romantic novels and romantic films remain bestsellers.

If romantic love is your desire, then perhaps you should consider carefully exactly what it is you want, for tragedy is often associated with romantic love... think of the tragic end to the romance of Romeo and Juliet in Shakespeare's famous play.

Comfort, soft lights, cool wine and sweet music is another kind of romantic love that is enjoyed by many people.

BARBARA CARTLAND

At the age of 85, this best-selling British writer of romantic novels was still turning out two per month.

Born in 1901, her lifestyle, blonde hair, green eye-shadow and fluffy pink clothes are romance personified. "Women can't have sex without getting emotionally involved," she has said, "and emotions get upset when you sleep around, which makes you sick." Since you can't have great love affairs unless you are healthy, sexual permissiveness does nothing for women. Nor, she maintains, does pornography.

MARRIED LOVE

This is an exclusive form of promised love between a man and a woman that is declared before witnesses and bound by a legal agreement.

Traditionally, married love is sexually consummated after the ceremony, though it is modern practice in many countries to have sexual intercourse beforehand. In some countries, the married couple neither make love nor live together until they have built a house or completed the furnishing of the new home.

Married love is a commitment to one person with whom you build a financial security, create a home and often have a family of children. Marriage can become a mutual love that grows over the years or a bondage of two unhappy people who stay together each for their separate reasons.

SHAH JAHAN AND MUMTAZ MAHAL

No other woman in the world ever had a monument built in her memory that has the sheer beauty and perfection of the Taj Mahal at Agra, India.

Her name, Mumtaz Mahal, means Chosen One of the Palace; Taj Mahal is a contraction of her name. She died in childbirth in 1631 after 19 years of marriage to Shah Jahan.

He spent as many years designing and building her memorial, which has often been described as "feminine" in style. It remains a lasting symbol of married love.

Love: areas of endeavor (cont.)

SACRIFICIAL LOVE
A love that is so sure of itself that a loss can be accepted without destroying that love can be called sacrificial love.

Sometimes the loss may involve death, as when Abraham sacrified his son Isaac, or when a parent sacrifices his or her own life to save a child from a dangerous situation.

Sacrificial love has a quality of true courage. Men and women who risk themselves, physically, mentally or emotionally without reward, often sacrifice their comfort, pleasures, status, health or finances as they give their total, loving attention to someone whose need at that moment is greater than their own.

Sacrificial love reaches its limit when the balance is tipped and the sacrifice outweighs the love.

HÉLOISE AND ABÉLARD
In the 12th century in France, Peter Abélard, a religious philospher, and Héloise, the young niece of Canon Fulbert, fell in love and married secretly.

Realizing that their marriage threatened Peter's career, Héloise sacrificed her desires and returned to her uncle's house. Unfortunately, the damage had already been done. Her uncle had Peter beaten up and castrated, while Héloise entered a nunnery.

Perhaps their sacrifice was not in vain, for their letters and poems remain an inspiration to all lovers.

EROTIC LOVE
Physical and emotional involvement leads to erotic love. The word itself is derived from Eros, the mythological god of love, whose arrows of love strike at random to the very heart of human beings.

Sensuality, sex, pleasure and trust are typical of erotic love. The most powerful and passionate form of love, it is also the kind of love that stimulates guilt in those who can't believe they have the right to enjoy so much simple, earthy, pleasure.

Erotic love strikes fear in those who dare not let go and discover the depths of their own human being in case they find something nasty; hence they express their fears as sadism, rape, disgust or satisfy their need for erotic love through voyeurism or by having loveless sex with those they can control or who are dependent on them.

ELIZABETH SMART
In 1945, this Canadian writer published one of the world's masterpieces of poetic prose: *By Grand Central Station I Sat Down and Wept*.

In this true story of erotic love, the juxtaposition of the intense and the ordinary adds humor, without which love can turn into an irreversible tragedy.

It is not graphic lovemaking scenes that make this novel great, for there are none. It is Elizabeth Smart's verbal images that make the reading an experience of erotic love, for those who dare to feel it.

DIVINE LOVE
This is the love that does not overcome fears but faces them and consequently makes life less complicated and simpler. The simplicity of those who are able to achieve a state of divinity is alarming to most people and not easy to achieve.

Innocence is not the route to divine love; experience of the realities of the darkest sides of human nature is a prerequisite.

The honesty without rancor, the gentleness and quiet strength of those who have this kind of love, is not born of sympathy or acquired by withdrawal from the world but rather of a deep compassion for and understanding of the world.

Those who have love divine have lived fully on earth and without compromise.

St. FRANCIS OF ASSISI
Born into a rich family in 1182, Francis was a well traveled man of rakish temperament, fond of women and given to cursing beggars... until one day it occurred to him that he, too, may sometime have to beg someone for help.

This is when he began to face his fears, even to the extent of kissing the hand of a leper, facing the horror he most feared. In this way he learnt the meaning of divine love and eventually founded the Franciscan Order of monks who lived very simple lives.

DEVOTED LOVE

Devotion is concentrating your attention, effort and abilities exclusively on one main interest or activity. Loyalty is love devoted to only one person, one family or one cause.

No matter what the outcome, those who devote themselves wholeheartedly want the loved one or the loved cause to succeed. Devoted people give total support through all the ups and downs of life.

Devotion involves believing totally in what you are doing; if you devote your love to the care, well-being or success of another person, you give yourself, your talents, your time and your money in the name of love and you create yourself in the process.

Devotion grows from conviction; it is a love that can overcome any adversity, whether it is love of a person, of an occupation or a country.

JENNY MARX

Eleanor Marx, the daughter of Karl and Jenny Marx, once said of her father, "He would have been nothing without his wife."

Born into a rich, German family, Jenny Marx could have lived a life of luxury. Instead she devoted herself totally to her husband and his work of revolution, her love always true even though three of their children died in squalid conditions in Soho. Jenny herself survived smallpox, but her beauty was severely scarred.

On her death, her husband described her as his "vital and luminous wife."

PLATONIC LOVE

The word platonic derives from Plato, the great philosopher, and there is an element of philosophy or theory about platonic love. The theory is that two people can be very deeply involved with each other without doing anything physical about it.

Platonic love is love without active sexual intercourse although the erotic potential may be present. For example, two friends who have known each other for years may, due to a change of circumstances, fall in love.

On the other hand two people may actively touch each other, care about each other and have an unspoken commitment but never cross that fine line between sensuality and sexual intercourse.

Platonic love often exists between friends, working partners, brothers, sisters and other relatives.

BUTCH CASSIDY

Leader of The Wild Bunch, a group of American cowboys who outlawed themselves in Wyoming when they took to robbery, Butch Cassidy had one close companion, Henry Longabough, known as The Sundance Kid.

Butch and Henry were always loyal to each other, no matter what they did or where they went. Theirs was the tough, unspoken kind of platonic love that grows between people who have thrown in their lot together. In 1902 they fled to S. America and died together, shot by soldiers in Bolivia.

SELF-LOVE

If you don't love yourself, how on earth can you expect someone else to love you? Loving yourself means having an honest regard and respect for yourself and it has often been said that until you love yourself you cannot love another person.

If you love yourself you will not always approve of or like your own actions; you may even get a little angry with yourself too, but on the whole you will like yourself and appreciate the way you are.

Many people are very self-critical, always trying to make themselves perfect, while others are pompous and boastful; neither should be confused with an urge towards genuine self-improvement.

If you love yourself, you do not need others to prove you are lovable; you genuinely believe in yourself and are glad to be who you are.

THE UGLY DUCKLING

In the fairy tale, the ungainly, little duckling sees his own reflection in a pool and is scornful of his ugliness, believing no one could ever love him looking like that.

It takes a lot to convince him that he, too, is destined to grow into a graceful swan. And, of course, his self-esteem gets a boost when he does grow up!

In contrast, the Greek god, Narcissus, was made to fall in love with his own reflection because he scorned the love of a water nymph. As a result, he wasted away, gazing at himself!

Love: the advantages and pitfalls

Love is the expression of a powerful feeling; hence we are all aware of "the power of love" which can heal, support, endure adversities and make you feel young again. Because love has this power, it also has many pitfalls when denied, unrequited or when it simply fades away in the natural course of events.

The denial of love is the denial of one of the most fundamental feelings common to all kinds of human beings. While some kinds of love are sexual and others are more concerned with other kinds of activities, all forms of love create a bond between the one who loves and the one who is loved.

THE BONDS OF LOVE
Bonding between people is common. The feeling that attracts and links two people together may be very strong, as between a parent and a child, or it may be less strongly felt as between two friends who have just met.

Bonding is a form of attachment, so the quality of the bond may also be important. A bond can be like glue or like gossamer; the difference is not in the importance of the link between two people but in how much they rely on each other.

People who always stick together in a face-to-face clinch, with their backs to the rest of the world, may have problems when one breaks away or disappears. If you lean on someone too heavily, you are likely to fall over when they move! On the other hand, it is natural to grieve for the loss of someone you love, and essential for your full recovery afterwards.

Bonds can be formed between people and animals, places, cars, trinkets, food, books, flowers and even a collection of old junk, kept in the loft just in case it might come in useful one day.

ADVANTAGES AND PITFALLS OF BONDING
Love forms a bond, which has great advantages, such as a sense of belonging, an outlet for enthusiasm, a partner for sex, emotional satisfaction and many other mutual benefits.

The pitfalls of bonding mainly occur when the link turns into an exclusive attachment without which you fear you wouldn't survive, one way or another. In the majority of cases this is never true.

When a bond is broken, for whatever reason, adjustment is inevitable, but the changes that take place also bring you fresh opportunities to explore the world anew and make new links with people or interests you hardly knew existed.

Each kind of loving has its own advantages and pitfalls, which are listed here.

HEROIC LOVE is rescuing others and giving them aid or protection when they are in need.

ADVANTAGES
The excitement and intrigue of being the person who saves the situation and earns gratitude in return.
PITFALLS
Danger; looking a fool if you fail; the permanent attachment of the one rescued; your own need for love.

CARING LOVE is giving attention to the practical needs of the loved one over a long period of time.

ADVANTAGES
Long-term satisfaction and reciprocation; a sense of purpose; feeling needed; friendship and firm bonds.
PITFALLS
Love turning into a chore or a duty; denial of your own needs; increasing demands from the loved one.

FREE LOVE is the pleasure of loving many people and all of nature without exclusive commitments.

ADVANTAGES
Discovering the truth and joys of love without jealousy or permanent attachment; do as you please.
PITFALLS
Reactions from others who are angry or hurt; expecting loyalty and devotion without giving it; insecurity.

HUMANITARIAN LOVE is working in a practical way for the general good of humanity.

ADVANTAGES
Sharing with others the satisfaction of making something good happen to many people.
PITFALLS
Disregarding minorities for the greater good of the majority; becoming a "messiah" in the eyes of others.

ROMANTIC LOVE is the dream of an ideal love, undisturbed by problems, jealousies or practicalities.

ADVANTAGES
Pleasure, relaxation, and control through exclusivity; confirmation of your dreams and your own lovableness.
PITFALLS
Things that disturb the perfection, like the telephone ringing just when you've got him/her charmed with the magic of wine, sweet lights and soft music.

DIVINE LOVE is a simple love uncomplicated by needs or jealousies because the deepest fears have been faced.

ADVANTAGES
Strength; understanding and compassion; honesty; no need to continue the rat race; self-acceptance.
PITFALLS
Reactions from others who are wary of someone who no longer participates in the struggle to be somebody.

MARRIED LOVE is a promise between two people to share love, sex, money, a home and children throughout life.

ADVANTAGES
Security, status, exclusivity, emotional support, state benefits, social advantages, respectability.
PITFALLS
Failure to make adjustments as each partner develops; unfaithfulness; widowhood; financial burdens.

DEVOTED LOVE is loyal and beneficial attention given to one activity or to one person.

ADVANTAGES
Creating yourself through an activity or another person who is greater because of your contribution.
PITFALLS
The activity or person to whom you are devoted does not have sufficient resources of their own.

SACRIFICIAL LOVE is disregarding personal needs or safety for someone whose need is greater.

ADVANTAGES
Strengthens the bond of love; self-confirmation; enables the other to survive or live more happily.
PITFALLS
Continuing when the sacrifice has become too great to bear; masochism which can turn to hatred of the other.

PLATONIC LOVE is an unspoken commitment to friendship without erotic involvement.

ADVANTAGES
Long-term contact with another; someone to rely on at work or in a joint enterprise. No sexual problems.
PITFALLS
When erotic stirrings occur; jealousy of spouse; gossip failure to resolve differences at work.

EROTIC LOVE is passionate physical and emotional involvement with another person.

ADVANTAGES
Sensual and sexual pleasure and fulfillment; trust; stimulation of energy; a focal point in your life.
PITFALLS
When the involvement of your partner is not so intense as your own or not reciprocated at all; misery.

SELF-LOVE is having an honest and caring respect for yourself and your place in the world.

ADVANTAGES
Confidence without illusions; urge for genuine self-improvement; able both to stand alone and to relate.
PITFALLS
Failure to ask for help or lean on others when necessary; addiction to gazing in mirrors!

How loving are you?

You can answer this question for yourself by completing this exercise, which is an analysis of your loves. There are no right or wrong answers and no comparisons to be made with other people. The way in which we love and the intensity of feelings of love are different for different people.

What is love?
Love is an active feeling of connection with or attachment to, for example, a person, a group of people, a job, a hobby, an animal, a place, a season, a belief, an idea, a piece of music, a picture, a film or a particular object. Feelings of love make you want to do something, for example, kiss your lover, listen to your favorite music, stroke your pet, play with the children, learn more about your job, discuss your favorite topic, etc.

IDENTIFYING YOUR LOVES
In the table (*below*), make a note in pencil of the names of your past, present and long-term loves, according to the definitions. Include both intense and milder ones.

Definitions of past, present and long-term loves.
A past love is one that is no longer active; that no longer has the excitement, attraction or satisfaction that it once had. It is natural that feelings change in this way. Of course, you may still have very happy memories of a past love, such as with someone who died or with a place you no longer visit.

A present love is one that is currently active, but has only recently begun within the last year or so.

A long-term love is an active feeling that has been there over a very long period of time; sometimes it may have been stronger or more involving than at other times but it has always been there.

MY LOVES

My past loves	My present loves	My long-term loves

ANALYZING YOUR LOVES
To find out which kind of loves are your's, first classify your list of loves according to the strength of the bond or link, calling them STRONG, AVERAGE or MILD, and writing their names under the appropriate headings in the table (*below*). (See the previous page for a description of bonding.)

When naming your loves, try to be very specific, for example, if music is one of your loves, then do you mean ALL music or do you mean a particular kind, the work of one composer or one special piece of music?

When you have completed this list, go down it again and mark with a check under the appropriate column to

WHICH KIND OF LOVE ARE MY LOVES?	Heroic Love (rescuing)	Caring Love (attending)
My strongest feelings of love		
My average feelings of love		
My mildest feelings of love		

show which kind of love it is. You may need to check more than one column for one love. For example, if you have listed your spouse, you may want to check the columns headed: CARING, MARRIED, EROTIC and ROMANTIC or your love for your car might be: CARING, EROTIC, DIVINE and DEVOTED!

You may like to add other kinds of love or your personal definitions, so a few empty columns have been left for this purpose. (For descriptions of the twelve loves refer to: **Love: areas of endeavor** (pp.64-7).)

Understanding your analysis
The completed table will show which kinds of bonds you form with different people, activities and things. The concentration or absence of checks will show your preferences. You may then like to consider adding to your list in the future or changing the way you love. If so, the exercise on the next page may be helpful.

The real answer to the original question: How loving are you? lies with yourself. There are no rules and no shoulds; love, attachment and bonding is a personal matter. Problems only arise when the balance of love or the kind of love between two people is very different. So you may find it interesting to compare notes with those people in your life whom you love.

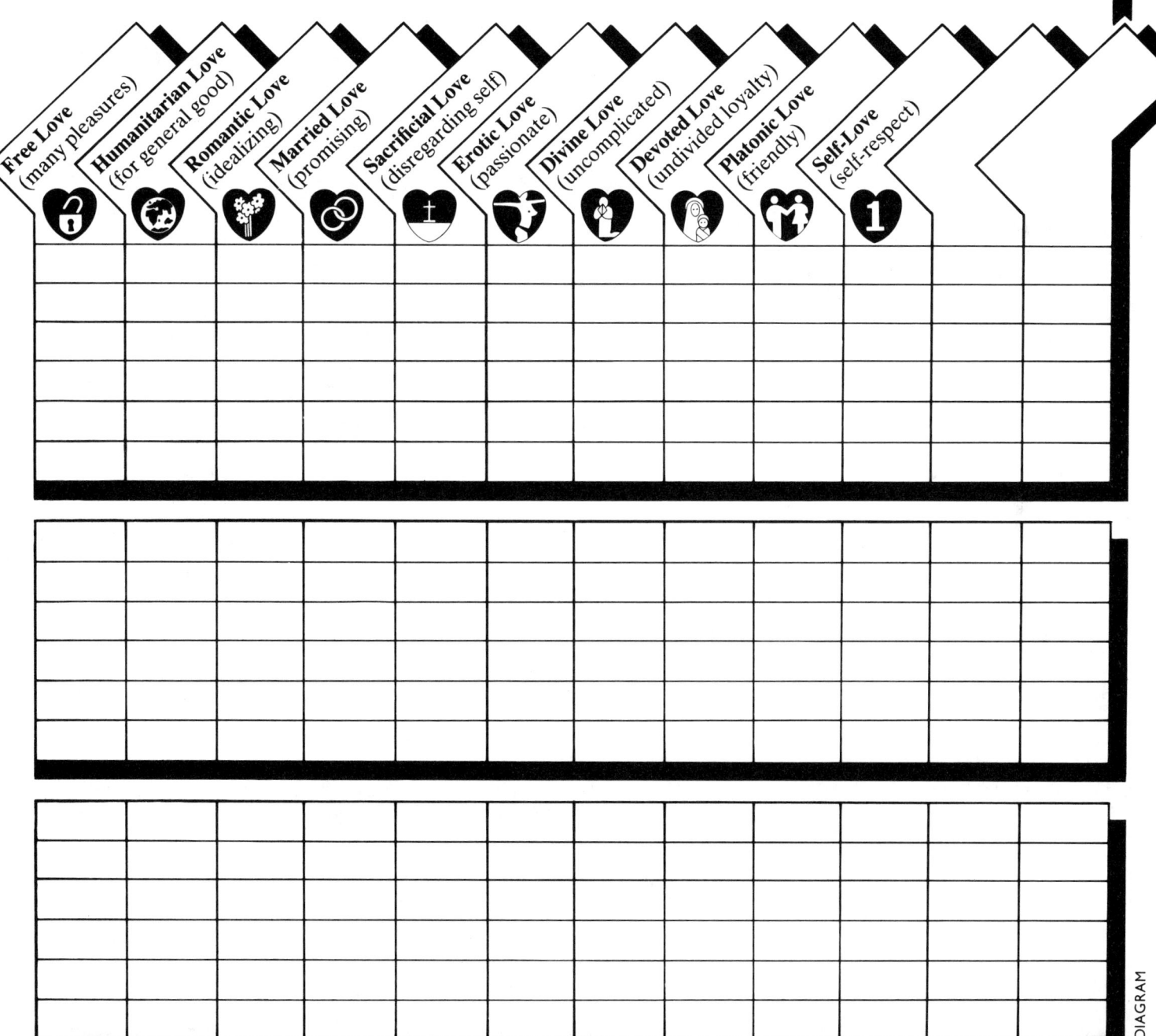

Which kind of love do you want?

In love relationships between people, love has a habit of happening or of not happening regardless of what you want. So the question really has two parts:
1. How to find love
2. How do you want an existing love to develop?
The analysis of your past, present and long-term loves on the previous page may also help you to answer these questions.

How to find love
Love is a relationship between you and another person, an activity or an object. Unless you begin a relationship, nothing at all will happen. First you have to find the people, activities or objects you want a love relationship with. This is something you cannot sit at home and decide; you have to get up and do something about it and the relationship will find you!

What to do to find a love relationship
1. To find a love with a person: go out and participate in the world, taking an interest in everyone you meet. Don't look for someone to love; just meet all kinds and all ages of people and listen to them, appreciate them and do things together with them. Share yourself, your thoughts and your skills with others. This way you will find out which kind of people you like and show yourself to other people.

There are two obstacles: believing that you are not lovable yourself or believing that you are the most attractive person for miles around! It is often true that when you stop looking, love will find you.

If you set out with fixed ideas about what kind of person you want to meet, you will either end up with no one or waste a lot of time trying to make someone behave the way you want them to be, which will kill love before it begins.

2. To find love with an activity or an object: go out and try as many new hobbies, skills or jobs as you can. Watch other people at work, try a new place for a holiday, borrow a boat, explore what is on offer in the way of classes or clubs in your local area, watch TV programs you have never seen before or take a trip round the shops. Again, something will arouse your interest; follow it up, just as you would with a person.

REFERENCES
If you are short of energy to do all these things, then find out how your energy may be draining away by reading:
SECTION ONE **Do you want to be more powerful?** (pp. 30-1)

HOW DO YOU WANT AN EXISTING LOVE TO DEVELOP?
Once there is an attraction between you and another person, or once you have had your interest aroused in a new hobby, then how the relationship develops is up to you.

The characteristics and desires of the other person have to be taken into account, just as you would expect them to take yours into account. Similarly a hobby offers both opportunities and limitations.

Make a list of the people, activities and things you love in your life on the table (*right*). Consider each one in turn and decide in which of the following ways (*below*) you would like the relationship to develop. Write the key letters by the interest on your list.

How would you like your relationship to develop?
A I want to feel I am helping and protecting.
B I want to attend to more practical details.
C I want variety and no long-term commitments.
D I want to do something worthwhile.
E I want to be blissfully happy in this relationship.
F I want to make a long-term commitment.
G I will give up anything for this relationship.
H I want the relationship to satisfy my sexual needs.
I I want a totally honest and open relationship.
J Faithfulness and complete loyalty are what I want.
K I want friendship without sexual involvement.
L I want this relationship to make me feel good.

Now compare the key letters you have chosen with the key list of loves (*far right*). This will indicate the kind of love into which you want your current relationships to develop. You will find full descriptions in: **Love: areas of endeavor** (pp. 64-7).

TABLE OF MY CURRENT INTERESTS	Key letters

KEY LIST OF LOVES

 A Heroic Love

 B Caring Love

 C Free Love

 D Humanitarian Love

E Romantic Love

F Married Love

G Sacrificial Love

H Erotic Love

I Divine Love

J Devoted Love

K Platonic Love

 L Self-Love

REFERENCES

To examine a power balance between the sexes, or the dependency relationship between you and another person, turn to:
SECTION ONE **Which kind of power do you want?** (pp. 32-3)
For more about relationships, turn to:
SECTION THREE **Intimate relationships** (pp. 122-3)
Displacing your hang-ups (pp. 144-5)

Does age make any difference?

In general, most people experience a change roughly every seven years; in the table (*right*), each seven year stage has been given a name and a brief description. The fifteen stages illustrated are not distinct, but are a continuum, one stage flowing into the next almost imperceptibly. Quite often it is easier to recognize the stages in retrospect rather than when they are happening.

Each stage brings different kinds of opportunities, so it is useful to be aware of the lifestages and take them as opportunities.

In which stage are you currently involved?
Try to identify the stages you have already passed through and note the ones you think you have missed on the way. You will probably find an opportunity to experience a missed stage will occur during the next phase. It is often helpful to make a note of particular events in the appropriate age range, always remembering that the ages given are only approximate.

The meaning of the repeating periods
Each lifestage of approximately seven years is part of a cycle of five phases, each phase having three distinct periods.

First there is an action period during which there is great activity, often stimulated by upheavals during the previous transition period.

The period of action is followed by a productive period, consolidating and stabilizing the earlier activity.

Finally, new stirrings begin to disturb the calm and stability, as the period of consolidation comes to an end and a new transition period begins... transition from one phase of life to the next, when the past twenty or so years have to be left behind and the future takes its place. Transition periods often stimulate new ideas and bring increasing awareness; consequently some emotional upheaval can be expected.

The fifteen lifestages rarely fit into neat seven year blocks; sometimes a stage is missed, delayed or lasts longer. Some people pass through several stages at once, experiencing either intensely productive years or a period of difficult upheaval.

On pages 76-77 you will find examples of what some people achieved during each of the fifteen stages.

TABLE OF FIFTEEN LIFESTAGES

	ACTION PERIODS	CONSOLIDATION PERIODS	TRANSITION PERIODS
PHASE ONE YOUTH **The years of growing up.**	**AGE 0-7** EAGER INFANCY Intense learning and rapid growth.	**AGE 7-14** GROOVY CHILDHOOD Acquiring facts and imitating adults.	**AGE 14-21** TEARAWAY TEENAGE The search for identity away from the family.
PHASE TWO DEADLINE ADULTHOOD **The urgent years of trying to become somebody.**	**AGE 21-28** TRY HARD TWENTIES The urge to establish oneself in the world of adults.	**AGE 28-35** AMBITIOUS THIRTIES Acquiring money, status, power and direction.	**AGE 35-42** CRITICAL MIDLIFE The search for meaning and lost youth.
PHASE THREE REBOUND ADULTHOOD **The time for getting comfortable with yourself.**	**AGE 42-49** FIGHTING FORTIES The urge to achieve ambition or fulfillment.	**AGE 49-56** FREELANCE FIFTIES Acquiring recognition and freedom of action.	**AGE 56-63** TEARAWAY PEAK The search for a new direction and lost time.
PHASE FOUR MATURE ADULTHOOD **The time for discovering real priorities.**	**AGE 63-70** FRESH START SIXTIES The urge to fulfill lost dreams and enjoy life.	**AGE 70-77** INDEPENDENT SEVENTIES Acquiring satisfaction, maturity and ease.	**AGE 77-84** CRITICAL LATELIFE The search for spiritual freedom.
PHASE FIVE WISE OLD AGE **The time for doing exactly what pleases you.**	**AGE 84-91** SURPRISING EIGHTIES The urge to remember and understand.	**AGE 91-98** DAY-TO-DAY NINETIES Acquiring yet another day to enjoy.	**AGE 98-105+** TEARAWAY CENTURY The search for lost spectacles!

Lifestage achievements

Is there a human age-limit?
The oldest person in the UK in 1986 was John Evans, aged 109, who still went about his daily tasks in his native Welsh village. Remote tribal cultures in the high Andes are reputed to expect people to live to reach 120, and elderly people of 90 years and more are to be found baking bread and tending the animals.

According to ancient Chinese philosophers, a person does not reach full maturity until the age of 57 and then begins the second half of life.

For a considerable fee, you can now have your body freeze-dried and "put on ice" until a future date when medical science has found the elixir of life.

The lifestages do not always occur at fixed ages.
It is worth remembering that if you have missed a stage or one has been delayed, quite often it can appear at a later age. For example, if you had little opportunity to enjoy a tearaway teenage lifestage, you may find elements of that stage appearing during your critical midlife or even during a later transition period.

Women who spend their twenties and early thirties bringing up children may be fired by ambition during their later thirties, adding power to their critical midlife period.

Men who follow the same career for years in order to support a family, pay the mortgage and perhaps enjoy an expensive personal hobby, such as motor racing, may find themselves trying hard to fulfill the dreams they shelved during their twenties, by making a fresh start, when they retire, in their sixties.

Physical capacities
Every physical activity has a peak age but, apart from natural wear and tear, there is no evidence to support the common fear that age inevitably means physical incapacity. Indeed some grand masters of the martial arts are still performing at a peak in their seventies and eighties. Duncan MacLean, a Scottish runner, was still breaking records at the age of 91, and many people in the Wise Old Age phase of life are still enjoying the pleasures of sexual activity.

WELL-KNOWN LIFESTAGE ACHIEVEMENTS
ACTION PERIODS

PHASE ONE
YOUTH

AGE 0-7
EAGER INFANCY
Wolfgang Amadeus Mozart
An Austrian composer, born 1756, was already writing music and playing the harpsichord with accomplishment at the age of 6.

PHASE TWO
DEADLINE ADULTHOOD

AGE 21-28
TRY HARD TWENTIES
Princess Diana
She acquired wealth, status and a title by marrying the heir to the British throne in 1981, and by her middle twenties had two children and a career in public life.

PHASE THREE
REBOUND ADULTHOOD

AGE 42-49
FIGHTING FORTIES
James Joyce
An Irish writer who, between the ages of 41 and 49, followed the success of *Ulysses* with *Finnegan's Wake*, which also explored the ultimate depths of human experience.

PHASE FOUR
MATURE ADULTHOOD

AGE 63-70
FRESH START SIXTIES
General Charles de Gaulle
After twelve years of retirement during which he wrote his memoirs, de Gaulle became the President of the Fifth Republic of France in January, 1958, aged 68.

PHASE FIVE
WISE OLD AGE

AGE 84-91
SURPRISING EIGHTIES
Elizabeth the Queen Mother
Wherever she went in 1986, and especially at the wedding of her grandson, Prince Andrew, she was indeed surprisingly spritely for her 86 years of age.

CONSOLIDATION PERIODS

AGE 7-14

GROOVY CHILDHOOD

Genghis Khan
Born as Temujine in 1162, he became Chief of Mongolia at the age of 13, quickly proving his worth among the elders and eventually creating an Asian empire.

AGE 28-35

AMBITIOUS THIRTIES

Wilbur & Orville Wright
On December 17th, 1903, at the ages of 36 and 32 respectively, these American brothers made the first powered flights at Kitty Hawk, North Carolina.

AGE 49-56

FREELANCE FIFTIES

Dr. Margaret Mead
An American anthropologist who, by the age of 50, had already had a career, love affairs and marriage, she then began to consolidate her new career in mental health.

AGE 70-77

INDEPENDENT SEVENTIES

Frank Lloyd Wright
The originator of the idea of "organic architecture," this great American architect created some of his most independent work during his seventies.

AGE 91-98

DAY-TO-DAY NINETIES

George Bernard Shaw
At the age of 93, and still writing every day, the Irish wit of this prodigious playwright was still as sharp and as exasperating as ever.

TRANSITION PERIODS

AGE 14-21

TEARAWAY TEENAGE

The Beatles
John Lennon, Ringo Starr, George Harrison and Paul McCartney were the teenagers who gave birth to the new pop music culture at The Cavern in Liverpool in 1956.

AGE 35-42

CRITICAL MIDLIFE

Gottlieb Daimler
The German inventor of the first motorbike, he was 38 when he finally perfected the design of a four-stroke engine made by his partner Nicholas Otto.

AGE 56-63

TEARAWAY PEAK

Queen Elizabeth II
As she passed her sixtieth birthday in 1986, it became clear that, far from retiring, the Queen was in very good form, especially on her visit to China.

AGE 77-84

CRITICAL LATELIFE

Pope John
Cardinal Roncalli was elected to be Pope John XXIII at the age of 77 and, in the 4½ years before his death, led the Catholic Church through profound changes.

AGE 98-105+

TEARAWAY CENTURY

Methuselah
He was a patriarch who lived before the time of Noah and is mentioned in the bible, Genesis 5 verse 27, as having lived for 969 years.

Reviewing your choices

Here are the 72 areas of human endeavor which have been described in this section. From these 72 areas, you made your first choices at the beginning of this section (pp. 12-3). Without referring back to your first selection, make your choices afresh by checking the areas that definitely appeal to you on the six lists (*below*).

WEALTH

- [ ] A PERSONAL FORTUNE
- [ ] A DYNASTY
- [ ] PROMISSORY WEALTH
- [ ] BUSINESS
- [ ] TERRITORY
- [ ] MARRIAGE
- [ ] ARBITRAGE
- [ ] CHANCE
- [ ] ENTITLEMENT
- [ ] PROPERTY
- [ ] EQUITY
- [ ] PATRONAGE

POWER

- [ ] ASSERTIVE POWER
- [ ] PHYSICAL POWER
- [ ] INTELLECTUAL POWER
- [ ] EMOTIONAL POWER
- [ ] EXECUTIVE POWER
- [ ] INFLUENTIAL POWER
- [ ] POLITICAL POWER
- [ ] SEXUAL POWER
- [ ] EVANGELICAL POWER
- [ ] REFORMATIVE POWER
- [ ] CONGRUENT POWER
- [ ] IMAGINATIVE POWER

STATUS

- [ ] FIRST POSITION
- [ ] LEGENDARY STATUS
- [ ] UNCONVENTIONAL STATUS
- [ ] THE BOSS
- [ ] STARDOM
- [ ] THE REPRESENTATIVE
- [ ] THE MEDIATOR
- [ ] THE WINNER
- [ ] THE GURU
- [ ] THE CONTROLLER
- [ ] THE SPECIALIST
- [ ] SAINTHOOD

CHALLENGE

- [ ] TO PIONEER
- [ ] TO BUILD
- [ ] TO DISCOVER
- [ ] TO NURTURE
- [ ] TO CREATE
- [ ] TO MASTER
- [ ] TO INVENT
- [ ] TO SOLVE
- [ ] TO EXPLORE
- [ ] TO OVERCOME
- [ ] TO RISK
- [ ] TO SELF-ACTUALIZE

WELL-BEING

- [ ] ENERGY
- [ ] BEAUTY
- [ ] YOUTH
- [ ] HOME
- [ ] A LITTLE APPLAUSE
- [ ] AN OCCUPATION
- [ ] AWARENESS
- [ ] PURPOSE
- [ ] OPPORTUNITY
- [ ] LONG LIFE
- [ ] INTEGRITY
- [ ] FREEDOM

LOVE

- [ ] HEROIC LOVE
- [ ] CARING LOVE
- [ ] FREE LOVE
- [ ] HUMANITARIAN LOVE
- [ ] ROMANTIC LOVE
- [ ] MARRIED LOVE
- [ ] SACRIFICIAL LOVE
- [ ] EROTIC LOVE
- [ ] DIVINE LOVE
- [ ] DEVOTED LOVE
- [ ] PLATONIC LOVE
- [ ] SELF-LOVE

ORDERING AND SPECIFYING YOUR SELECTION
1 In the spaces provided (*below*), enter the three most appealing areas in their order of importance to you, regardless of whether or not you think they are possible for you to achieve. Place the most important in first position and the least important in 3rd place.
2 Return to your first selection at the beginning of this section (pp. 12-3) and mark with a dot, on the six lists (*left*), the areas you chose originally. Do any of them coincide with the ones you have just chosen? If so, you may like to consider if they should be included among your first three choices (*below*).
3 Now consider each area in turn, specifying all the different ways in which you think you would personally carry out your venture.

If you have difficulty thinking up ideas, refer to: SECTION TWO **Generating ideas** (pp. 84-5).

MY FIRST CHOICE ....

MY SPECIFIC IDEAS

MY SECOND CHOICE ....

MY SPECIFIC IDEAS

MY THIRD CHOICE ....

MY SPECIFIC IDEAS

Confirming your selection
By reading SECTION TWO **What does it take to succeed?** (pp. 82-3), you can decide if, in general, you have what it takes to succeed in each one of the specific suggestions you have made.

A further way to confirm your selection is to leave your suggestions for a day or two, think them over, make a few enquiries and then return to them again.

When you are sure of not more than three ventures you want to undertake, then move on to the planning stage: SECTION TWO **Basic planning** (pp. 86-7).

Section Two
PLANNING

How can you plan for success? Planning is the first move into action; the planning process is regarded as an essentially practical part of your new venture. A plan is of no value unless it can be implemented.

In this section you can generate viable ideas and make plans that are functional. Good planning also involves anticipating snags, failures and other limitations. Becoming aware both of your resources and the problems you may encounter is an integral part of the planning activities suggested in this section.

81

What does it take to succeed?

Passion, persistence and commonsense are the essential qualities most frequently quoted in reply to this question. Every person who is successful, in whatever they set out to do in this life, has the PPC syndrome: those three qualities which, combined, will transform you into who you want to be.

What is passion?
Is it enthusiasm, drive or power, or is it courage and motivation? It is all of these but, of course, you can get along fairly well without much passion; many people do. Thousands have built bookshelves, marriages and bank balances without much passion. It is also true that such people have been heard to complain of gaining little satisfaction from their endeavors.

If you rarely feel passionate about anything, then life becomes dull and meaningless; understanding the link between passion and fear may help you.

The link between passion and fear
The key to understanding passion lies in taking risks, which involves anxiety... or to put it in plainer terms: fear. Fear is what adds the spice to life. Just the right amount of anticipatory fear will give you the fighting edge you need to succeed with satisfaction.

It was with typical comic seriousness that Woody Allen once said, "Early in life I was visited by the bluebird of anxiety." And when asked how to be successful, Helen Gurly Brown of the magazine *Cosmopolitan* said, "Feel fear!"

Nervous excitement is the fuel for passion
It is the thrill of anxious excitement that motivates us to achieve far beyond our expectations. Everyone experiences anxiety; check it out for yourself. Is it not true that when you make use of your anxieties, when you push through them, instead of letting them get you down, that you feel fully alive, on top of the world and confident? When we achieve something despite feeling 'nervous' or anxious, it is the resulting relief and pleasure that fuel the passion which keeps us going.

Excitement is the positive flip-side of fear
Unfortunately, fear and its young brother, anxiety, are most often regarded as exclusively negative feelings, to be avoided at all costs.

Legitimate fear causes a temporary shut-down, called shock, such as happens when we receive very bad news or are in an accident.

Unfortunately most of us accumulate dozens of small, unnecessary anxieties and paralyze ourselves. For example, we feel afraid to speak up in a discussion and the longer we stay silent, the more difficult it becomes to begin to speak. It is then we begin to feel depressed or frustrated, believing there ought to be more to life.

Typical among the anxieties that leave us devoid of passion and excitement are: fear of saying what we really mean; fear of looking a fool; fear of not performing to expected standards; fear of criticism, impotence or vulnerability; fear of not being loved, liked or appreciated and the fear of loss and failure.

Passion comes of taking risks
If you want to be truly successful, you not only have to accept fears and anxieties, but actually court them by taking risks; fear then becomes transformed into positive excitement.

To learn how to release your passions by taking small risks, step by step, refer to:
SECTION THREE **Courting failure** (pp. 108-9)

Responsible and irresponsible risk-taking
You could rightly argue that many people take irresponsible risks, for example by displacing their aggression into their cars and driving like maniacs. But do they know what they are doing? People who have a real passion for driving don't use their cars to express their frustration.

Anyone who drives is automatically taking risks. Successful drivers take responsible risks to improve and enjoy their skills. They are also aware of chance risks, which can prove fatal, but they don't waste energy on what might happen.

Responsibility demands persistence and commonsense
There could have been no doubt in Blondin's mind of the risks involved in crossing Niagara Falls on a tightrope! Well researched information, practised skills and sensible preparation reduced the risks he took to the bare minimum of chance risks. Every problem he came up against whilst planning his venture was tackled with persistence; he calculated and tested repeatedly until he got the balance right. Beyond that he chose to face the fear, fully aware of the implications of what he was doing.

Many people take psychological, emotional, political or financial risks, rather than physical risks. They too experience anticipatory anxiety. For example, those who perform to an audience will call their anxiety "stage fright", and the successful ones know that without it they couldn't perform at all. But they, too, leave it behind in the wings.

Transforming anticipatory fear into passion
So how do they do it, these people who take responsible risks? How do they handle the fear and transform it into a passion to succeed? They will give you a simple answer; they will tell you that they are too busy concentrating totally on the job in hand to have any time to spare. Activity keeps excitement positive, preventing it from degenerating into negative anxiety.

Beware of the chronically cool customer
A word of warning is appropriate here. There are some very energetic people about who nevertheless lack real passion. Their bodies function properly but they are no longer aware of what they feel. Consequently, such people, while they have energy, persistence and brain

Blondin crossing the Niagara Falls on a tightrope, 1859.

power, take irresponsible risks. These are the people whose persistence turns into foolhardy pig-headedness, and whose brainpower loses flexibility. Quite often, at heart, they are unhappy people, although they may appear to have everything.

Are you a relatively cool customer?
If you were totally cut-off from your feelings you wouldn't be reading this book, so you already have some awareness. All you need to do is become more aware of what you really feel before you begin to plan your new endeavor; then you will be able to find an enthusiasm and a purpose that gives you satisfaction. To do this, turn to:
SECTION ONE **Which kind of challenge do you want?** (pp. 52-3)
This will help you to identify your intuitive feelings, in particular the exercise: "How to access your intuition."
SECTION ONE **Do you want to be more powerful?** (pp. 30-1)
You may find the paragraph: "Is your power being drained?" especially helpful.

Cool customers come in all shapes and sizes and are often harder to detect than their counterparts, the bumbling enthusiasts.

Are you a bumbling enthusiast?
If you are, then you already have the passion that is the prerequisite to success. The rest you can learn. All you have to do is think clearly and plan efficiently. It is a pity to waste genuine passion because you don't know how to fulfill it.

If you follow the planning procedure in this section, and improve your strategies and skills by referring to SECTION THREE, you can become successful, whatever your endeavor.

SUMMARY
In order to succeed, the ability to feel fear, anxiety, stage fright, or call it whatever you like, is a golden nugget in your portfolio for success. We all get a dose of anxiety from time to time, perhaps in bed, at work or in a hundred daily activities. Be glad of it, that sinking feeling in your stomach, for it is the very stuff you need to fuel your passions, to endure with persistence, and to organize your activities with commonsense.

Passion, persistence and commonsense, the three qualities vital to success, together make the PPC syndrome. **HAVE YOU GOT IT?**

Generating ideas

Are you still unsure in which direction to move or do you want to be more specific about the area of endeavor you have chosen? Perhaps you just want to enlarge your range of choices or solve a minor problem.

Here are several methods for generating ideas. If one method doesn't work for you, try another, as different methods suit different people and different situations.

BORROWING IDEAS
New ideas are rarely new, so borrow ideas from other situations.
Example. An unemployed sales manager who wanted to find a top class job "borrowed" the idea of TV advertising and invested all his resources in selling himself on national TV at a peak viewing time. He received several telephone offers the same evening.

BRAINSTORMING
A group method to generate a large number of ideas to resolve any kind of clearly stated problems.
Procedure
1 Write the problem clearly on a large piece of paper.
2 Invite 4-8 people to participate, for example your family, a committee or your project team at work as appropriate. Couples can also do a brainstorm.
3 Create a relaxed atmosphere and supply pens and a dozen plain white cards per person.
4 Read out the problem and ask everyone to write down their immediate ideas in response to it, writing one idea on one card.
5 Ask each person in turn to read out their ideas; while this happens, make it clear that:
(a) Nobody criticizes any idea.
(b) A large number of ideas are wanted.
(c) Impossible, wild or crazy ideas are very welcome.
Encourage everyone to combine, alter or improve on the ideas they hear and continue noting down ideas as people read out what they have written.
6 Continue for about 20 minutes
7 Lay all the cards out on a table and sort or evaluate them as appropriate, discussing how particular ideas could be put into practice.

Brainstorm examples
Two sample problems are stated with a short selection from the ideas that might be suggested.
How could we cut our cost of travel to work?
Travel share. Smaller car. Jog to work. Go to live near work. Move work nearer to home. Buy discount tickets. Give up work. Buy a bus and charge others.
How could Jane improve her prospects?
Dye her hair black. Move to a larger city. Employ a housekeeper. Learn to speak in public. Get on local community committees. Go to college. Buy a computer.

MAKING NEW CONNECTIONS
Generate ideas and innovations by searching for connections and combinations between components that have not been made before by using an interaction net.
Example: procedure for re-designing a kitchen.
1 List all the component parts required.

Stove	Refrigerator	Worktop
Microwave	Kettle	Sink
Pans	Pots	Tools

2 Draw an interaction net, as illustrated, trying out new connections between items and marking them with lines. Things that need to be next to each other have lines connecting them.

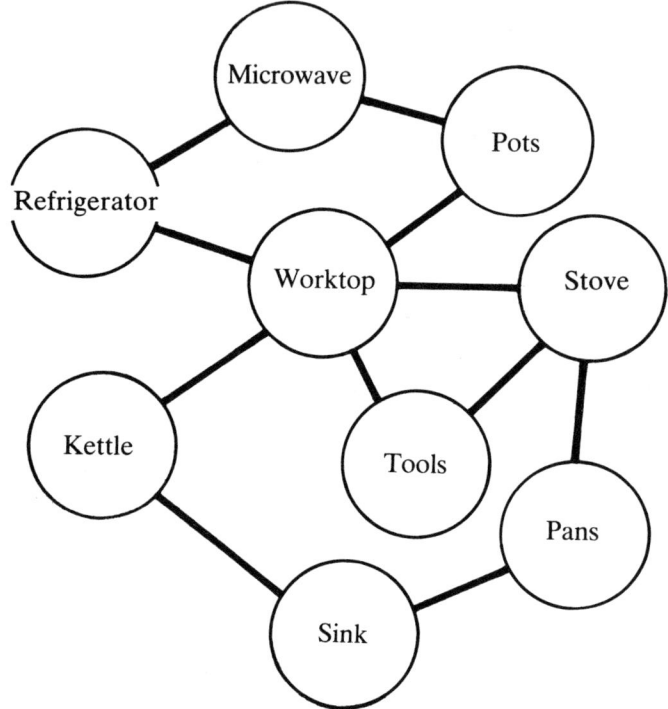

3 Make an outline floor plan which eliminates as far as possible all crossed lines.

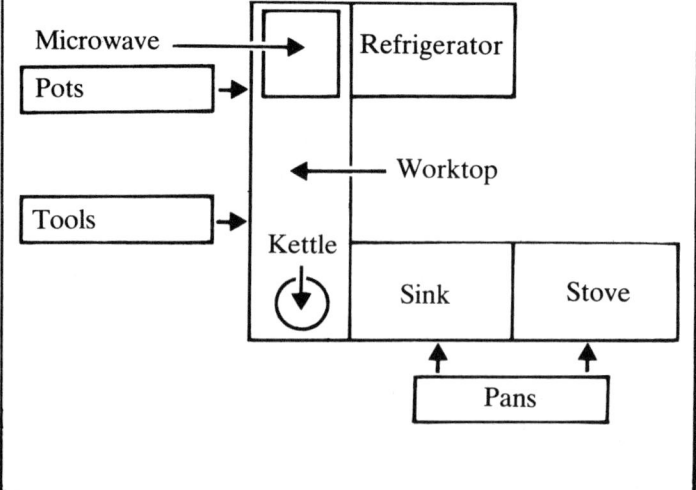

SYNECTICS

This is a creative process during which analogies are made which suggest new ideas. The aim is first to make what is familiar seem strange. Synectics involves four kinds of analogy. These can be illustrated using a problem: We have a very small flat; where is the best place to put a bed?

1 DIRECT ANALOGY. Think of the meaning of bed in different contexts... the sea-bed, a flower-bed, etc.
2 PERSONAL ANALOGY. Think as if you were a bed... "I am a strong but soft bed. I can move about, I can stand up or lie down, etc."
3 SYMBOLISM. Think of poetic images and abstract metaphors... the marriage bed, you made your bed you must lie in it, apple-pie bed, etc.
4 FANTASY. Imagine an impossible dream bed... a bed of floating bubbles that carries you high and hums you to sleep, etc.

The second stage of synectics is to combine some of these strange ideas and make them a practical reality.

The couple in the example suspended a platform from the ceiling for their bed, which they could raise and lower as they wished.

ASKING "WHY?"

Write down a statement that summarizes what you want to do and ask a series of questions beginning with why? This method will challenge your basic assumptions and can reveal your real objectives.

Example. A married couple wanted to explore their reasons for having children, so they wrote the following statement: We want to have a family. Then they each built a tree of questions and answers, which they compared and discussed later. The woman's question tree is shown (*below*).

You will notice that the woman has worded her "why" questions in the way that is important for her. Her answers to the last set of questions were similar to her husband's answers. Although they both genuinely wanted children, they were both mildly unhappy with their marriage. Consequently, they attended to their marriage first and later had a family.

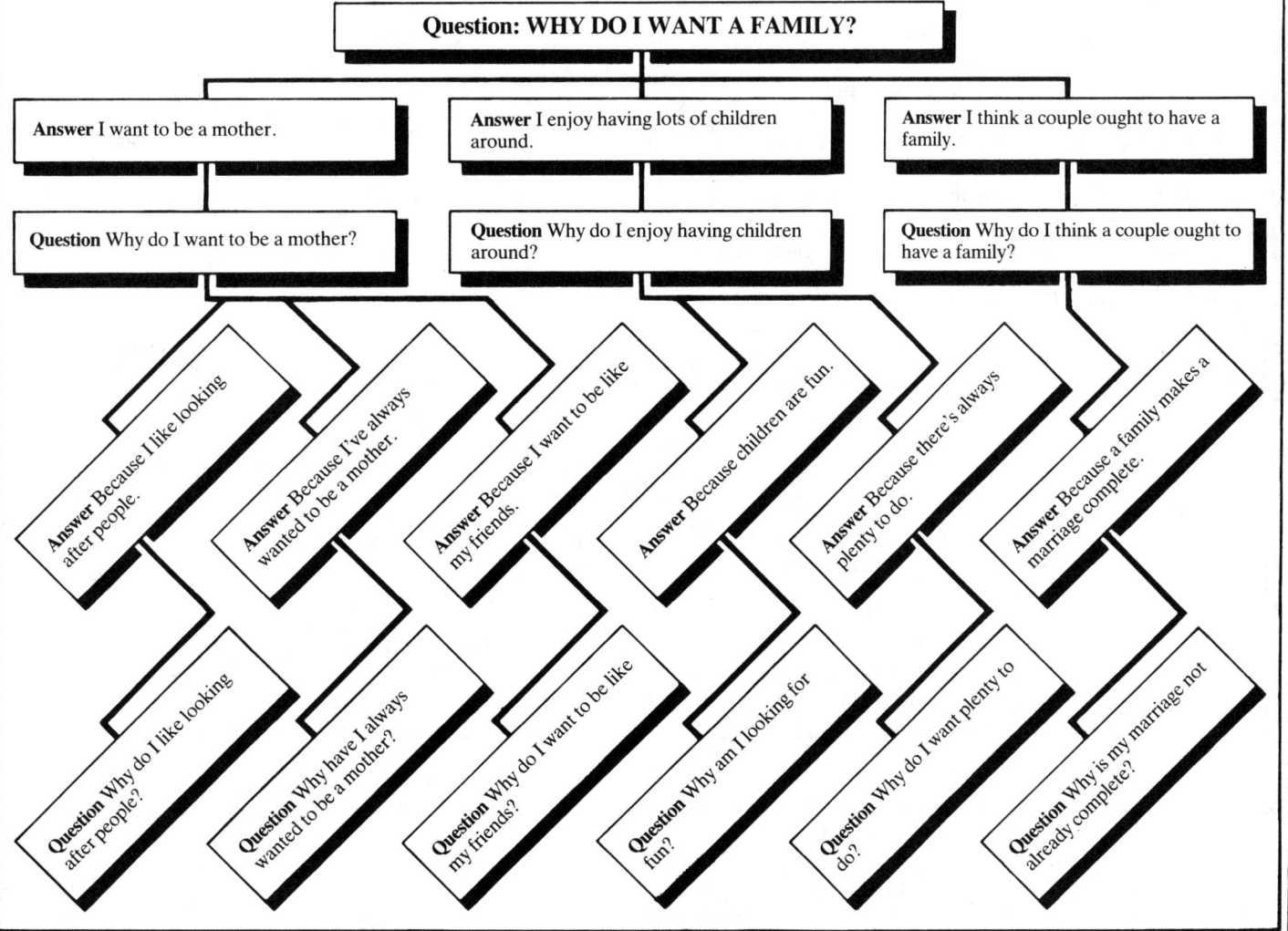

Basic planning

The purpose of planning is to find out what you have to do to achieve your aim.

All planning is active, whether for a short-term or long-term period. There are five steps (*below*), each of which may affect the others.

THE FIVE STEPS				
INTENTION: What, precisely, is my aim?	**METHOD:** How am I going to achieve it?	**RESOURCES:** Which resources do I need?	**FEEDBACK:** When shall I review progress?	**ADJUSTMENT:** Where do I need to make changes?

A short-term plan
The plan made by Jean (*above right*) for a very busy Monday will illustrate the five steps in a real context. Jean drew five columns on a sheet of paper, each headed with the name of the step.

There were ten jobs extra to her normal routine that she intended to complete. She sorted and numbered them in order of timing. Across the page she entered the method and the resources, which she collected as she made the list. Finally she made a note under feedback of when she had to review the situation. As the day proceeded she used the last column for re-planning or to indicate the item was completed.

Making a long-term plan
Too many plans fail because the aim has not been clearly stated in realistic terms. Looking too far ahead for too long can leave you suspended in never never land, or bogged down in rules, regulations and opposition from others that you didn't take into account.

FOUR DREAMS
For years Brian, single and a car salesman, had dreamt of building a boat and sailing round the world, while George, married and a mechanic, had his sights on owning his own chain of garages.

For years Mavis, married and an advertising executive, had dreamt of becoming the mother of a large family, while Carol, single and a computer programmer, had her sights on political achievement.

There is nothing in these examples to suggest that any of the four people *couldn't* achieve their dreams, except that they are all still at the dreaming stage!

Writing down a very clear, first intention is the way to begin any new venture. Then the method becomes clearer. This is how our four dreamers might begin.

The effect of clarity
BRIAN could not possibly achieve his dream without first acquiring the basic resources, one of which would need to be sailing skills.
GEORGE scaled his first objective to an attainable size and realized that his wife's opinion was important.
MAVIS isn't really sure if she wants children of her own; she and her husband haven't discussed the issue for a long time. She decides that first of all she wants to get involved with children and realizes that she has skills to offer the sports club.
CAROL realizes that she knows very little about local political affairs and has never attempted to participate fully. She feels it would be a good way to gain experience.

The first intentions of our dreamers

BRIAN
INTENTION: to learn how to sail. Start on Saturday.
METHOD: join beginners' course at sailing school.

GEORGE
INTENTION: to begin my repair service May 1st.
METHOD: discuss objective with my wife.
Make a plan for a small business.

MAVIS
INTENTION: to spend time each week with children.
METHOD: offer to coach at the sports center.

CAROL
INTENTION: gain place on union committee; January.
METHOD: attend all meetings; discuss; learn.

Using feedback
Feedback is essential not only when reviewing the whole situation but also throughout your venture.

Although a plan needs to be orderly, successful plans are not fixed. They constantly alter because of feedback. For example, if you intend to visit a friend on Tuesday, your plans may have to be adjusted for all kinds of reasons you weren't aware of when you first made them.

REFERENCES
The rest of SECTION TWO in the following pages will help you with specific parts of your plan.

JEAN'S PLAN FOR MONDAY

INTENTION	METHOD	RESOURCES	FEEDBACK	ADJUSTMENT
1 Get keys from John.	Note on mirror.	MEMORY!!!	Get duplicates.	Call at garage.
2 Rearrange weekend.	Phone.	098-9876 (diary).	Tell John.	21st April.
3 Settle accounts.	Go to bank.	Account book.	???	OK.
4 Collect prescription.	Go to drugstore.	Prescription.	Monday.	Carry forward.
5 Interview M. B. Jones.	Agency 11 a.m.	Take file.	Arrange meeting.	11 a.m. 24th.
6 Bake cake.	Use ready-mixed ingredients.	Buy icing.	Deadline 5 p.m.	OK.
7 Plan essay.	From notes.	Desk ready.	???	OK.
8 Pick up children.	Use van.	Keys from John.	Check gasoline.	OK.
9 Kid's party 5 p.m.	Plan on wall.	???	Ask kids.	GREAT!
10 Write essay.	Borrow typewriter.	Desk ready.	Tutor Tuesday 10 a.m.	???

MY BASIC PLAN

1 Define one of your own objectives.	2 List all the things you will need to do. Then number them in order of priority and put the date when you are going to begin.	3 List all the resources you can foresee you will need. Include information, skills, equipment, finance, other people, agreement, advice.	4 Decide the date on which you are going to review your progress.	5 As you work through your plan, note down any changes or adjustments you have to make.
INTENTION My objective is...	**METHOD** The steps I need to take are...	**RESOURCES** The things I need to acquire are...	**FEEDBACK** I shall review my progress on...	**ADJUSTMENTS** I have to change...

Appreciating yourself

How do you estimate your worth? Are you sensitive to your potential? How do you judge your skills? What value do you place on your experience?

Are you satisfied with yourself? Do you really know your strengths and weaknesses? Do you know how skilled you are?

To succeed in your chosen endeavor, you need faith in yourself, not as a paragon of virtue, but as a person of worth. If you don't believe in yourself, you will never convince an investor, an electorate or the one you love to have faith in your word, your skills and your integrity.

So how do you view yourself? Are you shamed into action by a sense of inadequacy or motivated by a desire to continually learn more, have more, do more or become more? Do you appreciate your own worth?

Self-worth
Appreciating yourself infers making a value-judgement. We often judge ourselves and our actions as worthy or unworthy, "good" or "bad." From these judgements, over the years, we build an image of how we see ourselves, but how close to reality is that self-image? We also build an image of an ideal self; so how close to our ideals are we?

The test (*right*) will help you discover a little more about your self-image. The results may surprise you or they may confirm what you already think.

REFERENCES
If you would like to discover more about your talents and your general situation in life, refer to:
SECTION TWO   **What are you good at?** (pp. 90-1)
              What are your limitations? (pp. 92-3)
              What advantages do you have? (pp. 94-5)
SECTION THREE **Getting feedback** (pp. 116-7)

HAVE YOU A POSITIVE SELF-IMAGE?
The table (*below*) comprises two columns of vertical boxes which are separated by a list of 25 adjectives which could be applied to you. The test is divided into two parts, and the instructions given (*right*) will enable you to determine which score number you should enter in each set of 25 boxes (*below*).

PART ONE SCORES	LIST OF ADJECTIVES	PART TWO SCORES
	Optimistic	
	Tactful	
	Responsible	
	Open-minded	
	Bright	
	Confident	
	Aware	
	Mature	
	Satisfied	
	Clear-thinking	
	Pleasant	
	Fair-minded	
	Presentable	
	Considerate	
	Sensible	
	Ambitious	
	Effective	
	Stable	
	Honest	
	Reasonable	
	Efficient	
	Purposeful	
	Warm-hearted	
	Normal	
	Understanding	
Part one total score	**Difference between scores**	**Part two total score**

PART ONE
Listed in the table (*left*) are 25 adjectives that could describe you. The first one is optimistic. It would fit into the sentence:

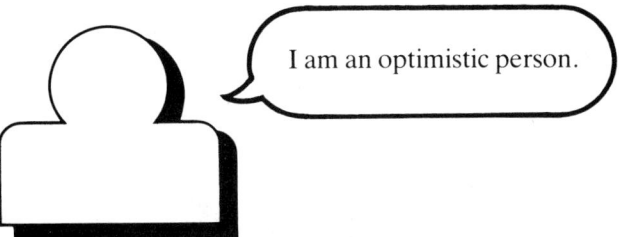
I am an optimistic person.

In the box to the left of the adjective (Optimistic), put a score to indicate how true this is of you. Use the following scale:

	Alotted score
NEVER I don't think I am ever like this.	2
SOMETIMES I am sometimes like this.	4
AVERAGE I am like this on average.	6
USUALLY Most of the time I am like this.	8
ALWAYS I think I am always like this.	10

Then go down the whole list of 25 adjectives, giving each one a score in the same way. Be as honest as you can. When you have finished, add up your total score for PART ONE and then read the instructions for PART TWO (*right*).

PART TWO
Using the same list of adjectives, decide how much you would like to be as described, fitting the adjectives into the sentence:

I would like to be an optimistic person.

In the box to the right of the adjective (Optimistic), put a score to indicate how true this is of you, using the following scale:

	Alotted score
NEVER I never want to be like this.	2
SOMETIMES I would sometimes like to be like this.	4
AVERAGE I'd like to be this about half the time.	6
USUALLY I'd like to be this most of the time.	8
ALWAYS I would like to be always like this.	10

When you have completed the whole list, add up your total score for PART TWO, calculate and insert in the center column the difference between each pair of scores (i.e. those for PART ONE and PART TWO) and then turn to the interpretations (*below*).

Interpreting your scores
Your total score for PART ONE represents your self-image. The higher your score, the more positive your self-image. Your total score for PART TWO represents your ideal image, i.e. how you would like to see yourself. The **SCORE KEY** (*below*) will show you where you have placed yourself.

SCORE KEY FOR PART ONE AND PART TWO
200+. You have a very positive self-image.
151 to 200. You have a generally positive self-image.
101 to 150. Your self-image is partly positive.
50 to 100. Yours is a generally negative self-image.

The difference between your self-image score (PART ONE) and your ideal-image score (PART TWO) usually indicates how contented you are with yourself. The less the difference, the more contented you are. The SCORE KEY (*right*) will show you where you have placed yourself.

SCORE KEY FOR DIFFERENCE
0 to 50. Contented with yourself.
50 to 100. Fairly contented with yourself.
101 to 150. Not really happy with yourself.
151 to 200. Very negative about yourself.

How close to reality is your self-image?
Sometimes we carry a self-image through life and do not adjust it to include all the many new experiences we have had. Self-discovery is one way to find out how close to present reality is our old self-image. Also, other people we trust can often give us a clearer view of ourselves if we ask them for feedback.

What are you good at?

Four lists, selected from the many activities we learn over the years, are given (*below*). To find out what kind of activities you are good at, read through each list and check those at which you know you are very competent.

Put a cross by those activities which you feel are not yet fully developed to an adequate level of competence. If in doubt about your competence, put a cross anyway.

MANIPULATING OBJECTS	ORGANIZING INFORMATION	RELATING WITH PEOPLE	CREATING IDEAS
☐ Use utensils correctly	☐ Find out facts	☐ Get people talking	☐ Make color schemes
☐ Visualize 3-dimensionally	☐ Keep accounts	☐ Organize people	☐ Write creatively
☐ Make things from scratch	☐ Solve problems	☐ Inspire people	☐ Listen to sounds
☐ Keep your balance	☐ Take stock	☐ Cooperate in a team	☐ Improvise & adapt
☐ Coordinate hand & eye	☐ Sort things	☐ Receive appreciation	☐ Be spontaneous
☐ Diagnose practical faults	☐ Do mental arithmetic	☐ Represent opinions	☐ Be witty
☐ Cook, serve & host meals	☐ Write or type clearly	☐ Give assistance	☐ Express feelings
☐ Do household D.I.Y. jobs	☐ Follow instructions	☐ Socialize with ease	☐ Develop ideas
☐ Do all kinds of housework	☐ Time things accurately	☐ Take a joke	☐ Size up situations
☐ Use tools correctly	☐ Analyze information	☐ Convey understanding	☐ Light rooms effectively
☐ Construct useful things	☐ Diagnose problems	☐ Open conversations	☐ Converse or discuss
☐ Mend things	☐ Evaluate facts	☐ Conduct meetings	☐ Draw pictures or plans
☐ Drive safely	☐ Remember things	☐ Show appreciation	☐ Design things to make
☐ Work with precision	☐ Make lists	☐ Negotiate effectively	☐ Compose tunes or songs
☐ Take measurements	☐ Budget financially	☐ Address a meeting	☐ Make up stories
☐ Cultivate plants	☐ Give reports	☐ Inform others	☐ Pick up ideas
☐ Service machinery	☐ Keep to routines	☐ Welcome visitors	☐ Use intuition
☐ Do the family shopping	☐ Observe details	☐ Keep a confidence	☐ Act or imitate

What are you best at?

Count the total number of checks and crosses in each of the lists (*left*) and enter them in the table (*right*).

You may find that you have more checks in one of the lists than in others. This list will indicate in which areas your particular interests and talents lie.

You can always improve your level of competence in activities marked with a cross by using them in a context where you are doing whatever you do best. If you read the description appropriate to your best skill (*below*), you will see how this can be done.

SUMMARY TABLE OF MY BASIC SKILLS	Total number of checks	Total number of crosses
Manipulating objects		
Organizing information		
Relating with people		
Creating ideas		

People who are best at manipulating objects
These people generally enjoy practical, realistic activities with machines, objects, plants, food, electronic circuits, animals, fabrics and other things they can handle.

They prefer doing things which involve using their hands, feet and bodies with skill. They are realistic people with a sense of practical application.

They organize information, create ideas and relate to people best when they are involved in manipulating objects.

People who are best at organizing information
These people generally enjoy reliable routines with figures, words, facts, timetables, computer systems, legal material and regulations that they can keep in order.

They prefer doing things which involve using their memories and their eye for details. They are well-organized people with a sense of logical application.

They manipulate objects, create ideas and relate to people best when they are involved in organizing information.

YOUR BEST SKILL

People who are best at creating ideas
These people generally enjoy spontaneous and varied activities in which they are free to focus on their feelings and respond to their intuition.

They prefer doing things that involve tossing ideas around, trying out results and developing unexpected angles. They are independent people with a sense of aesthetic application.

They manipulate objects, organize information and relate to people best when they are involved in creating ideas.

People who are best at relating with people
These people generally enjoy being involved with others as helpers, healers, teachers, leaders, instructors, bodyguards and other roles in which they can be helpful, supportive or concerned.

They prefer doing things that require tact and produce a response from others. They are sociable people with a sense of empathetic application.

They manipulate objects, organize information and create ideas best when they are involved in relating with other people.

Which basic skills does your new venture require?

Whatever project you undertake, it would be a good idea to check if the basic skills you will need match your natural inclinations.

If, for example, you find that relating with people is your area of least competence, then it might be unwise to start a venture that would rely entirely on social skills until you have prepared yourself, for example by taking some training.

REFERENCES
SECTION THREE **Learning and researching.** (pp. 134-5)
Getting yourself trained. (pp. 136-7)
You can choose other skills from SECTION THREE.

What are your limitations?

Limitations are like brick walls. The brick walls that prevent us from becoming successful appear to be solid. Some of them are solid, because they are outside our control, such as world events, the economy or some physical limitations we may have inherited, so we may just have to learn to climb over those walls.

Other walls are only as solid as we let them be, because they are partially under our control, such as the influence of our family or of other people, or the need to gain qualifications or skills.

The biggest and most solid wall of all is the one we build with our own attitudes and beliefs. This wall is totally under our own control.

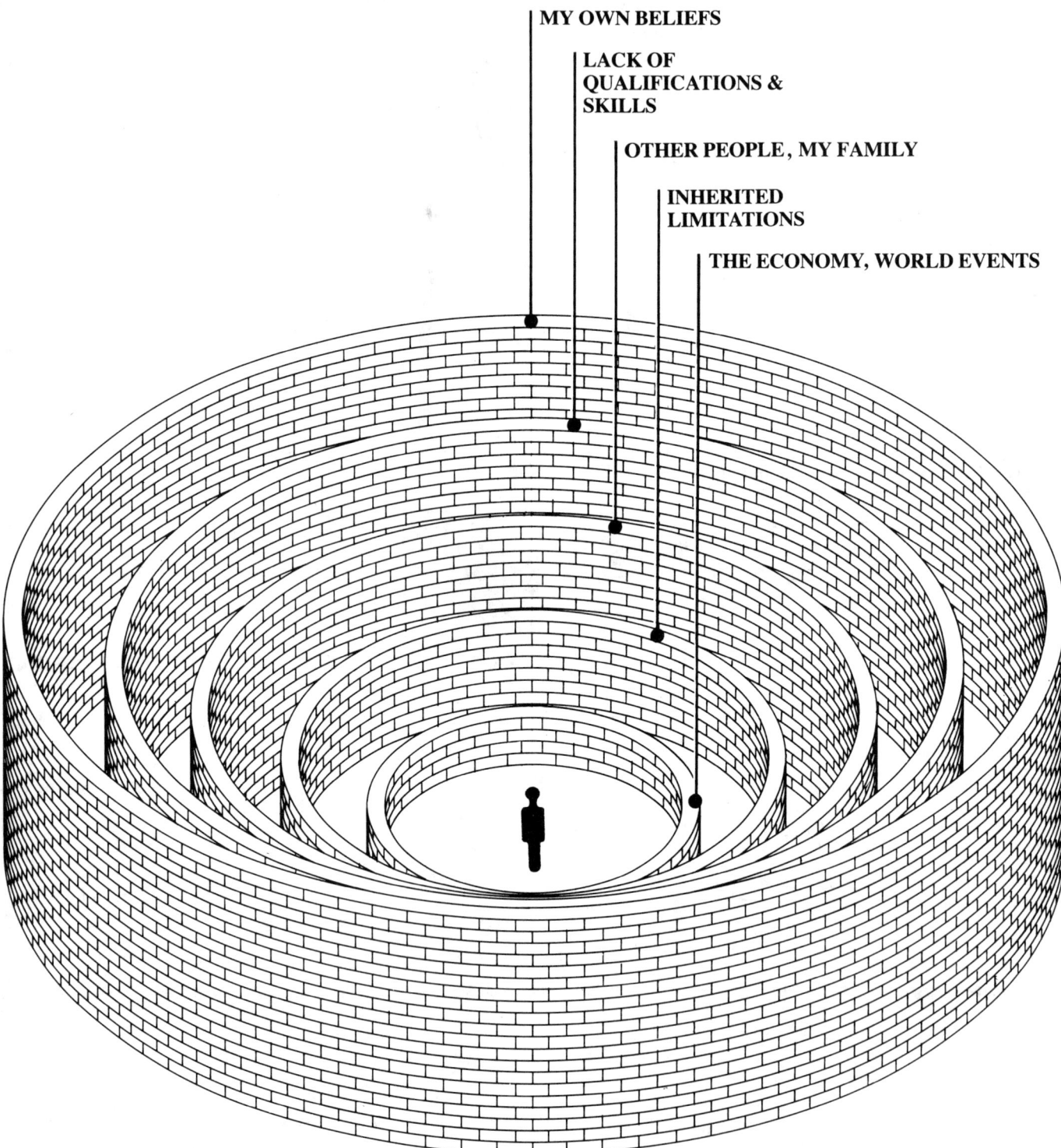

MY OWN BELIEFS
LACK OF QUALIFICATIONS & SKILLS
OTHER PEOPLE, MY FAMILY
INHERITED LIMITATIONS
THE ECONOMY, WORLD EVENTS

HOW TO EXAMINE YOUR OWN WALL OF BELIEFS

Here are eight bricks, interpretations of which are given *(below)*. Cross out the ones that are not applicable to you. Underneath each brick is the name of the skill or strategy you can use to knock those bricks out of your wall of beliefs.

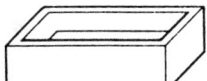

1. If I have problems I'm a failure.
SECTION THREE
Making decisions
(pp. 124-5)

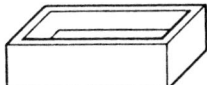

3. I can't live without...
SECTION THREE
Analyzing situations
(pp. 126-7)

5. SOMEWHERE in this world is...
SECTION THREE
Knowing what they want
(pp. 142-3)

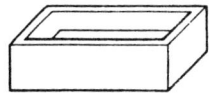

7. I don't know how to...
[Choose from SECTION THREE]

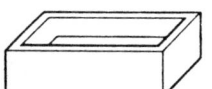

2. I ought to keep my problems to myself.
SECTION THREE
Getting feedback
(pp. 116-7)

4. I shouldn't have to push myself...
SECTION THREE
Presenting yourself
(pp. 138-9)

6. No matter what I do...
SECTION THREE
Courting failure
(pp. 108-9)

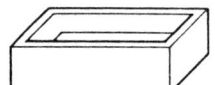

8. It's all right for...
SECTION THREE
Displacing your hang-ups
(pp. 144-5)

INTERPRETATIONS OF THE EIGHT BRICKS

1. If I have problems I'm a failure.
All normal people have problems. Successful people turn their problems into challenges and enjoy resolving them. They learn how to resolve conflicts and how to use an action tree, so they never get stuck in an impossible situation.

2. I ought to keep my problems to myself.
Not if you want to be successful you don't! It is true that some people like to talk things out and others prefer to think them out privately, but all research on success shows that it really is true that solving problems is usually improved by the contributions of other people.

3. I can't live without... money, position, love, etc.
How many times have you said something like this? It takes a brave person to sit down and analyze these kinds of statements; to challenge some of your own most fundamental beliefs about what you can and cannot live without.

Some of them are rather like a ball and chain that we drag around with us all our lives. Cut the chain, and we feel suddenly very vulnerable without that heavy, comfortable ball to drag us back, ensuring that we never become successful! If you have a pet ball and chain, try using analytical skills to find out if you really do need it anymore.

4. I shouldn't have to push myself or sell myself.
Many of us labor under the illusion that someday the great talent scout will bring us our due reward. We hope the "headhunter" will call us on the telephone, or that the "knight in shining armor" will rescue us. Fairy Godmothers do sometimes turn up, but having enough realistic confidence in yourself to bring your own talents out into the open is certain to bring success. Learning to present yourself is a basic skill available to everyone.

5. SOMEWHERE in this world is...
The perfect job, my one true love, the magic formula... if only. In truth there are many jobs, many loves and many formulas available to you... if only you take the trouble to go out and find them. Jobs and love affairs are mostly what you make of them.

6. No matter what I do it won't turn out right.
Well, some people do make a career of proving how worthless they are. Usually this is a fear of becoming successful, of not being perfect or of failing. If others get to know how good you are at doing something, they will expect you to continue. Someone once said that to be successful you have to fail frequently. This is how we learn to be successful. It is how you learned to walk successfully, all those years ago.

7. I don't know how to...
The short answer is... you are never too old to learn. If you are out of practice, start on something you really want to know about. Whatever you want to learn will come easily.

8. It's all right for... men, women, younger people, etc.
If one of your beliefs is that other people can do it because they are of the opposite sex or of a different age, take a close look at this belief by imagining yourself doing what is "all right for them." Often you will discover your belief is invalid, although it may be a widely held belief.

For example, many men believe it is all right for women to be soft and gentle, but not men. Many women believe it is all right for men to be assertive, but not women. Do you hold any invalid beliefs?

It is, of course, realistic to be aware of actual physical limitations, but these are facts, not beliefs.

What advantages do you have?

Some advantages are free gifts and, as with commercial offers of free gifts, you may have to make an effort to gain from them. You may have been born physically attractive, inherited a talent for detective work, been brought up as bilingual or be related to a very influential person. All are free gifts with potential advantage.

Some advantages are acquired by chance or created by effort. For example, you choose to learn a skill or you meet a potentially advantageous business contact by chance.

Other advantages come of turning a limitation into an advantage. For example, personal income tax is a financial limitation. By taking the trouble to investigate tax regulations, most people could gain legal tax advantages and avoid paying tax unnecessarily. (This is quite distinct from illegal tax evasion.)

Finally, in some circumstances, advantage can also be gained by resisting a free gift. For example, the son of a family of powerful politicians who broke with tradition and became a geophysicist would probably gain in personal confidence.

Where are advantages to be found?
There are five main sources of advantage. A brief description of each is given (*below and right*), together with references from SECTION THREE, in brackets, to help you focus upon that source of advantage.

1 YOUR BELIEFS.
Personal conviction can be a powerful advantage. For example, your belief in the purpose and policy of the organization that employs you, your belief in yourself or your belief in the best course of action after you have examined all the alternatives. [**On being assertive** (pp. 112-3), **Resolving conflicts** (pp. 148-9)]

2 YOUR ACQUIRED SKILLS.
A range of skills, knowledge, qualifications or experience is indisputably advantageous in a world that is changing rapidly and in an era that demands excellence in every area of endeavor. One of the most valuable skills is knowing how to learn. [**Learning and researching** (pp. 134-5), **Getting yourself trained** (pp. 136-7)]

3 OTHER PEOPLE.
The knowledge, skills, influence and situation of other people can be an invaluable advantage, just as yours can be of advantage to them.

It is always possible to enquire, even if you are not certain that someone else can help or would be willing to help. Although you may sometimes have to "return to favor," most people enjoy the feeling of worth they get when someone else asks for assistance or advice. [**Persuading others** (pp. 114-5), **Developing a network** (pp. 132-3)]

4 YOUR NATURAL PERSONALITY AND TALENTS
It is often said that human potential is, like an iceberg, 80% hidden beneath the surface. Personality traits that you take for granted, such as being a charming host or a reliable friend, are some of your natural advantages. Furthermore, everyone has untapped or undeveloped talents. [**Acquiring a positive attitude** (pp. 118-9), **Presenting yourself** (pp. 138-9)]

5 YOUR ENVIRONMENT
The furniture in the room, the locality in which you live, the economic climate and geographical features of the world you inhabit, are all a part of your immediate environment. The broader environment would include trends in fashion, politics, social awareness and other influences. All are sources of advantage once you become aware of them. [**Analyzing situations** (pp. 126-7), **Knowing your environment** (pp. 140-1)

What advantages do you have?
Quite often we forget our dormant advantages because we are busy trying to make something else happen. To set you thinking, find one advantage that would fit each of the boxes in the table (*below*).

For example, consider the five boxes along the top line which relate to wealth. Find an advantage to write in each box by asking the following five questions:
In an endeavor to gain wealth...
1 How are my own beliefs an advantage?
2 Which of my skills are advantageous?
3 What advantage can other people give me?
4 How can I use my natural personality to advantage?
5 What advantage can I gain from my environment?
Then proceed to fill in the second row of boxes that relate to power, by asking the same five questions, beginning:
In an endeavor to gain power...
Continue through all six areas of endeavor, looking for actual or potential advantages and making a note in each box. You may find that you have to leave some boxes empty until you have completed the rest. Try returning to them later to see if there is an advantage you have overlooked.

You will probably find that the exercise will stimulate your awareness of several advantages in one or two areas. Keep a note of all of them; they could be very helpful as your chosen venture moves into the action stage.

When you have completed the table, you will have a record of the many advantages at your disposal. If you have difficulty thinking of advantages, refer for help to:
SECTION ONE **The advantages and pitfalls** of each of the six areas of endeavor: **Wealth** (pp. 18-9), **Power** (pp. 28-9), **Status** (pp. 38-9), **Challenge** (pp. 48-9), **Well-being** (pp. 58-9), **Love** (pp. 68-9).
SECTION TWO **Generating ideas** (pp. 84-5), **What are you good at?** (pp. 90-1).

MY ADVANTAGES		SOURCES OF ADVANTAGE				
		My beliefs	My skills	Other people	My personality	The environment
AREAS OF ENDEAVOR	Wealth					
	Power					
	Status					
	Challenge					
	Well-being					
	Love					

Making a time-scale

MY TIME-SCALE for the week beginning: ....

	24·00	01·00	02·00	03·00	04·00	05·00	06·00	07·00	08·00	09·00	10·00	11·00	12·00
MONDAY													
TUESDAY													
WEDNESDAY													
THURSDAY													
FRIDAY													
SATURDAY													
SUNDAY													

A time-scale is a statement of when you are intending to do selected things, and for how long. Time-scales are measured in clock-time, ranging from fractions of a second to several years. A daily appointments diary or a seven-year development plan are examples of activities organized into a time-scale.

How to find the time
If you are starting a new project, you need to know how much time is needed for it and when you are going to find the time for it. For example, William made a basic plan for his new venture, estimating that it would require 15 hours a week of his time during the first few months. He already had a very busy schedule, so he had to look at his current weekly time-scale and reorganize it.

What is your current weekly time-scale?
The only way to be certain of how you spend your time during a typical week is to record your activities each day. If you try to record a whole week at once, it is unlikely that you will remember accurately. To find out how you spend your time, read the four steps (*below*), then fill in your time-scale (*above*).
1 Record each day how you spent your time during each hourly period. You may need to write across several hours if an activity lasted that long. Include even short breaks. If you want more space than is given here, draw a similar schedule on a large sheet of paper.
2 Write in the time for any pre-arranged appointment and note if you were able to keep to the time.
3 Use a watch – don't rely on guesswork.
4 When you have completed your time-scale for a typical week, complete the questionnaires (*right*). You may then like to rewrite your time-scale to include the time you need to spend on your new venture.

WHAT DOES YOUR TIME-SCALE FOR THE WEEK TELL YOU?

1 Is it a typical week? If not, how is it different?

	Yes	No

....

2 How many hours during the week were spent in my different activities? (You may find that some of these overlap and some may not be relevant to your life. Add or delete anything you wish.)

Activities	Number of hours per week
Providing income	
Resting & sleeping	
Washing & dressing	
Eating & drinking	
Selecting & shopping	
Traveling & walking	
Doing household jobs	
Being with spouse	
Being a parent	
Chatting & discussing	
Studying & learning	
Leisure activities	
Community activities	
Time alone	
Doing nothing	
Other activities	
Total number of hours per week	

	13·00	14·00	15·00	16·00	17·00	18·00	19·00	20·00	21·00	22·00	23·00	24·00	
													MONDAY
													TUESDAY
													WEDNESDAY
													THURSDAY
													FRIDAY
													SATURDAY
													SUNDAY

Time and motion

Most time-scales involve activities. Knowing how long is required for an activity will help you to make a reliable time-scale.

Cash flow is a very important financial time-scale; wealth in the form of fixed assets is useless when you need the cash next week to pay some bills.

Making a plan of when and how much cash is likely to come in and be paid out is essential in business and equally important when handling personal income. Colin's example (*below*) illustrates how to make a cash flow chart.

Part of Colin's cash flow chart for 1987

Items listed (*below*) can usefully be expanded in detail, for example car costs could be itemized as credit repayments, insurance, tax, gas, repairs, etc.

3 Which activities do I do by choice, and how long do I spend on each activity?	Number of hours per week

4 If I started a new venture that needed 15 hours a week, which time-slots could I make available?

Day of week	Time of day
....	.... to ....
....	.... to ....
....	.... to ....
....	.... to ....
....	.... to ....
....	.... to ....
....	.... to ....

	JANUARY			FEBRUARY			MARCH		
	In	Out	Bal*	In	Out	Bal*	In	Out	Bal*
Bf** from previous month:	900			1150			1100		
Net salary	1000			1000			1000		
Other income									
Sale of boat							500		
Mortgage		200			300			300	
House costs		150			250			150	
Car costs		250			300			350	
Personal		100			200			800	
Other expenses		50			–			–	
Medical treatment								300	
Totals	1,900	750	1150	2150	1050	1100	2600	1900	700
Cf*** to next month:			1150			1100			700

*Balance   **Brought forward   ***Carried forward

Setting standards

Standards are levels of achievement often set for reasons of safety, health, comfort and commonsense, and take into consideration moral, political and financial values. Standards affect the potential success of a venture.

How are standards determined?
In any endeavor there are four determinants of standards to be taken into account.
1. Statutory standards, as laid down by legislation. E.g. in Great Britain, touring caravans on a campsite must be parked at least 20 ft (6m) away from each other, a rule that will affect how many overnight rents can be charged on a campsite.

When deciding which regulations you may have to take into account, you should consult trade and professional bodies, lawyers and community advice centers.
2. Environmental standards, such as the laws of nature. E.g. a house built on the top of a receding cliff will eventually slip into the sea.

When deciding which laws of nature you may have to take into account, use your commonsense, consult reference libraries and get expert advice.

It would be commonsense, for example, to protect yourself against certain fatal diseases while exploring a tropical jungle; finding out what kind of protection against which diseases is a matter of taking proper expert advice.
3. Market standards, as determined by others. E.g. a restaurant is more likely to flourish when customers enjoy the food.

In order to decide which market demands to take into account, do some market research, consult other people with experience and above all be prepared to be flexible. Markets can be fickle.

If your endeavor was political power, then the electorate is your market. If marriage is your venture, then your intended spouse is your "market;" taking into account your partner's standards is crucial if a marriage is to succeed.
4. Personal standards, as decided by you. E.g. a refusal to be seen driving in anything other than a pure white Porsche car could stimulate an ambition to achieve a high income.

When deciding on your own standards, give careful thought to their rating. An essential standard that cannot be achieved will indicate that you should cut your losses and pull out of the venture, turning your attention to something more satisfying.

PLANNING FOR STANDARDS
While preparing to launch your new venture, standards will have to be taken into account. You can give consideration to these by consulting **Operating standards** (*below*), and then answering the questions raised in the table (*right*).
1. Write down your venture in the space provided.
2. Consider each question in turn, writing down your answers. If the question is not appropriate to your venture, ignore it. There is space for you to add anything extra at the bottom of the table.
3. When you have completed all the questions appropriate to your venture, decide if each standard is **essential, desirable** or **a bonus** – see **Definitions** (*below*) – and make a check in the appropriate column.
4. The completed table will form a useful reference point during the action stage of your venture and you may like to refer to it when checking your progress.

Operating standards
One of the most vital aspects of setting standards is their practicality. For example, it is fruitless to decide you will sell only pink umbrellas with green spots, since people who buy umbrellas want a choice and, the bigger the choice, the more you would sell.

An operating standard that says: "We will always pay local suppliers on delivery," is good for business, providing you have also set yourself some sensible cash flow standards.

Promises are no guarantee of standards. If you make a promise, always consider first how you are going to keep to your promise. Similarly, an agreement between a couple to behave according to a particular standard can only be kept if it works in practice.

You may like to reconsider the list you make, once you have tried out your standards in practice.

Definitions
Essential means that you could not go ahead unless this standard is achieved.
Desirable means that, although this standard would definitely enhance the situation, you could continue without it being achieved.
A bonus means that achieving this standard would be great if it happened, but would not be essential to success.
U.S.P is your unique selling proposition; i.e. what have you on offer that will make other people want your product more than they want the product of your competitors. A term usually used in business, it can be equally useful when climbing the status ladder, acquiring power or gaining in love.

REFERENCES
For further information, refer to:
SECTION TWO   Finding an outlet (pp. 102-3)
SECTION THREE Checking your progress (pp.150-1)

STANDARDS REFERENCE TABLE A summary of my venture:	Essential	Desirable	A bonus
STATUTORY STANDARDS Six legal requirements I should investigate are:			
1			
2			
3			
4			
5			
6			
ENVIRONMENTAL STANDARDS Six laws of nature I should take into account are:			
1			
2			
3			
4			
5			
6			
MARKET STANDARDS Six market demands I should take into account are:			
1			
2			
3			
4			
5			
6			
PERSONAL STANDARDS			
1 Which kind of wealth do I want?			
2 Which kind of status do I want?			
3 Which kind of power do I want?			
4 Which kind of challenge do I want?			
5 Which kind of well-being do I want?			
6 Which kind of love do I want?			
7 How much money am I prepared to invest?			
8 How much time am I prepared to invest?			

9 Which three benefits do I most want?
  (i)
  (ii)
  (iii)			

10 What is my U.S.P?			
11 What is my political standpoint?			
12 What is my moral standpoint?			
ANY OTHER QUESTIONS OF STANDARD:			
1			
2			

Enlisting help

Understanding what help you may need and knowing how and when to get it is part of the planning process. By completing the exercise (*below*), you can clarify what help you will need, where you are going to get it, how much it will cost and the order of its importance in your plan of action.

WHAT KIND OF HELP WILL YOU NEED?
With your chosen venture in mind, answer **Yes** or **No** to each of the ten questions in the table (*below*). When you have finished answering, look again at all the ones you have marked **Yes** and, in the spaces given below the questions, write precisely what help you will need and from whom or where you will get it. Include all other kinds of help you will need in the blank spaces at the bottom of the table.

Order of importance
Under the column bearing this heading, number the kinds of help you require in order of chronological importance. For example, you may have to obtain the consent of your spouse before offering your home as collateral against a loan, or you may need the help of a designer before you can being to explore potential markets for your idea.

The cost of help
Under the three columns bearing this heading, consider carefully how you will have to pay for the help you enlist. Will you have to pay in money, for example by paying interest on a financial loan, or by paying wages for labor? Will you need to pay in services, for example by returning a favor? Or will you have to pay by commitment, for example by fulfilling a contractual agreement or by remaining faithful to the spouse who gives emotional or material support? Place a check in the appropriate column.

THE HELP I WILL NEED My chosen venture			Order of importance	Money	Services	Commitment
Do I need help from members of my family?	Yes	No				
Do I need financial help, such as loans?	Yes	No				
Do I need the help of an expert to teach me skills?	Yes	No				
Do I need the help of legal consultants?	Yes	No				
Do I need the help of marketing consultants?	Yes	No				
Do I need help in the design stage?	Yes	No				
Do I need help to sell myself, my idea or product?	Yes	No				
Might I need specific counseling services?	Yes	No				
Might I need to obtain equipment or supplies, or to gain access to information or places?	Yes	No				
Are there other kinds of help I will need?						

Losers: do you really need them?
You can end up drained, financially or emotionally, if you accept help from or give help to a loser. The presence or absence of wealth, qualifications and status does not necessarily distinguish winners from losers. Losers aim to either become dependant on you or make you permanently dependant on them.

So, when enlisting help, or giving it, choose a winner. Winners can be detected by their response. If you give the help that is needed by a winner, they will use the help you give and not become a long-term drain on your financial or emotional resources. If you enlist the help you need from a winner, they will offer the best they can, at a price that is reasonable and not waste your time or theirs.

Winners offer you temporary structures on which you can depend; losers want you to need them for ever.

Help and support are temporary structures
No amount of help or support can give you the firm foundation skills and faith in yourself that you need to succeed in your venture. Help and support are temporary structures, enlisted to enable you to take another step forward which would otherwise be difficult or impossible.

WHICH HELP WOULD YOU ACCEPT?
Each illustration (*below*) shows help being given, either by a winner or by a loser. Check the ones you think are useful, temporary structures on offer from a winner and put a cross by those that would have a very negative effect eventually because the help is being offered by a loser who is trying to make you permanently dependant (the only way a loser can win in the long run).

Which choices did you make?
A, B and **C** are situations in which a loser is trying to make you permanently dependant by being helpful.
A is giving you support in such a way that if you move away he would fall down. He is reckoning that you wouldn't do that because you know that if he had withdrawn his support in your moment of need, you would have fallen down.
B is helping by making life so comfortable that you won't want to move away and leave her.
C helped you to get up there and now has you in his power because you can't see him hidden away, keeping you up there.

D, E and **F** are situations in which a winner is giving a helping hand to another winner. Sometimes the situation could be reversed. Each knows the other can be depended upon in a moment of need because each person has a firm foundation of their own. The dependency is temporary.
D is offering to make the last pull up the cliff a little easier.
E is offering temporary balance as you leap from the last stepping stone.
F is casting the rope that tied you to the shore to give you a better start on your trip across the lake.

Finding an outlet

Whatever your endeavor... making money, finding love, winning an election, exploring, inventing, increasing your power, gaining social position or improving your personal well-being... sooner or later you will need an outlet.

The outlets for products, services, skills, love, power, status and challenges will all be different but equally essential. It is useless planning to make a profit selling certain gadgets if nobody wants to buy them; it is fruitless to transform your whole way of being unless you interact with the outside world; and a rich imagination would remain dormant without a medium for expression.

A market for your endeavor
Marketing is an activity normally associated with business; the concepts are equally applicable to any kind of endeavor.

A market is the medium through which you channel your endeavor and it is the sounding board that feeds back a response. Success is a positive and satisfying response from your market. Failure is a negative response from your market, which you can use to improve your endeavors.

If a market does not exist or cannot be created, then your endeavor will remain barren, frustrated and neither a success nor a failure.

WHICH MARKET OUTLET?

MARKETS REQUIRED FOR CREATING WEALTH

- **A PERSONAL FORTUNE** — Someone to pay for your talent.
- **A DYNASTY** — A large, talented, ambitious family.
- **PROMISSORY WEALTH** — A patent or contract with royalties.
- **BUSINESS** — Customers to buy your goods or services.
- **TERRITORY** — People who want your land or its resources.
- **MARRIAGE** — A rich bachelor or spinster to marry.
- **ARBITRAGE** — Stock market membership or inside information...
- **CHANCE** — A gambling casino or bingo, etc.
- **ENTITLEMENT** — A vacancy in an occupation with high income and perks.
- **PROPERTY** — People to rent or lease your property.
- **EQUITY** — Profitable ventures requiring your investment.
- **PATRONAGE** — A patron whose image you could enhance.

MARKETS THROUGH WHICH TO DEVELOP YOUR POWERS

- **ASSERTIVE POWER** — Issues to confront.
- **PHYSICAL POWER** — A physical sport or activity to pursue.
- **INTELLECTUAL POWER** — A problem requiring extensive, structured thought.
- **EMOTIONAL POWER** — A situation about which you have very strong feelings.
- **EXECUTIVE POWER** — An activity requiring leadership decisions.
- **INFLUENTIAL POWER** — A situation or person available to your influence.
- **POLITICAL POWER** — A political candidacy.
- **SEXUAL POWER** — A sexual partner who has something you want.
- **EVANGELICAL POWER** — People who need convincing of their self-worth.
- **REFORMATIVE POWER** — A situation requiring long-term improvements.
- **CONGRUENT POWER** — An activity that matches your personal beliefs.
- **IMAGINATIVE POWER** — A medium to give form to your imagination.

MARKETS THROUGH WHICH TO ACQUIRE STATUS

- **FIRST POSITION** — Something that has never been done before.
- **LEGENDARY STATUS** — A popular interest in your kind of lifestyle.
- **UNCONVENTIONAL STATUS** — A lifestyle contrary to conventional expectations.
- **THE BOSS** — An organization of which to take charge.
- **STARDOM** — A potentially huge fan club.
- **THE REPRESENTATIVE** — A collective point of view requiring expression.
- **THE MEDIATOR** — A conflict in which to mediate.
- **THE WINNER** — A competition to win.
- **THE GURU** — A group of people needing spiritual direction.
- **THE CONTROLLER** — A situation requiring an outsider to control it.
- **THE SPECIALIST** — People requiring your specialist skills.
- **SAINTHOOD** — Appreciation, in the future, of your virtues.

What kind of market outlet do you need?
Look under the area of your endeavor (*below*) and select from the list of markets the one (or ones) that you need to find. If your endeavor embraces more than one area, select from each area.

Is there a market for your endeavor?
Only you can answer this question when you have researched your markets.

Power is a very flexible commodity; if you can't find an outlet for your power in politics, you could always redirect your power, for example, into intellectual pursuits.

Markets for your aspirations to wealth or status may require careful analysis. There are often clearly structured routes that must be taken to achieve status, and several well-proven methods of market research for those who plan to trade. There are many books and agencies available to provide advice for your particular circumstances.

REFERENCES
For further useful information, refer to:
SECTION THREE **Developing a network** (pp. 132-3)
Learning and researching (pp. 134-5)

MARKETS REPRESENTING A CHALLENGE

- TO PIONEER
  A totally new way of doing something.
- TO BUILD
  Something requiring long-term construction.
- TO DISCOVER
  An unknown place, substance, process or person, etc.
- TO NURTURE
  Something that needs long-term help to develop.
- TO CREATE
  A medium through which to express your creativity.
- TO MASTER
  A discipline to learn, practice and use.
- TO INVENT
  A practical application for your ideas.
- TO SOLVE
  An unsolved puzzle, problem, mystery or impasse, etc.
- TO EXPLORE
  A known place, concept or activity to investigate.
- TO OVERCOME
  A difficulty, adversity, handicap or opposition, etc.
- TO RISK
  An activity involving danger by chance.
- TO SELF-ACTUALIZE
  Willingness to develop fully your own personality.

MARKETS OFFERING OPPORTUNITY FOR WELL-BEING

- ENERGY
  Activities offering stimulation and mild anxiety.
- BEAUTY
  Beauty salons, health clubs, dance routines, etc.
- YOUTH
  Contact with fresh ideas and new processes, etc.
- HOME
  A place almost anywhere that feels safe and familiar.
- A LITTLE APPLAUSE
  An appreciative audience.
- AN OCCUPATION
  An attractive activity demanding commitment.
- AWARENESS
  Experiences to observe, question and sense, etc.
- PURPOSE
  A clear aim, goal or objective.
- OPPORTUNITY
  A set of propitious circumstances.
- LONG LIFE
  A constant succession of interests and ventures.
- INTEGRITY
  Something to do that you honestly believe is right.
- FREEDOM
  Choices to make for which you take full responsibility.

MARKETS THROUGH WHICH TO GIVE EXPRESSION TO YOUR LOVE

- HEROIC LOVE
  A brave deed to be undertaken for someone else.
- CARING LOVE
  A situation that needs your unselfish devotion.
- FREE LOVE
  Others who need love temporarily.
- HUMANITARIAN LOVE
  A human cause in need of help and support.
- ROMANTIC LOVE
  A perfect time, place and person for sensual pleasure.
- MARRIED LOVE
  A financial and sexual contract with one partner.
- SACRIFICIAL LOVE
  Someone whose need is greater than yours.
- EROTIC LOVE
  A long-term sensual, sexual partner.
- DIVINE LOVE
  A complex personal lifestyle to reform.
- DEVOTED LOVE
  Someone who cannot be successful without your love.
- PLATONIC LOVE
  People who could reciprocate your friendship.
- SELF-LOVE
  Faith in your own self worth and adequacy.

Section Three
ACTION

How can you achieve your aims? The answer is to have a clear strategy and the skills that are needed to implement your policies. A strategy is a long-term policy or direction. A skill is a practical method for accomplishing something in the short-term.

An overall strategy does have its pitfalls. The more committed you are to one direction, the less inclined you may be to change when circumstances demand it. Learning a variety of skills ensures flexibility of strategy. The more skills you acquire the easier it becomes to adjust your general direction as necessary, thus ensuring ultimate success.

Nine basic strategies and fourteen practical skills are contained in this section. References from the previous sections guide you to the ones most likely to be appropriate to your new project.

Four ways to change a situation

There are four basic strategies for managing in a situation that you wish to change.
1. **Change the situation** or parts of the situation and make it as you want it to be.
2. **Change yourself** perhaps by taking a different attitude to the situation.
3. **Live with it creatively** by getting the very best out of what there is and reducing the disadvantages.
4. **Leave the situation** completely by dropping it, moving away and making a permanent exit.

Working out your options
To illustrate the way you can work out your options in more detail, three examples are given (*below*). You will notice that all four strategies for change are taken into consideration before a final choice can be made. Every option is listed under each strategy, regardless of whether it is either possible or desirable. Evaluation can take place after all the options have been listed. If you have difficulty thinking of options refer to SECTION TWO **Generating ideas** (pp. 84-5).

More often than not, a combination of any of the first three strategies can be useful. The fourth one, leaving or moving away, inevitably includes the question: Moving towards what?

PETER'S EXAMPLE
Peter finds his job is no longer satisfying and wants to make a change. These are the options he listed.

1 Change the situation
A Negotiate a change of responsibilities.
B Reorganize my team membership.
C Suggest new projects.
D Suggest how my routine can be better organized.

2 Change myself
A Update my knowledge.
B Attend the international conference.
C Investigate my potential career pattern.
D Lower my expectations.

3 Live with it creatively
A Take up a new outside interest.
B Negotiate job-sharing and take another job.
C Reorganize how I spend my time.
D Take a fresh look at my colleagues.

4 Leave
A Transfer to another department or branch.
B Get a new job elsewhere.
C Quit my job.
D Get leave of absence.

MARGARET'S EXAMPLE
Margaret's marriage to Gerald is no longer satisfying and she wants to make a change.

1 Change the situation
A Make time for us to talk privately.
B Control our financial commitments.
C Suggest we join the marriage counseling group.
D Arrange a week's holiday without the children.

2 Change myself
A Turn my complaints into constructive action.
B Learn how to communicate more clearly.
C Examine my attitudes to each member of the family.
D Re-assess my expectations.

3 Live with it creatively
A Get retrained.
B Get a job.
C Concentrate more on the children.
D Go out to social events without Gerald.

4 Leave
A Go away on my own for six months.
B Leave and get a job in another town.
C Join an expedition to China.
D Take the children and live with mother.

TOM'S EXAMPLE
Tom owns a restaurant which has recently lost some business and he wants to make a change.

1 Change the situation
A Expand the business.
B Change the image and style.
C Establish a bar.
D Take professional advice.

2 Change myself
A Take a more personal interest in the customers.
B Be more adventurous with my recipes.
C Learn some management skills.
D Keep my accounts properly.

3 Live with it creatively
A Cut down on costs.
B Take a part-time job and put Mary in charge.
C Concentrate on developing the take-away side.
D Lower my expectations.

4 Leave
A Cut my losses and sell out immediately.
B Offer Mary a lease for two years.
C Close down and sell my assets.
D Turn the property into a shop.

THE POSITION I WANT TO CHANGE
When you are in a situation you want to change, use the spaces provided (*below*) to list your options in response to the questions asked.

1 How can I change the situation itself?

A ....
B ....
C ....
D ....

2 How can I change myself?

A ....
B ....
C ....
D ....

3 How can I live with the situation creatively?

A ....
B ....
C ....
D ....

4 How can I exit from the situation and where do I go?

A ....
B ....
C ....
D ....

Evaluating your options
It is useful to select several options, put them in chronological order, and prepare your ground before you start to apply any of them. Any personal changes you make should be designed to have an effect upon the situation.

Preparing for the worst
Things don't always work out; other people, external events or your own mistakes will often prevent or postpone success. The challenge is how well you can respond in a situation that really cannot be changed.

REFERENCES
To explore alternatives return to SECTION ONE.
To assess a situation, formulate back-up plans or improve your personal skills, turn to:
SECTION TWO **Basic planning** (pp. 86-7)
SECTION THREE **Negotiating for what you want** (pp. 110-1)
　　　　　　　Making decisions (pp. 124-5)
　　　　　　　Analyzing situations (pp. 126-7)
To cope with disappointment, turn to:
SECTION THREE **Acquiring a positive attitude** (pp. 118-9)

Courting failure

Whatever you do in life, you know that the moment you set out to achieve something, you are risking failure. Courting failure is a way of reducing that risk.

Just like courting the one you love, courting failure is a stimulating and exciting activity. Courting reduces the risk of being unsuccessful and, whatever the outcome, makes the process much more interesting and satisfying.

How to court failure
The short answer is by doing something differently than you have been doing it for the last five or ten years or so. In fact, there comes a time when the way we have been doing things for years no longer works, if it ever did. So, to court failure, change unproductive behavior. This may involve changing what you do or how you do it. One of the most effective changes is to work on the pleasure principle.

The pleasure principle
Simply stated, the pleasure principle means have fun and *enjoy* whatever you set out to do. When your prime motivation is pleasure, depression and stress vanish, energy is released and time is never a major problem. As Robert Townsend, former Chairman of Avis Rent-a-

THE STREET OF LIFE

The street of life is busy, exciting and hazardous, rather like a city thoroughfare. In our example (*far right*), four people, who all want to buy some fruit, are walking along the street. Across the road is an attractive fruit and flower stall.

Three people react unproductively, while the fourth, Raymond, gets exactly what he wants, and in a just and fair manner, having fun in the process. We all behave like Raymond sometimes.

Read the descriptions (*below*) of how each person behaves in this situation. Then ask yourself this question: Do I ever behave like Nancy, Ronnie or Annie when the outcome is vitally important?

If your answer is yes, then you may like to try courting failure by changing your behavior in the manner suggested for each of the three people.

 Annie the acceptor

Annie likes to feel involved with life as much as possible. She does this by enthusiastically accepting every opportunity without question.

When Annie sees the fruit stall, her eyes light up; if she doesn't hurry they will all be gone, so she dashes across the road. Too late she realizes she should have stopped to look if the road was clear. This time she was lucky to end up in hospital with only broken bones, but she does get a bunch of flowers from her boyfriend when he visits her.

Annie is used to having to pay dearly for anything she wants in this life. In the long term she avoids getting what she really wants by offering too high a price for too small a return.

 Ronnie the rejector

Ronnie likes to control life as much as possible. He does this by deliberating at length before taking action and rejecting most things on logical grounds.

He'd been wanting apples for a long time and sees the fruit stall which looks attractive from this distance. He eventually crosses the road carefully. On closer inspection the apples don't look so good and are much too expensive. He goes home convincing himself that perhaps tomorrow he will find some better apples.

Ronnie is used to never finding what he really wants; he hardly expects it anymore. Next time he probably won't even risk crossing the street, preferring to admire unattainable apples from a distance.

 Nancy the neutralizer

Nancy avoids getting too emotionally involved in life as much as possible. She does this by neutralizing any stimulus that comes her way, which is why she often wears dark glasses.

Although she had it in mind to get some apples, she carefully ignores the fruit stall, and arrives home empty-handed, looking terribly overworked. Her best friend always feels sorry for Nancy and goes out to get some fruit for her.

Nancy attracts people who will provide for her, so she doesn't have to risk going out to get what she really wants for herself, because that would be both an ungrateful way of behaving and far too complicated and involving.

 Raymond the responder

Raymond enjoys being involved in life. He does this by responding to opportunities, taking a little time to consider the best course of action and savors the experience as he goes into action.

He sees the fruit stall, decides it is worth a visit, crosses the street where it is safe and spends a little time browsing, finally selecting the apples he wants. He doesn't expect perfection and he knows what would be a fair price to pay. He might even buy one to try before purchasing more, at the same time enjoying a brief conversation with the salesman.

Raymond enjoys putting some effort into getting what he wants, knows how much risk he is prepared to take and treats himself and others fairly.

Car, once said: "If you're not in business for fun and profit, what the hell are you doing here?"

If you have difficulty finding pleasure in what you do, then either you don't want to do it or you are being driven by redundant beliefs (injunctions). To check out your injunctions, refer to SECTION ONE **Do you want to be more powerful?** (pp. 30-1).

Unproductive behavior
There are three kinds of unproductive behavior; we may get stuck with any one of them, or even a combination. Each behavior has served, in the past, to protect us from failing (and all the consequences of failure, such as looking a fool). Unfortunately, avoiding failure almost inevitably means avoiding success. Thus, a very effective way to court failure (and increase our chances for success) is to change the behavior that we use to avoid failing. The street of life is a way of illustrating these three kinds of unproductive behavior and a fourth, more effective way of doing things.

REFERENCES
For further help or understanding turn to:
SECTION TWO **What does it take to succeed?** (pp. 82-3)
What are your limitations? (pp. 92-3)

Courting failure by changing unproductive behavior
Nancy, Ronnie and Annie all invite failure, by trying, even unconsciously, to avoid it. To invite success, they each have to court failure by changing their current unproductive behavior. In other words, they would each have to risk not getting fruit except by their own responsible efforts.

How Nancy could court failure
Nancy could take off her dark glasses, take notice of the fruit stall and risk feeling involved in the world by buying some apples which she and her best friend could enjoy sharing. Of course, she may have to risk losing her best friend if the best friend can't exist without Nancy's continued dependency.

How Ronnie could court failure
Ronnie could let go of some of his control by asking the salesman, a friend or another purchaser to recommend apples. He could also buy one of each kind of apple, take them home and decide which tastes best to him. Of course, he would have to risk relying on other people and on his senses, as well as his logic.

How Annie could court failure
Annie could count to thirty, breathing evenly, before jumping into anything. Once relaxed, she could think through what to do next, find a safe crossing and take her time choosing apples. Of course she would have to risk pleasing herself and getting what she wants by paying only the going rate.

Negotiating for what you want

Negotiation is a transaction between two parties to agree a price, a time or a set of circumstances. For example, negotiations take place when selling a car, buying a house, arranging time off work, making an employment contract or agreeing an international treaty.

Unlike persuasion and assertion, the negotiated transaction always involves the active participation of at least two parties, such as between buyer and seller, employer and employee or nation and nation. Couples, friends, parents and children also negotiate.

Assertion and persuasion
These two activities are described later in this section (pp. 112-5) and should not be confused with negotiation, although assertiveness and persuasiveness may be used by one or other party during a negotiation.

How do YOU define negotiation?
1 A fair and equal give and take.
2 Finding a reasonable compromise.
3 Coming to an agreement that satisfies as far as possible the interests of both parties.

The realistic negotiator would choose number **3**.

Image
The image presented often influences the price charged and the price commanded. Clever negotiators never let big, luxurious images intimidate them. If you sometimes feel intimidated, refer to: **On being assertive** (pp. 112-3).

HOW EFFECTIVE ARE YOU AS A NEGOTIATOR?
Rarely do any two people agree on a price, a time or a set of circumstances without discussion. Success in any endeavor depends largely on your ability to negotiate effectively for what you want. Choose which you think is the best response in each situation described (*below*). Then score your choices from the key.

A For the first time, you have been asked to take the lead role in a new musical. You are offered low rates on the grounds that it is your first starring role and will help you to make a name and get much higher rates in the future. Would you:

☐ 1 Accept, because it is the opportunity you've been wanting and it will enhance your career prospects?

☐ 2 Refuse because you feel insulted?

☐ 3 Demand you are paid the top rate?

B A university abroad in a very attractive location has asked you to give the annual valedictory lecture on your recent research and wants to know how much you would charge. Would you:

☐ 1 Accept and quote your standard fee plus expenses?

☐ 2 Ask for more details of the event, such as who will be there and how many people?

☐ 3 Quote twice your normal fee, which will cover economy travel and still leave you in pocket?

C QUESTION FOR MEN. You are married and have a well paid job that you enjoy. Your wife says that now the children are at school she would like to restart her professional career. Would you:

☐ 1 Agree to her doing this on condition that she pays from her salary for a housekeeper?

☐ 2 Question her timing and suggest that she does a little part-time work for a couple of years?

☐ 3 Discuss what changes this would imply for the whole family and negotiate how to resolve them?

C QUESTION FOR WOMEN. You are married with school-age children. Your husband says that he would like to make a change of career that will involve giving up his job and taking a year's retraining. Would you:

☐ 1 Agree to getting a job to support the family providing he looks after the house while he is studying?

☐ 2 Question his timing and suggest that he keeps his job and does the course part-time over the next two years?

☐ 3 Discuss the changes this woud imply for the whole family and negotiate how to resolve them?

D You have quoted your price and terms for a bulk purchase of essential raw materials. The buyer says that he has more attractive prices from your competitors and you will have to do better than that. Would you:

☐ 1 Ask which features of your proposal he finds attractive?

☐ 2 Ask for details of the other offers?

☐ 3 Offer to increase the size of the delivery at the same price?

E Your young son wants a ball he sees in a shop window. He has already spent his pocket money and threatens to scream right there in public if you don't buy it for him. Would you:

☐ 1 Buy it to keep the peace?

☐ 2 Say NO very firmly and threaten retribution if he screams?

☐ 3 Ask him how he could raise the cash to buy the ball himself?

F You want to sell your vintage car and know you would be very fortunate to get more than $20,000 for it. An eager enthusiast has heard you are interested in selling and offers you $25,000 cash on the spot. Would you:

☐ 1 Accept immediately?

☐ 2 Start haggling over the price?

☐ 3 Accept and throw in some spare parts?

G You have an old caravan cluttering up your space. You think it would probably fetch $200. Which price would you ask in your advertisement.

☐ 1 $240?

☐ 2 $200 or nearest offer

☐ 3 Any offers?

Scoring key
The following are the options that would be chosen by a good negotiator. Score 10 for each one you choose. **A3, B2, C3, D1, E3, F2, G1.** Maximum score 70.

If your score is below 50, reading the following comments will give you some ideas on how to improve your negotiating strategies.

A3 Never undersell yourself
You have been offered a leading role and you should expect to get paid for it. However, demanding the top rate does not ensure you will get it under the circumstances, but it does leave room to negotiate. Even if you have to accept a small drop from the top level, you still gain and show that you are not an easy pushover. If you accept the low rate, you can hardly expect anything better when the next lead role comes along; worse still, your employer may even think he has misjudged your ability if you accept a low rate.

B2 Create an impact
Asking for information not only gives you some facts and leaves room for negotiation, but it creates an impression on your prospective client. Even if the client questions your subsequent quotation, you have already prepared the ground for confirming you are well worth the price you ask and for convincing him that you will make a good impact on the audience.

C3 Everything is negotiable
Even a fixed, traditional contract is negotiable so long as both parties are willing to negotiate and that applies as much to marriage contracts as to any other kind of contract. A spouse who accepts your conditions without discussion may already be a doormat and could pull the mat from under your feet one day.

Timing is a valid item for discussion but is a blackmail weapon otherwise.

D1 Generosity is a sign of weakness
By asking what the buyer finds attractive in your proposal you can open negotiations on the whole package without reducing your price. It may lead to a discussion of the differences between the offers of your competitors. Price is not the only variable; delivery dates, method of payment, etc., are all part of the package.

E3 Encourage the other party to negotiate
Conceding or threatening for the sake of temporary peace always leads to future difficulties. You will either have to give bigger and bigger concessions or make (and keep) harsher threats in the future. Neither is good for adults or children. If you teach your children to think for themselves and negotiate, you will show them the path to future success.

F2 Never accept the first offer
If you accept the enthusiast's first offer he will immediately think he could have got the car for less and will feel unsatisfied, maybe complain or push you to include the spare parts anyway. Haggling makes him feel he has got a bargain; in any case you could even raise the price or at least get a separate price for the spare parts.

G1 Leave yourself room to negotiate
The phrase o.n.o. means "I will drop my price." Always create a space for negotiations; it is more likely to be profitable and certainly more enjoyable than feeling afterwards that you could have got more if only you had made the effort.

On being assertive

Assertion is self-expressive power that stems directly from a personal conviction; it is not aggression, which is a form of attack. Unfortunately the two are often confused.

To assert yourself means to insist on your opinion being heard or your rights being acknowledged. Assertive power can be felt; some people quietly insist while others assert themselves more actively.

Either way, those who are on the receiving end of assertive power are stimulated to respond because an honest impression or impact is made. Being assertive involves revealing yourself.

Because the reality of the other person is always recognized, being assertive carries responsibilities, not least of which is the obligation to listen to the other person's reply and make a further response yourself... and so on.

Absence of assertion
When personal, expressive power is inhibited or restricted, the result is inevitably a mess. Then pseudo-assertion may be used or a weary, indeterminate lack of interest makes nonsense of any attempt to communicate with clarity and warmth.

ASSERTION AND PERCEPTION
When you are being assertive, you are revealing your personal perceptions of reality. Your perceptions may be right, wrong or simply different; by asserting yourself, you demonstrate your convictions about how you perceive the world.

Included among your convictions are your political, social and religious beliefs, your prejudices, hopes and ideas, your views on current issues, your attitudes towards others and your own self-image, i.e. how you see yourself.

A The assertive person in a sports competition

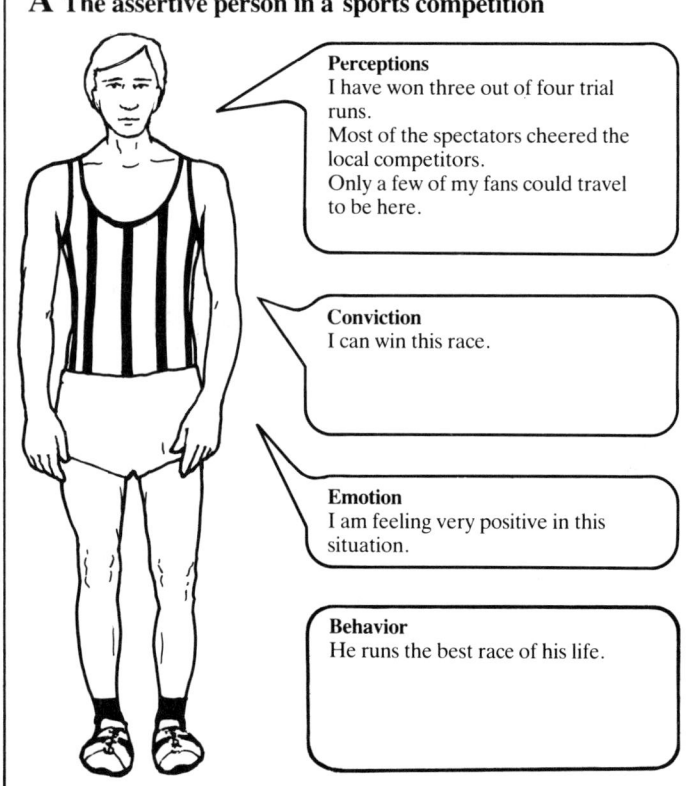

Perceptions
I have won three out of four trial runs.
Most of the spectators cheered the local competitors.
Only a few of my fans could travel to be here.

Conviction
I can win this race.

Emotion
I am feeling very positive in this situation.

Behavior
He runs the best race of his life.

B The non-assertive person in a sports competition

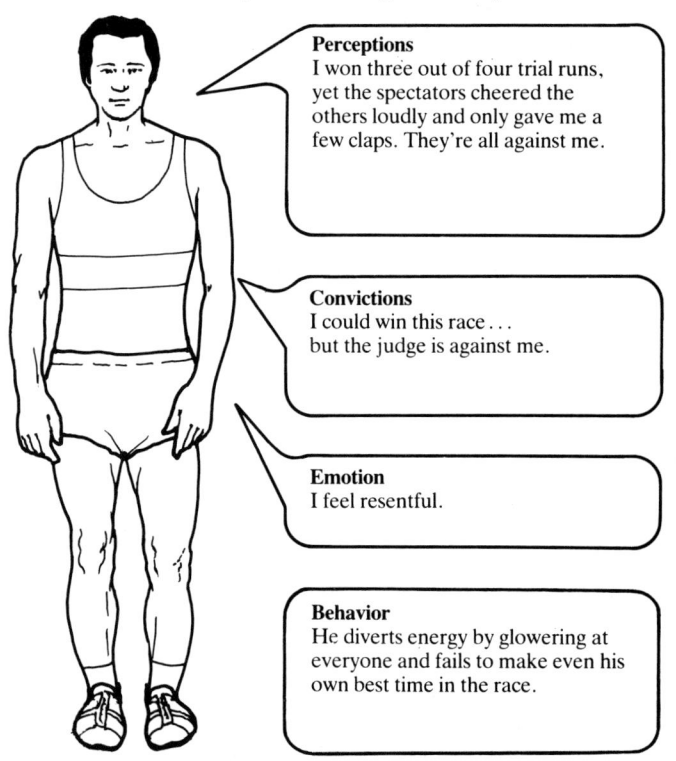

Perceptions
I won three out of four trial runs, yet the spectators cheered the others loudly and only gave me a few claps. They're all against me.

Convictions
I could win this race...
but the judge is against me.

Emotion
I feel resentful.

Behavior
He diverts energy by glowering at everyone and fails to make even his own best time in the race.

How to become more assertive
As illustrated in the diagrams (*above*), a change of perception can change your eventual behavior. New perceptions alter basic convictions, which themselves create different emotions and consequently alter behavior.

Some people advocate deliberately changing behavior, and others encourage the release of emotions to clear the air.

While both of these may be helpful in particular situations, unless you change your fundamental convictions you are likely to be constantly fighting a battle with yourself.

Unfortunately, once we have an entrenched belief, we tend to make our perceptions match! It is useful to write down the facts and then several possible interpretations of this reality. In this way you can begin to loosen entrenched beliefs, prejudices or attitudes that are

How to recognize when you are being assertive
If you are being assertive, you will feel warm and alive; it is the warmth that stimulates the other person. Consider the following statements:

1 I love you.
2 I will accept the job on the terms agreed.
3 The work will be completed before Friday.
4 I like the way you have decorated this room.
5 Would you like to come over on Tuesday?

How would you know if these are honest remarks? Only by the way they are spoken. Any of them could be a lie.

Our perceptions form convictions that shape our emotions, which in turn determine how we behave. Assertion travels a direct route from perceptions through to behavior – see diagrams **A** and **C** (*below*). A failure to respect some realities causes conflict... we become torn between one conviction and another. In order to cope with this inner split, we then practice pseudo-assertive gamesmanship or show a non-assertive lack of interest – see diagrams **B** and **D** (*below*).

C The assertive sales person

Perceptions
They sell a million packets of our products every month through their hypermarkets.
The buyer is trying to get us to reduce our price by threatening to place his order elsewhere.

Conviction
They must have a lot of happy customers they wouldn't want to disappoint by taking our product off the shelves.

Emotion
I enjoy working in this kind of situation.

Behavior
She smiles at the buyer and says: "No."

D The pseudo-assertive sales person

Perceptions
They sell a million packets of our products every month through their hypermarkets.
The buyer is threatening me.

Convictions
If I lose this order, my job's at stake...
but he's trying to make a fool of me.

Emotion
I feel frightened.

Behavior
First she tries to dominate the buyer who, sensing her uncertainty, takes the advantage and eventually gets a price reduction.

counter-productive, and take a more flexible approach to life.

When examining your convictions, never confuse your intrinsic self-worth with your skills or lack of them. Because you can't spell, for example, doesn't make you a bad person. Similarly, because you can spell, doesn't make you a good person!

Finally, remember that whatever else reality may be... it is never fair.

REFERENCES

SECTION ONE   **Power: areas of endeavor** (pp. 24-7)
              Do you want to be more powerful? (pp. 30-1)

SECTION THREE **Negotiating for what you want** (pp. 110-1)
              Resolving conflicts (pp. 148-9)

Persuading others

Persuasion is a strategy to induce one or more people to believe something and act accordingly. Akin to manipulation, which works because someone already believes, persuasion involves reinforcing an old belief or restructuring it into a new one so effectively that people persuade themselves they are taking the right course of action.

Persuasion is a one way process. Advertising that increases sales is a prime example of the art of successful persuasion. Political manifestos, evangelical mass gatherings, major conferences, protest meetings and one track logic are all designed to persuade people to take a predetermined line of action.

Persuaders and hidden persuaders
The sharing of information is often accompanied by an element of persuasion. When the dangers of the AIDS virus became known, the British Government sponsored a TV campaign; spoken and written information were combined with visual shock tactics. To be persuaded, people had to believe a simple truth... that the AIDS virus would kill.

Fear of death was the overt persuader in that campaign; the hidden persuaders were the many and varied beliefs already widely held, such as beliefs arising from age old sexual guilts, attitudes toward homosexual men who had been singled out for attention, and alarm on the part of heterosexuals who had more than one sexual partner... or who feared their spouse might be having an affair.

We are all manipulators from time to time, but if you intend to use persuasive strategies for whatever purpose, moral or immoral, be aware that beliefs are the real persuaders, both overt and hidden.

The difference between persuasion and negotiation
Persuasion is an inducement during which one party has an impact on the other; negotiation is a transaction during which both parties have an impact on each other. To use the art of persuasion, you have to temporarily regard the other person as some kind of puppet whose strings of belief you can pull.

To negotiate you have to risk confrontation, which involves both people feeling the effect of the other's presence. Persuasion will only fail if you pull the wrong string at the wrong moment or in the wrong direction. Negotiation will only fail if there is a deadlock and even that can be loosened by asking how the other sees the situation, thus reopening negotiations.

TOP DOG AND UNDER DOG

The late Fritz Perls, a Gestalt psychologist, used to call the two sides of ourselves the **Top Dog** and the **Under Dog**.

Paul Newman shoots pool to reach the top in *The Hustler* (1961).

Winning the bet is cold comfort for Paul Newman in *Cool Hand Luke* (1967).

Top Dog is the creative and active side of us that enjoys the lively impact of negotiation. Our Top Dog listens, considers, learns, changes and is too busy enjoying life to want to bother overmuch with persuasive games.

Under Dog is the compliant and submissive side of us that fears the impact of others and tries to make us behave like a helpless puppet, moaning and groaning to our Top Dog, persuading us to build an image and wallow privately in our unfulfilled miseries.

Some characteristics of Top Dogs
 ENJOYS NEGOTIATING

1 Is transparently honest, genuine and authentic.
2 Aware; listens, looks and is interested.
3 In charge of, and takes responsibility for, own life.
4 Trusts self and others to cope with life.
5 Values him/herself; has compassion for Under Dog.
6 Laughs, expresses anger, love, and grief naturally.

Some characteristics of Under Dogs
 ENJOYS PERSUADING

1 Pretends, plays parts and is unauthentic.
2 Unaware, bored; has tunnel vision and fixed views.
3 Controls own life, conceals motives and is bored.
4 Cynical and distrusting; tries to control others.
5 Does not value self or others; fears creativity.
6 Expresses feelings chosen to suit the occasion.

Since we all try to persuade and manipulate sometimes, it is wise to be aware of when we are doing it and when someone else is doing it to us. We do have a choice. Natural life itself isn't fair and there is nothing we can do about that, but we can change some of the unfairnesses of social life by letting our Top Dogs have a bigger say in how we go about things.

REFERENCES

SECTION ONE — **Do you want to be more powerful?** (pp. 30-1)
Which kind of power do you want? (pp. 32-3)

SECTION THREE — **Negotiating for what you want** (pp. 110-1)
On being assertive (pp. 112-3)

Getting feedback

Feedback is information about the effect of an action, which is then used to adjust the action.

The value of feedback
All new learning depends on feedback, and the only route to successful achievement in any human endeavor is learning how to improve the action you take to reach a goal or a state of satisfaction.

Some feedback, of course, can be very discouraging; feedback from a dismal failure is something we often ignore, because we want to forget the failure. However, T.J. Watson, the founder of IBM, once said, "The way to succeed is to double your rate of failure."

Success itself, while invigorating and satisfying, teaches us very little, because what worked on one occasion isn't always appropriate on another.

FEEDBACK CAN BE INTERNAL
You turn on the tap and put your hands under the water to wash them. The effect is a burning sensation in your fingers, because the water is too hot. You quickly pull your hands away from the water. You have adjusted your actions because you got immediate internal feedback in the form of a burning sensation.

FEEDBACK CAN BE EXTERNAL
You are rowing a dinghy across a lake. Jim, sitting opposite to you in the stern, is the only one who can see where you are going. He can see the effect as you pull on the oars and feeds back to you the effect your rowing is having on the direction of the boat. The adjustment you make is too much, so he feeds back more information, and so on, until you get it right.

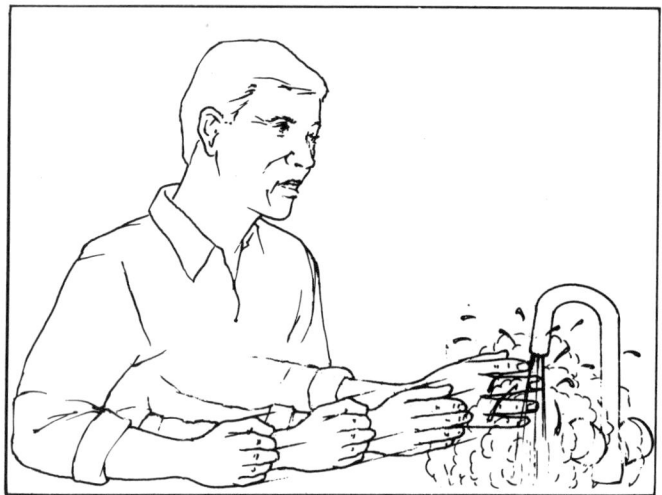

Two ways to get internal feedback
1 **Responding to your immediate felt-experiences while you are in action.** This is learning by actively experimenting by trial and error as you proceed. For example, during negotiation, during lovemaking or during a game of tennis.
2 **Reflecting privately upon an activity you have recently completed.** This is learning by reflecting on your own ideas about how to proceed in the future.

Two ways to get external feedback
1 **Asking for information from others while you are in action.** This is learning by the practical experience of adjusting as you proceed. For example, during a coaching session, during a training program, or during a team activity.
2 **Asking for the observations of others about an activity you have recently completed.** This is learning by accepting an idea from someone else about how to proceed in future.

USING NEGATIVE FEEDBACK
There is an old proverb that goes something like this: "If one man tells you you are an ass, ignore him. If two men say you are an ass, you may still take no notice; but if three men separately tell you that you are an ass, you should check it out. They may be seeing things more clearly than you."

The same proverb can be applied to internal feedback. For example, jumping to the conclusion that you will never be able to ride a bike because you fall off once. Even when you have fallen off three times, it would be more profitable to examine your whole approach to bike-riding before abandoning your ambition to ride a bike.

In the final analysis, it is sometimes wise to abandon a project and try something else before you either break your neck or thoroughly convince yourself you are never going to succeed at doing anything!

Instructions are not feedback
If, at a crossroads, you ask someone to give you directions to Cambridge, you would be asking for directions, not feedback. However, if you asked "What would happen if I took a right turn here?", the reply would be anticipatory feedback; for example: "If you turn right you'll be heading for Cambridge.

ANTICIPATORY FEEDBACK
Anticipatory feedback is information you get, from yourself or from others, about what is likely to be the result of your actions in a given situation. Then either change your approach when you repeat an activity, or decide the best course of action to take in a new situation.

Some examples of anticipatory feedback
Asking a friend for feedback on an application form you have written for a job is finding out what the effect of your application would be on one other person. This is a much more useful exercise than asking for help to fill in the application form in the first place.

Similarly, asking for feedback during a trial run of a speech you have to give, or the draft copy of a report or a business plan, will give you valuable information to help you make improvements.

Putting your application form away for a while and re-reading it later, or tape-recording the trial run of your speech, will also give you some useful feedback.

USING FEEDBACK POSITIVELY
A restaurant asked for feedback from its customers by providing cards with questions about their menus and service. Customers were asked to check or cross items they liked or disliked. Much praise was received for the food but the timing was heavily criticized.

To serve food of that kind required time. What should the restaurant do about the situation? Changing the menu and serving fast food would change the nature of the restaurant and be a negative use of the feedback.

The restaurant used the feedback positively by stating on the menu how long it would take to personally cook and serve each dish (and kept to the time stated), and by serving each table, all free of charge, with a variety of "dips" and a choice of bread-sticks, celery and sliced carrots, etc., as the customers arrived. The result was amazing. Everyone was happy to wait for their main course to be personally cooked, *and* the number of customers increased.

CONDITIONED FEEDBACK
At its very worst, conditioned feedback turns into a phobia. For example, claustrophobia... a physical fear of being shut in. However, most conditioned feedback is open to change, once you know of its existence. Very typical of conditioned feedback are beliefs (or injunctions) that we learned in the past and are no longer valid. For more information about injunctions, refer to: SECTION ONE **Do you want to be more powerful?** (pp. 30-1)

Acquiring a positive attitude

When things don't work out to our satisfaction, we may find ourselves in a negative situation feeling depressed or frustrated. Battling through, regardless, is not always helpful since stress might increase.

There are four areas in which we can take action to turn negatives into positives. They are connected, as shown in the diagram (*below*); dealing with one area will help in another area, as shown by the directional arrows.

FOUR ACTION AREAS

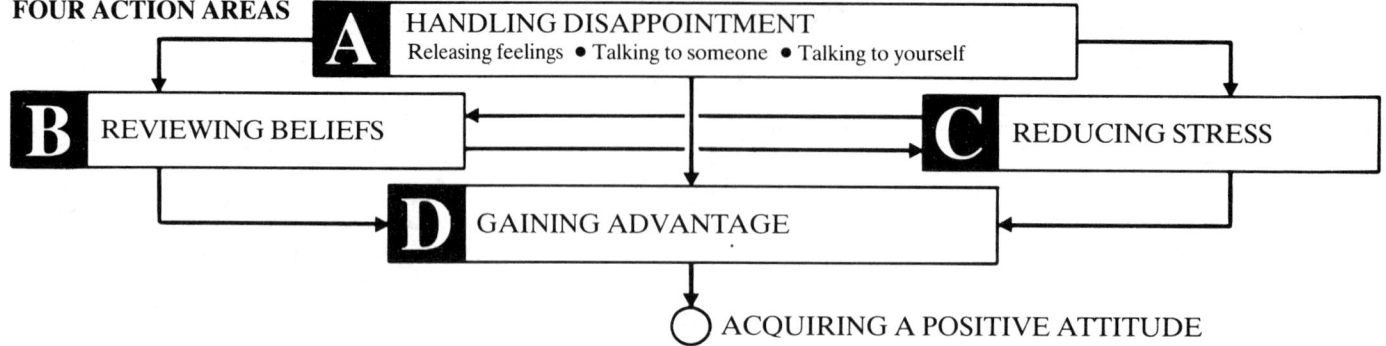

A   HANDLING DISAPPOINTMENT
Releasing feelings • Talking to someone • Talking to yourself

B   REVIEWING BELIEFS

C   REDUCING STRESS

D   GAINING ADVANTAGE

○ ACQUIRING A POSITIVE ATTITUDE

A   HANDLING DISAPPOINTMENT

1 BY RELEASING NEGATIVE FEELINGS. The first thing that happens after a disappointment is an emotional reaction; for example: anger, frustration, grief.

An outlet for these feelings is important. Sobbing your heart out into a pillow or shouting your anger while punching a thick cushion is healthy and very relaxing. Laughter, too, is a life-saver.

Physical activity can help to release emotions, so long as you do not use it on someone else. Picking a fight, kicking the dog or seeking relief through sex will alienate you.

If you habitually repress emotion, you may prefer to seek professional help. Feelings that are not immediately and properly expressed grow out of proportion and remain potent for years, preventing progress, causing illness or endangering others.

2 BY TALKING TO SOMEONE. Since time immemorial, talking to someone we trust to be non-judgemental has been recognized as a helpful way of expressing disappointments and joys.

A spouse, friend or close relative may be the automatic choice, but we cannot expect the same person to fulfill all our needs.

Your network might include formal help, such as support groups, counselors, people at work, a doctor, religious minister, tutor, psychotherapist, bank manager or laywer.

The stranger you meet by chance on a journey may be just the non-involved listener you need sometimes.

One person will be ideal to challenge you, another will listen and understand, while others will be helpful when sharing good news.

3 BY TALKING TO YOURSELF. A chat with yourself can be a real tonic. If you aren't used to listening to the positive, creative side of yourself, the following examples will give you some ideas. If you can't find something good to say to yourself, you will need to review the beliefs that are holding you back.

A very good technique for talking to yourself is to talk out loud to something that doesn't answer back, such as a dog, a tree or your favorite photo of yourself. This will give you instant feedback from your own subconscious. If you feel silly talking to yourself in this way, then perhaps you don't take yourself seriously on important matters.

Clarissa is feeling angry that she has been passed over for promotion.
CLARISSA'S NEGATIVE SELF-TALK: "My boss is prejudiced against women. I hate these chauvinists who put me down. I'll not risk applying for promotion again."
CLARISSA'S POSITIVE SELF-TALK: "My boss may be prejudiced against women or I may need some further training. I'll check out both possibilities and make a clear plan for when the next promotion opportunity arises in six months' time."

Martin is feeling upset after the death of his mother.
MARTIN'S NEGATIVE SELF-TALK: "It's all my fault; if only I had been there when she was rushed into hospital. I'm so depressed."
MARTIN'S POSITIVE SELF-TALK: "I shall let myself cry when I feel the need. It's natural to grieve. I have a lovely memory of the last time we had tea together before I left for my business trip abroad. I'm just very sad I couldn't be with her at the end. Perhaps my father and I can help each other."

In both these examples, the positive self-talk results in some positive action that can be taken. Clarissa can gain some advantage from the situation and Martin can reduce stress and perhaps develop his relationship with his father.

REFERENCES
SECTION TWO   **Enlisting help** (pp. 100-1)
SECTION THREE   **Developing a network** (pp. 132-3)

B REVIEWING BELIEFS

Beliefs about ourselves, other people and the world in general can help or block our progress. Everything we do is based upon a belief system. If some of your beliefs are self-defeating, disappointments will be hard to handle.

If you believe you have to be perfect, then you will always be a failure as perfection is unattainable. If you have a racial prejudice, it will affect your choices. On the other hand, if one of your moral values is honesty, you will not be hampered by having to keep a lie going.

To review your self-defeating beliefs, refer to:

SECTION ONE **Does age make any difference?** (pp. 74-5)
SECTION TWO **Appreciating yourself** (pp. 88-9)
What are your limitations? (pp. 92-3)

C REDUCING STRESS

If you are already in a chronically stressful condition when a disappointment or disaster happens, the extra stress will be quite incapacitating. Is your normal stress level within safety limits? Find out by answering **Yes** or **No** to the statements (*below*).

Yes No

☐ ☐ I take regular exercise naturally or have a personal fitness program.
☐ ☐ I eat balanced meals regularly and never have more than two spoons of sugar a day.
☐ ☐ I do not smoke more than twice a day.
☐ ☐ I have a regular daily schedule.
☐ ☐ I do not watch TV for over two hours a day.
☐ ☐ I do not drink more than one glass of alcohol a day.
☐ ☐ I have a method of relaxing and use it.
☐ ☐ When away from home I make sure I get all I need to reduce stress and be comfortable.
☐ ☐ I never drive for longer than two hours without stopping for a proper break.
☐ ☐ I can say **No** to things I don't want.
☐ ☐ I have a place at home where I can be undisturbed.
☐ ☐ I never work until I have rested after a time-lag trip by plane.
☐ ☐ There are no relationship or family problems that I am ignoring.
☐ ☐ I get enough sleep and wake refreshed.

☐ Total number of **No** answers

Interpreting your score

Ignore the statements that are not applicable to you and count the ones to which you have answered **No**. Any score higher than three indicates that you are probably under some stress which could be reduced.

A score higher than five could mean problems if sudden, extra stress occurs. You can do something about the ones marked **No** to ensure you are fit enough to handle both unforeseen stress and the pleasant events in your life that are also stressful, such as going on holiday or getting a new job.

D GAINING ADVANTAGE

Getting the best out of a disappointing situation is rather like understanding how to take tax advantage. If you have to pay tax, then it is wise to know how to make best use of the tax regulations.

It is helpful at the planning stage to consider questions such as "What if . . . ?" – then you will be prepared. However, not every disappointment can be anticipated.

During the process of handling the disappointment, some positive gains can emerge, as illustrated in the previous examples. The reduction of stress results in more energy becoming available to take action, as does the removal of self-defeating beliefs. Now you are ready to gain advantage from the situation.

How to proceed

1 List the positive ideas that have emerged from the first three processes (**A**, **B** and **C**) and consider your other advantages by referring to:
SECTION TWO **What advantages do you have?** (pp. 94-5)
2 Analyze the situation thoroughly by referring to:
SECTION THREE **Analyzing situations** (pp. 126-7)
3 Proceed to decide what should be abandoned and what can be transformed. Be quite firm about this. For example, if a business is in serious trouble, closing down may be the best advantage, rather than continuing by borrowing more money, no matter how tempting that may be. In a situation of impending unemployment, there are many advantages to be gained if you take the trouble to find out. It may be a complete waste of time, effort and money to fight against unemployment when your efforts could produce results in an entirely new direction.
Refer to SECTION THREE **Making decisions** (pp. 124-5)
4 Using the information, make a new plan for a new venture. Refer to:
SECTION ONE **What do you want out of life?** (pp. 10-1)
SECTION TWO **Generating ideas** (pp. 84-5)
Basic planning (pp. 86-7)
. . . and enjoy yourself.

A happier home life

Your home is where you base yourself; from home you move out into the world. Three main areas make up home life.
1 HOME IS YOU.
2 HOME IS YOUR FAMILY or others with whom you share.
3 HOME IS A PLACE you can call your own.
Home may be based in a house, an apartment, a hospital, a barracks, a ship, a communal dwelling, a hotel, a caravan, a tent, or in a changing location. Homelessness implies that a person or family have no physical base to call their own.

Sometimes people who do have a physical base feel homesick when away from it. This is often just a yearning for familiar surroundings when in strange, foreign places.

Are you happy with your home?
Here are some tests you can use to decide if an area of your home life needs improvement. The tests themselves give some indication of how to set about making a happier home life.

HOME IS YOU
Read each statement. Check **Yes** if it is true on the whole; check **No** if you have any doubts.

	Yes	No
I like myself.		
I take care of myself.		
I am honest with myself.		
I can laugh at myself.		
I often make mistakes.		
I am glad to be alive.		
I feel love, anger, grief, joy and fear.		
I have interesting things to do.		
I accept responsibility for my actions.		
I have several prejudices.		
I am an optimistic person.		
I learn something new every day.		

Total number of statements answered Yes [ ]

Interpreting your score
Home is always where YOU are, so if your total is nine or more, you have the most important basis for a happy home life...you feel happy with yourself as a normal, growing, living person.

If your score is lower, then pay attention to the statements you indicated **No** and your home life will become happier.

If your score is six or less, then perhaps you have too many self-doubts. Are you taking yourself too seriously or trying to become a perfectionist?

The greatest contributor to a happy home life is you. An unhappy person once said: "Wherever I go, I take myself with me...and that spoils everything!"

For more information, refer to:
SECTION TWO **Appreciating yourself** (pp. 88-9)

HOME IS YOUR FAMILY or others who share with you
A happy home life involves healthy relationships with your family or other people who come into your home.

A checklist for healthy relating
This list is derived from the work of psychologist Erich Fromm and is often called the R.R.T.U.C.H. list of six qualities that help to build healthy relationships.

Think of the relationship between yourself and each person involved in your home life separately. Relationships in a happy home have at least five of the qualities listed (*below*). It should be noted that people from happy homes quite often have arguments. Happiness has its ups and downs; it is how the arguments are handled that matters.

R = RESPECT for the other person. Re-spect means "look again." Do you frequently look at your family with fresh eyes? Can you see things from their point of view? Can you allow them to be who they are or do you tend to try and take them over? Is anyone not giving you respect?

R = RESPONSIBILITY in thought, feeling and action for yourself. Responsibility means the ability to respond appropriately to others, rather than react according to some old pattern or conditioning. Do you and your family respond to each other or automatically react the same way every time something happens?

T = TRUST of yourself and therefore other people. Trust means believing in the basic goodness and humanity of your family, accepting that mistakes are often made. Do you and your family trust each other? Is there someone you distrust?

U = UNDERSTANDING of what makes other people tick. Understanding literally means standing on something firm underneath. Do you know what motivates your family? Are you aware of their concerns and beliefs? Do you give them support to develop a firm base? Do they understand your point of view?

C = CONCERN for your family. Concern means caring...loving concern and angry concern are both a part of genuine caring. Are you concerned for others in your home? Do you ever confuse protection or possessiveness with concern? Does your family show concern for you?

H = HONESTY about your own blind spots and hidden secrets. Honesty means saying what you really mean and encouraging others to be honest with you. Are you honest with your family? Do you give them honest appreciation? Do you also tell them, courteously, the things you don't like?

For more information about relationships refer to:
SECTION THREE **Intimate relationships** (pp. 122-3)
Knowing what they want (pp. 142-3)

HOME IS A PLACE you can call your own
The place may be your reply to the question: "Where do you live?" Where you live is important. While a move to another place will not improve your view of yourself or solve relationship problems, home life will be happier if you are living in a location that offers what you want. What kind of amenities do you want? Which things are important to you and your family?

Some items for you to consider are listed (*below*). Add any others in the blank spaces. Then select the ten most important items and place them in rank order in the table (*right*). For example, if the type of house is more important than anything else, place it at number ten. Whatever is the least important item in your selection, place at number one.

TYPE OF HOUSE/APARTMENT	POLITICAL CLIMATE
CULTURAL AMENITIES	RELIGIOUS ETHOS
SPORTS FACILITIES	MORAL CLIMATE
MEDICAL FACILITIES	EMPLOYMENT PROSPECTS
SHOPS & SERVICES	PROXIMITY TO RELATIVES
TRANSPORT FACILITIES	PROXIMITY TO FRIENDS
CLIMATE	INCOME LEVELS
SCHOOLS & COLLEGES	COST OF HOUSING/RENTS
CITY, TOWN, COUNTRY, etc.	

....
....
....
....
....

Rating your selection
Rate each item by deciding how well satisfied you are in your present location.

2 means completely satisfied on the whole.

1 means tolerable.

0 means not satisfied.

For each item, multiply its rank order by the present rating you have given it to obtain the score. For example:

WHAT I WANT FROM THE PLACE WHERE I LIVE		
Rank order	Present rating	Score
10 Cost of housing	× 1	= 10
9 Transport facilities	× 2	= 18
8 Type of house	× 2	= 16
7 Shops & Services	× 0	= 0

Then total your scores to find out how much the place in which you live is contributing to a happy home life. The maximum score would be 110, the minimum 0.

WHAT I WANT FROM THE PLACE WHERE I LIVE		
Rank order	Present rating	Score
10	×	= ....
9	×	= ....
8	×	= ....
7	×	= ....
6	×	= ....
5	×	= ....
4	×	= ....
3	×	= ....
2	×	= ....
1	×	= ....
TOTAL SCORE		

Interpreting your TOTAL SCORE
110 to 88
On the whole you are happy where you are. The place where you live is making a large contribution to a happy home life.

87 to 66
The place where you live is satisfactory in many ways although there may be one or two items that don't suit you, but these are compensated for by others.

65 to 44
The place where you live isn't the cause of any great unhappiness although if other aspects of your home life are not satisfactory, you may sometimes think that a move would improve the situation. The upheaval is unlikely to make home life any happier in the long run.

43 to 22
You are not very happy in the place where you are living. Would a move elsewhere improve the situation? You can use the rating to check out places where you might think of moving.

below 21
The place where you live is contributing little or nothing to your happiness. What is keeping you where you are? Do you want to stay there?

Intimate relationships

Intimacy occurs when any two people know each other very well, especially their good and bad points, including those vulnerabilities and personal habits that are not normally revealed in public life.

Marriages, parents and children, working partnerships and boss/secretary, tutor/student or doctor/patient relationships all have a greater or lesser degree of intimacy. Intimacy can occur between close friends, people who share personal living space and people whose work obliges them to know each other well.

Games in intimate relationships
The greater the intimacy, the more dangerous the situation for people who feel at all uncertain or vulnerable, which applies to most of us to some extent. Hence we begin to play power games and set up situations in which one person is dependent on the other, who in turn becomes dependent upon that dependency.

Games in marriage relationships
Dan Kiley and Colette Dowling both wrote books describing some of the most common fairy tale games that can destroy a marriage. These games also occur between any two people, but mostly between men and women.

Dr. Kiley suggests that some men are like Peter Pan, the little boy who didn't want to grow up. Terrified his wife may realize what he is really like, he compensates for any loss of power in his marriage by playing the part of Prince Charming. He keeps her in luxury and shares his high status with her, in return for a few favors, such as cooking, sex, emotional support and her undying loyalty, devotion and uncritical admiration. He turns his wife into a Wendy figure, who, in James Barrie's immortal story, was the little girl who mothered Peter Pan.

Colette Dowling suggests that some women are like Cinderella, the helpless little kitchen maid who thought so little of herself that she had to rely on external magic (in the form of a fairy godmother) to make her beautiful enough to be chosen. When Cinderella settles down to feather her nest and bring up her children under the protection of the man she has turned into a Prince Charming, she tries to compensate for her lack of power in the outside world by taking control in the home. She readily responds to her Peter Pan by becoming his Wendy figure.

Both Kiley and Dowling recognize that it is easy to turn the traditional marriage structure into a Peter Pan and Wendy situation. When only one partner plays the game, arguments ensue which may save the marriage; when both partners play the game, they may stay together for ever... unhappily.

REFERENCES
SECTION ONE	**Do you want to be more powerful?** (pp. 30-1)
	Which kind of power do you want? (pp. 32-3)
SECTION THREE	**Knowing what they want** (pp. 142-3)

IS YOUR MARRIAGE FOUNDED ON A FAIRY TALE?
Here are two tests (*right*), one for wives and the other for husbands. There are twenty descriptions of how your mate could be behaving. Rate each of them as follows:

0 This behavior NEVER happens with you.
1 This behavior happens only OCCASIONALLY.
2 This behavior ALWAYS happens.

How do you and your partner rate?
Score of 0 to 10: Your spouse is not living a fairy tale. You may like to note which items you scored and see if he/she would agree and perhaps would like to do something about it.
Score of 11 to 20: Some indication of fairy tale behavior; the higher the score the more likely it is that your marriage is entering never never land. First check out your own behavior. If your spouse is playing a part, then either you are responding with the matching part or you are already aware something is going wrong.

Consider how your spouse rated you and use both test results to discuss how to get your marriage back on to a realistic footing.
Score of 21 to 40: Either your marriage is in jeopardy or you are both very happy, content and completely fullfilled by your fairy tale existence. Unfortunately, it is more likely that one partner, at least, is very unhappy.

Begin by looking at your own part in the game, as with this kind of score both partners are involved.

You should also consider very carefully if you care. If you have reached the stage of no longer caring about the marriage, or how much you care for your spouse is now less than your dislike of his/her behavior, then seriously consider ending what can only be an unproductive situation for both of you and damaging for children if you have any.

If you do care, take action slowly, change one thing at a time, beginning with your own behavior. Give your partner every support in his/her effort to change. Don't expect miracles overnight and never aim for perfection.

If you find yourself in any kind of fairy tale relationship, begin by looking at the part you play and change that. Inevitably the other person will have to adjust. Parents who play fairy tale games with their children are not helping them to face reality.

DESCRIPTIONS TO BE RATED BY WIVES	HUSBAND'S SCORE 0 1 2	WIFE'S SCORE 2 1 0	DESCRIPTIONS TO BE RATED BY HUSBANDS
When he makes a mistake, he makes excuses or blames himself only for lack of anticipation.			When she makes a mistake, she regards herself as silly or stupid and often makes more mistakes. She may even look helpless and expect you to haul her out.
He forgets important anniversaries and expects you to write cards from both of you and keep in touch with mutual friends.			She always remembers dates and automatically writes cards and buys presents from both of you.
At parties or during social outings, he does his best to impress other women and pointedly ignores you.			At parties or social functions, she expects you to stay with her the whole time or waits around for you.
He does not say he is sorry without fuss.			She buys your clothes for you and keeps them organized, though you'd rather do it yourself.
He expects you to have sexual intercourse when he wants it or controls how much foreplay.			She doesn't take the initiative in sex, tries to avoid it or appears to be detached during intercourse.
He does special little jobs for friends and ignores, delays or complains when you ask for jobs to be done.			She looks after the home very well, but she treats you more like one of the children than a partner.
From time to time he makes an enormous effort to please you, gives gifts or writes messages that don't feel real to you.			She listens to your problems and other people's problems but rarely divulges her own inner feelings, though she may well talk about her concerns for you and the children.
You have to point out his indifference before he shows concern for your problems.			She makes demands on you on behalf of the children or the house, but rarely on her own behalf.
He regards his earnings as all his money, although you may have a joint account.			She expects you to ring her when you are away.
He would like to be closer to his father.			She complains nobody helps in the house but usually says she can do it quicker herself.
He never argues with his mother and accepts her wishes.			She is in total control in the kitchen and she finds it hard to share it or to leave it to someone else.
He has difficulty listening to opinions that are different from his own.			She expects you to do things she could easily learn, like backing the car out for her.
He has sudden, irrational flashes of rage, or threatens to blow up, or he tends to hit out instead.			She gives you the impression that she thinks you couldn't manage without her.
He complains about his job but doesn't change things.			She does not go away overnight without you or the family.
Warmth and expression of feelings are missing, especially in his relationship with his eldest son.			She is obsessed with her weight, whatever it is.
He tends to drink more than he thinks he does or he is obsessively teetotal. He demonstrates bravado.			She either avoids doing any training or remains convinced she is no good after endless successes.
He likes to go out with "the boys" and hates to miss the fun.			She seems more interested in her son/s than in you.
He has a hobby that he expects, or needs, you to participate in whether you like it or not.			She either cries or goes cold when she is quite evidently angry.
He accuses you of being too emotional; he may send you crazy because he reacts with cool, stony silence.			She is underemployed; her work does not stretch her.
He is chauvinistic, yet also seems to lack confidence or have fears he won't talk about.			She is terrified of living alone.
Totals			**Totals**
Husband's total score			**Wife's total score**

Making decisions

We only need to make decisions when we are uncertain of what to do next. Even simple either/or decisions can cause much thought. How can we know which is the best choice?

It is said that nothing succeeds like success; if you apply this idea to the process of making a decision, then you are more likely to make the best decisions for you and ones which are successfully put into action as you make them.

Active decision-making has many advantages; pitfalls are anticipated, consequences can be estimated, risks can be reduced. It is easier and quicker to find out if what you want is realistically possible and how to gain any cooperation you need from other people. Alternatives can be included, giving yourself more options. Active decision-making is, itself, a series of mini successes.

Active decisions are made by a series of steps and adjustments on an action tree. Commonsense, a little imagination and some hard facts are required. If you are one of those people who think they can't think, or imagine they have no imagination, here is the opportunity to learn how to build an action tree... and to enjoy success as you proceed.

HOW TO BUILD AND USE AN ACTION TREE
The illustration (*right*) shows the steps you must take in order to build and use an action tree successfully.
STEP 1
Clarify why you are going to make a decision.
Find out how much time is available.
Write down a starting aim and a time limit.
STEP 2
Begin your action tree with your starting aim.
Collect information about the situation.
List what options may be open to you.
STEP 3
List the implications and consequences of each option, which may require collecting more information.
Eliminate options that are either unrealistic or ones you definitely don't want.
STEP 4
Follow each option to its conclusion.
You can often follow more than one option at once.
Don't waste time if you reach a dead end.
STEP 5
Add alternatives and new information as you proceed.
STEP 6
When you have achieved your starting aim, write down your next aims and new time limits; proceed from STEP 2.
STEP 7
When you have achieved your final aim, you will be well on the way to final success.

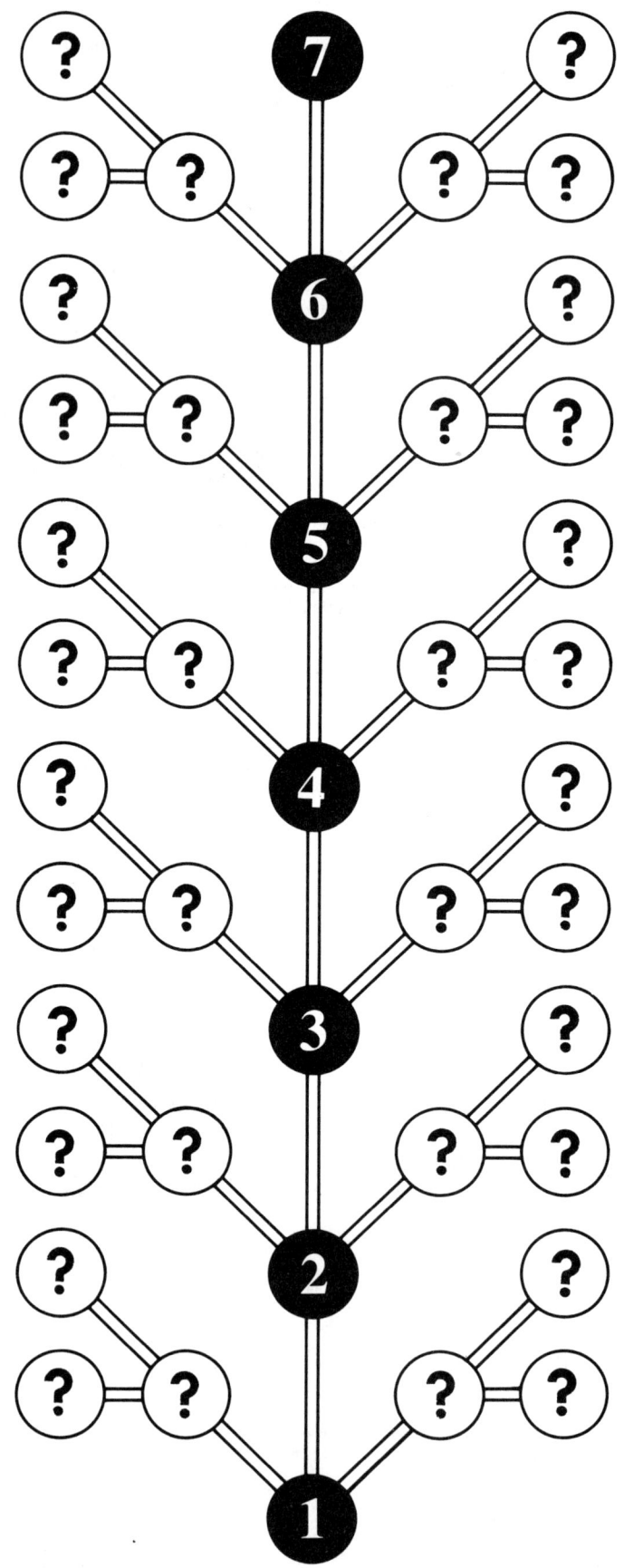

A SAMPLE ACTION-TREE
The events relating to Maria are given (*below*) so that you can see exactly how the concept of an action tree works in practice.

Maria is a member of a professional team of five. Holidays have to be taken by agreed rota. When asked by her boss if she has preferences, Maria normally replies, "I don't mind, I'll fit in with everyone else." The holiday year begins April 1st: so far, Maria has taken some of her statutory holidays in October and December and has had no holiday break during the summer.

In January, it is Maria's turn to attend a four day training course; she is furious and hurt to discover that her remaining eight day's holiday have been scheduled to start on the Monday immediately following the end of the course.

On the third day of the course, Maria complains to a friend that her boss has not given her a fair deal. Her friend points out that if she had taken the trouble to make her own decisions about which holiday periods she wanted, she would have got a fair deal. (This is one of the consequences of delay.)

Maria decides she wants to do something about the situation. Since it is Thursday and her final holiday period is due to start on Monday, in reality she only has two days to achieve satisfaction. This is the action tree she built and used.

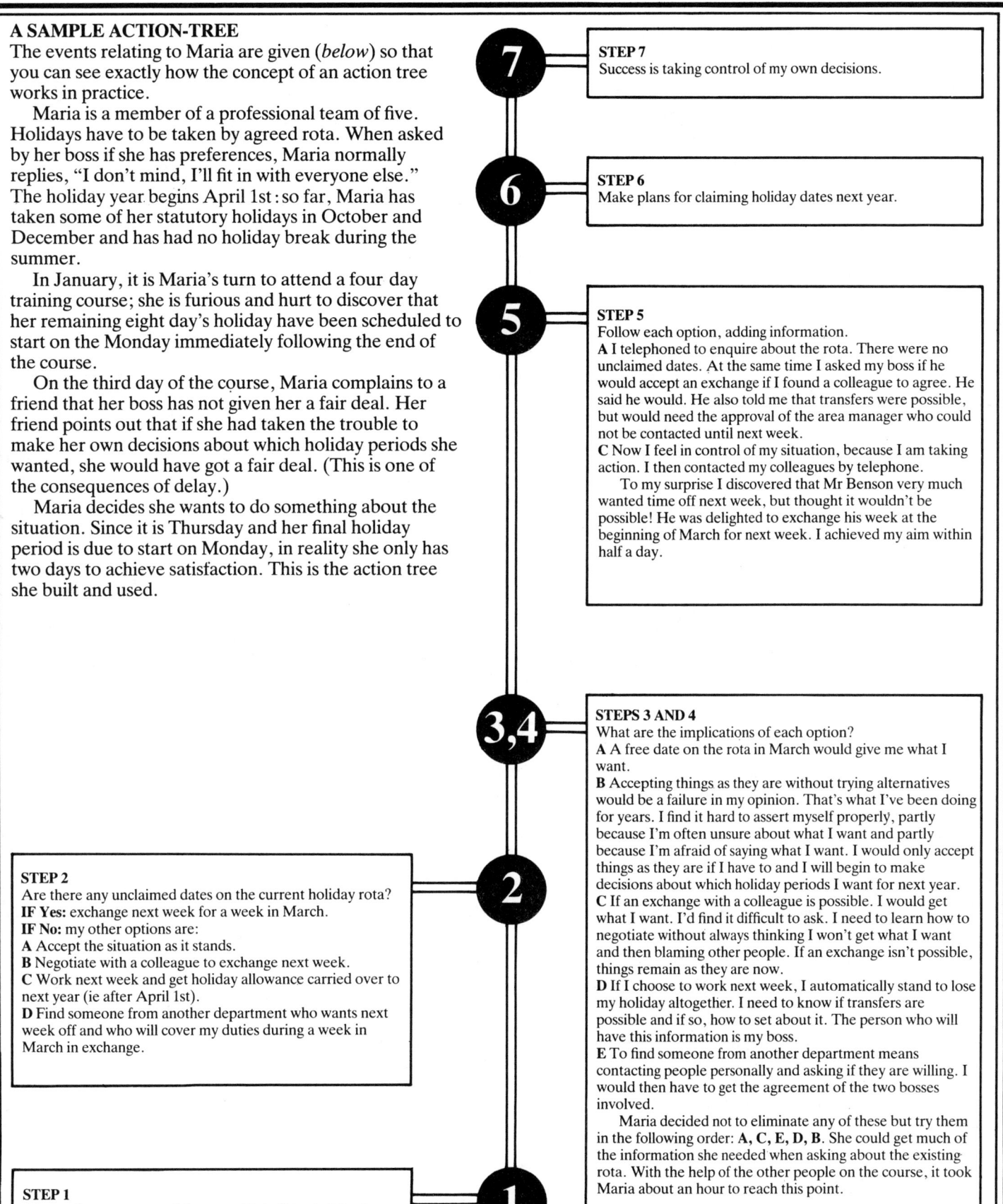

STEP 7
Success is taking control of my own decisions.

STEP 6
Make plans for claiming holiday dates next year.

STEP 5
Follow each option, adding information.
A I telephoned to enquire about the rota. There were no unclaimed dates. At the same time I asked my boss if he would accept an exchange if I found a colleague to agree. He said he would. He also told me that transfers were possible, but would need the approval of the area manager who could not be contacted until next week.
C Now I feel in control of my situation, because I am taking action. I then contacted my colleagues by telephone.
To my surprise I discovered that Mr Benson very much wanted time off next week, but thought it wouldn't be possible! He was delighted to exchange his week at the beginning of March for next week. I achieved my aim within half a day.

STEPS 3 AND 4
What are the implications of each option?
A A free date on the rota in March would give me what I want.
B Accepting things as they are without trying alternatives would be a failure in my opinion. That's what I've been doing for years. I find it hard to assert myself properly, partly because I'm often unsure about what I want and partly because I'm afraid of saying what I want. I would only accept things as they are if I have to and I will begin to make decisions about which holiday periods I want for next year.
C If an exchange with a colleague is possible. I would get what I want. I'd find it difficult to ask. I need to learn how to negotiate without always thinking I won't get what I want and then blaming other people. If an exchange isn't possible, things remain as they are now.
D If I choose to work next week, I automatically stand to lose my holiday altogether. I need to know if transfers are possible and if so, how to set about it. The person who will have this information is my boss.
E To find someone from another department means contacting people personally and asking if they are willing. I would then have to get the agreement of the two bosses involved.

Maria decided not to eliminate any of these but try them in the following order: **A, C, E, D, B**. She could get much of the information she needed when asking about the existing rota. With the help of the other people on the course, it took Maria about an hour to reach this point.

STEP 2
Are there any unclaimed dates on the current holiday rota?
IF Yes: exchange next week for a week in March.
IF No: my other options are:
A Accept the situation as it stands.
B Negotiate with a colleague to exchange next week.
C Work next week and get holiday allowance carried over to next year (ie after April 1st).
D Find someone from another department who wants next week off and who will cover my duties during a week in March in exchange.

STEP 1
Aim to change next week for a week's holiday in March.

© DIAGRAM

Analyzing situations

To analyze means to list all the small elements or simple components of an object or a situation. For example, the results of sporting events are often analyzed in detail, showing all the cumulative scores and times, while commentators spend hours analyzing results of an election.

The purpose of analysis is to understand how and why something happened and is often used to predict future events. For example, doctors diagnose illness by matching the results of past analyses with the present symptoms, and companies use financial analyses when deciding upon future policy.

Analysis is useful when a situation is complex and you want to find out what would happen if you changed one or two elements. "What if...?" is a useful question to ask in many situations, for example when planning a new road system or the arrangement of furniture in a room.

Interpreting facts
Detectives collect facts by listing what they see, asking questions and taking samples for further analysis in a laboratory. Their aim is to find out what happened and to gather evidence in support.

Many facts prove unimportant and others have to be questioned because circumstantial evidence can be misleading. For example, if a dead man has a gun in his hand, this is a fact, but it is not proof that he was the one who fired it, if it was fired at all.

Psychological facts are even more difficult to analyze than material facts as, for example, when trying to determine a motive.

HOW DO YOU INTERPRET THESE FACTS?
Two different situations with the material facts are listed (*below*). What do you think happened?

THE GARDEN	
Material facts	What has been going on in the garden?
1 Grass 2 Large carrot 3 Six pieces of coal 4 Woolly hat	Left behind when the snow melted, the carrot was a snowman's nose, the coal formed two eyes and four buttons and the hat was on his head.

THE EMPTY CELLAR	
Material facts	How did the man hang himself?
1 Five centimeters of water 2 No window 3 Door locked from inside	He locked the door and stood on a block of ice which melted.

How to analyze your present life situation
The main areas of life are listed in the first column of the table on the opposite page. Not all the areas will be applicable to you, so blank spaces have been left for you to make further entries if necessary. Write the facts relevant to your (area of) life in the second column, then check one of the last three columns (**A**, **B** and **C**) as follows:
Column **A**: I am very happy with this situation.
Column **B**: I am satisfied on average in this situation.
Column **C**: I am not at all satisfied in this situation.

"What if...?" is a vital question when considering making a change in your life. You would want to know if you would be better off and how other people are likely to respond. When you have completed your analysis, select the life areas for which you have checked Column C and consider what changes you want to make and what would be the likely outcome if you did make those changes.

REFERENCES
SECTION ONE   **Choosing your areas of endeavor** (pp. 12-3)
   Does age make any difference? (pp. 74-5)
SECTION TWO   **What does it take to succeed?** (pp. 82-3)
SECTION THREE   **Making decisions** (pp. 124-5)
You may also find it useful to record how you feel; if so, refer to: **Rating your progress** (pp. 152-3).

MY PRESENT LIFE SITUATION		A	B	C
Areas of life	My life facts			
Spouse				
Children				
Relatives				
Confidante				
Lover				
Friends				
Enemies				
Colleagues				
Hobbies				
Sports				
Health				
Handicaps				
Fitness				
Age & gender				
Appearance				
Skills – practical				
Skills – social				
Skills – intellectual				
Skills – creative				
Skills – emotional				
Sense of humor				
Memory				
Qualifications				
Training				
Paid work				
Unpaid work				
Use of time				
Possessions				
Home				
Membership of clubs, etc.				
Religion				
Income				
Savings				
Debts				
Status				
Power				
Ambitions				
Fears				
Guilts				
Achievements				
Pleasures				
Outlets				
....				
....				

Understanding finance

PROFIT AND LOSS ACCOUNT FOR THE SMITH FAMILY
For the year January 1st 1985 to January 1st 1986

INCOME	Budget	Actual	OUTGOINGS: Direct costs	Budget	Actual
John's net salary	9,000	9,785	**Labor**		
Mary's net wages	3,500	3,300	For Adam's jobs in house	150	190
Cake sales	1,500	2,000	For Eve's jobs in house	150	200
Newspaper delivery	80	80	John's personal allowance	540	540
Sales of dolls' dresses	40	60	Mary's personal allowance	540	540
Joseph's pension	1,000	1,000	Joseph's personal allowance	440	440
Carpentry jobs	500	650	**Materials**		
Students' accommodation charge	1,600	1,600	Food & other consumables	4,000	3,800
From colleague for gasoline	250	250	For cake-making	500	630
Sale of Mary's magazine article		100	For carpentry	200	290
TOTAL FAMILY INCOME for year:	**17,470**	**18,825**	For dolls' clothes	10	5
			Gasoline for traveling to work	500	500
			TOTAL DIRECT COSTS	**7,030**	**7,135**

If appropriate, child allowance should be included. Also any perks that go with John or Mary's job, e.g. travel expenses or luncheon vouchers.

Whatever your chosen project, money will be required. A properly planned profit and loss account, such as the one shown (*above*), will give you a good start. Once your project has begun, careful control over your cash flow will help you to stay in business.

The same principles apply whether your business is an international corporation, a small private company, a charitable trust, a workers' cooperative, a marriage partnership or the management of your personal or household income. If your project is to start your own business, you should always seek professional advice.

Making a profit and loss account
To find out if your chosen project is financially viable, a budget is essential. In the example (*above*), figures are adapted from several real families to produce a fictional Smith family budget. The actual figures are also shown so that the family could compare their budget with their actual expenditure.

If you wish to make a family budget of your own, use the same main headings, but include the items that are appropriate for your family or household. The main headings are explained under **DEFINITIONS** (*above right*).

The Smith family
The family consists of John and Mary Smith, their two school-age children, Adam and Eve, and John's elderly father, Joseph. They accommodate two students during term times.

John has a full-time job and shares his car with a colleague who pays for half of the gasoline. Mary's part-time job is seasonal so she also makes and sells cakes. Adam delivers newspapers, Eve makes dresses for dolls, and Joseph still does some carpentry jobs and has a small pension.

Everyone does basic household tasks, but the children earn money for doing specific jobs, such as gardening and cleaning the car. John and Mary taught their children to manage money from an early age and their contribution was always included in the family budget.

Comment on the account
The Smiths could see clearly from the figures (*above*) their real position for the year and would use this information when making a budget for the next year.

While they had hoped to save $1,000 toward a new car, their profit did not reach this figure. But they actually spent much more than they estimated in their

OUTGOINGS: Indirect costs	Budget	Actual
House		
Rent/mortgage	2,400	2,600
Rates/local taxes	500	500
Insurance/repairs & renewals	350	330
Hire purchase/rental/licenses	520	520
Purchases (e.g. furniture)	150	140
Fuel & services		
Gas/oil/electricity	1,000	1,100
Telephone	400	590
Upkeep of car and appliances	860	865
Leisure		
Holidays	600	580
Family maintenance		
Children's clothes	300	350
Medical expenses	200	450
Miscellaneous & life insurances	350	320
Unforeseen events	200	220
TOTAL INDIRECT COSTS	**7,830**	**8,565**
TOTAL DIRECT COSTS	**7,030**	**7,135**
TOTAL OUTGOINGS	**14,860**	**15,700**

SUMMARY	Budget	Actual
TOTAL INCOME	17,470	18,825
TOTAL OUTGOINGS	14,860	15,700
Profit before extra taxes	**2,610**	**3,125**

DEFINITIONS
Budget: A forecast of how much you will need to spend.
Income: Everything the family earn. In this example, the net amount is shown, which has had taxes, etc., deducted.
Outgoings: Everything that is spent.
Direct costs: Spending on labor and materials to generate the income.
Indirect costs or overheads: Things that have to be paid for regardless of how much income is made. Food and other consumables could be included as an overhead, but as the amount spent on food will vary with the income in the Smith's household, this item should be regarded as a direct cost. For example, if the students leave, income drops and so does the amount of food required.

Each family would have to decide in which category to place each item.

budget, and they could see exactly where the money went: on the mortgage, fuel, medical expenses and the telephone.

Thus, they could plan ahead for the next year with information that would be useful. A medical insurance might be considered, care with the fuel and the installation of a pay-as-you-call telephone system could control the situation.

John's and Mary's earnings
They would take into account that John was unlikely to gain another increase in salary at present and that Mary's part-time job was slowly disappearing. When Mary made a separate account for her cake sales, she discovered that if she could double her sales, her costs only increased by a very small amount.

Mary decided to find out if there would be a market for more cake and other special dishes. She discovered a big local outlet through several restaurants, so she spent 1986 launching a small business.

In a business, depreciation of the value of a car or equipment, such as a stove, would also be taken into account.

Time on your side

Time is a resource in any endeavor, yet many people feel short of time, while others find that time seems to pass slowly one day and very quickly the next.

How do you perceive time?
In general, our perception of time is related to:
1 How much has to be done in a given time.
2 How much we are enjoying what we are doing.
3 How old we are in years.
Therefore, when planning ahead, our view of time is likely to be affected by our attitude to each of these three things: clocks, personal rhythms and age.

Clock time on your side
Some people like to estimate how much time is needed and plan accordingly. They get time on their side by adjusting their personal rhythms to timetables and favor a desk diary or keeping track with a stopwatch. Over the short-term, their output is fairly even and regular, although over a longer period their output is less reliable.
 To plan ahead, using a timetable, refer to:
SECTION TWO **Making a time-scale** (pp. 96-7)

Personal time on your side
Some people pace their activities according to an inner rhythm which rarely coincides with clock time. They get time on their side by following the dictates of their personal rhythms and prefer to live without clocks and watches. Over the short-term their output is fairly uneven and irregular, although over a longer period their output is more reliable.

Planning the use of personal time
Although a diary or calendar will be useful for those few, important clock timed events that have to be remembered, a different approach is required for personal timing. The easiest way to plan for personal timing is to make a job table (*below*) rather than a time-scale.
 A job table can be simply a list or it can be a more organized network (*right*). With either method you can look back and see with satisfaction the many things you have done.
 Retrospection will also give you confidence when a timetable becomes necessary, because it puts a long-term personal rhythm into a long-term clock time perspective. It can also prove that you have achieved just as much as a person who has been working to clock time.

Age time on your side
Younger people tend to view older people as becoming too old to learn, achieve, make love, start a new venture or change direction, etc. When people become older, they discover this view is incorrect, although it is true that some physical changes take place.
 Older people also discover a reality that is evident all

MAKING A JOB TABLE BY LISTING
1 Use a large notebook.
2 List all the things you intend to do. Number each item. Add new things whenever they occur to you.
3 Check off each job when it is done.
4 Use the rectangular boxes on the far left of the jobs to note final completion dates of whole jobs.
5 Sometimes a job has to be repeated. Mark it with a large R in the square boxes on the left of the jobs, and add it to the bottom of the list.
6 Sometimes a job gets ignored. Put a cross in the square boxes on the left of the jobs, and carry it forward to the end of the list.
7 At the beginning of each week (or each month), enter the current date as part of your list.

SAMPLE PAGE FROM ROBERT'S JOB TABLE

W/e Aug 7th, 1986.
- ✓ 1 Redesign back bedroom.
- ✓ 2 Buy paint, etc.
- R 3 Mend doorknob.
- ✓ 4 Design bookshelves.
- ✓ 5 Borrow ladders.
- [Aug 14th] ✓ 6 Buy a puppy.
- ✗ 7 Research microwave ovens.
- [Aug 11th] ✓ 8 Join squash club.

W/e Aug 14th, 1986.
- ✓ 1 Start dog training.
- ✓ 2 Order furniture.
- ✓ 3 Prepare for painting.
- ✓ 4 Buy wood for shelves.
- [Aug 30th] ✓ 5 Decorate bedroom.

W/e Aug 21st, 1986.
- ✓ 1 Teach dog to STAY
- ☐ 2 Research microwave ovens.
- [Aug 31st] ✓ 3 Make bookshelves.

our lives: there really is a time limit. Consequently, most older people learn very quickly how to make best use of their time and eliminate many of those useless activities to which they have been tied all their lives. To have the physical capacities of youth combined with the wisdom of age would seem to be the ideal!

At every stage of life, there is something new to be enjoyed, providing you are willing to let go of the past. For information about lifestages, refer to:
SECTION ONE **Does age make any difference?**
(pp. 74-5)
Lifestage achievements (pp. 76-7)

MAKING A NETWORK PLAN
Robert could have made a network to plan his activities which may have helped him to be a little better organized.

When taking stock, a network plan for the use of personal time can give the same information as a list. For further information about how to make a network, refer to:
SECTION THREE **Developing a network** (pp. 132-3)

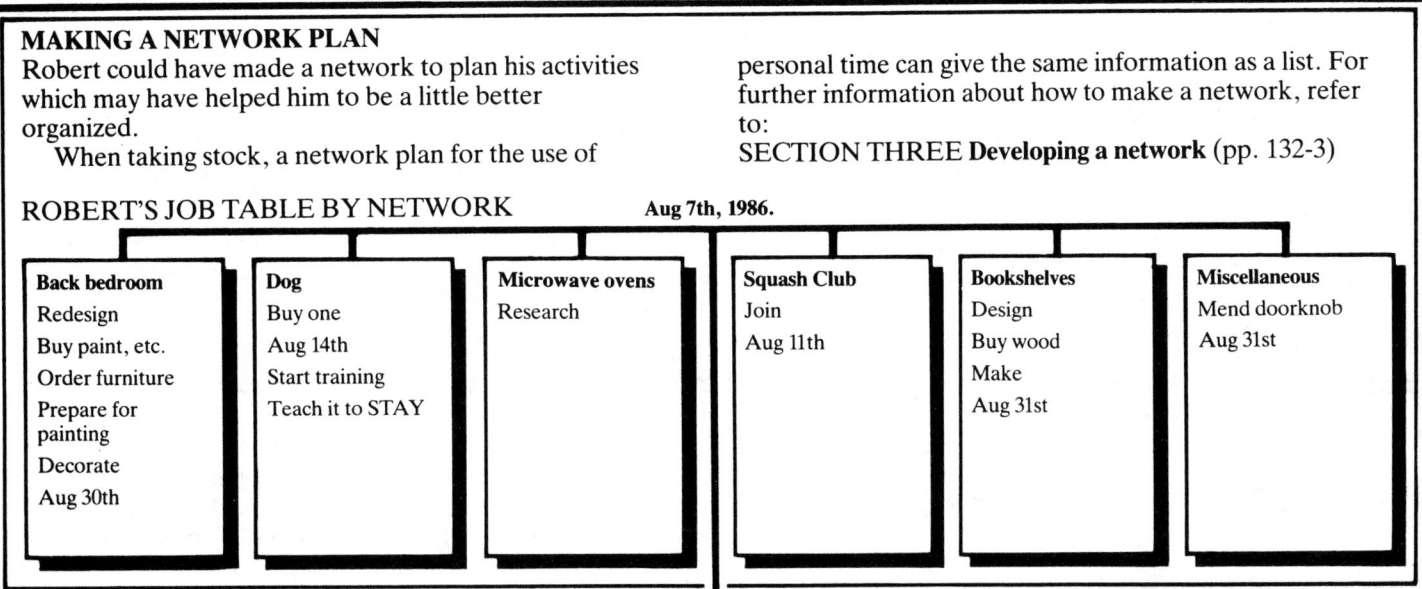

ROBERT'S JOB TABLE BY NETWORK   Aug 7th, 1986.

Sep 4th, 1986.

8 Take stock annually.
 (a) How many jobs you have actually accomplished? (Count the number of completion dates.)
 (b) How many jobs did you get through in a week or month? (Count the jobs between dates.)
 (c) How often you have to do a job twice through lack of proper organization? (Look for the R.)

 (d) Which items did you keep delaying and carrying forward? (Look for the crosses.)

With practice, you will find other valuable information during your annual, personal stocktake.

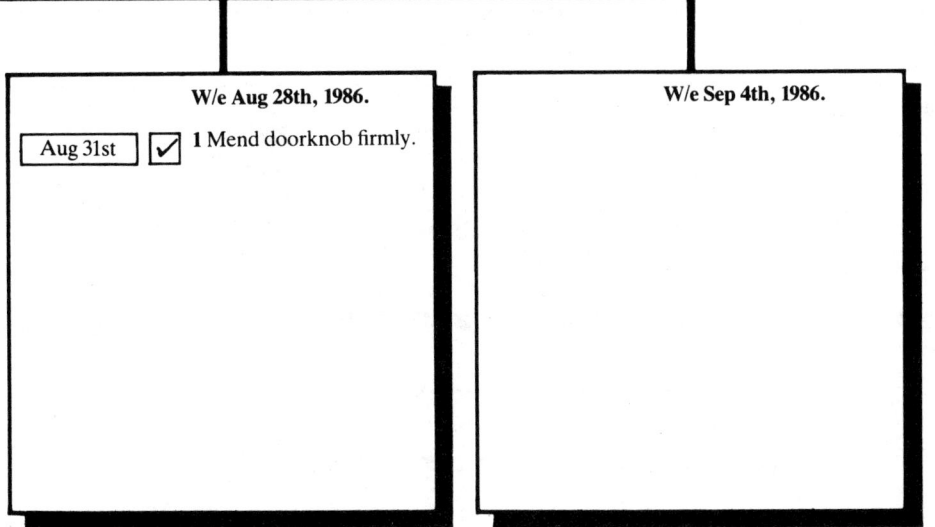

...and so Robert's list continued. To date he had accomplished 14 jobs, as shown by the checks, and had completed 5 major projects, as shown by the completion dates. He had to mend the doorknob twice and put off researching microwave ovens as he wasn't sure how to go about choosing which one he was going to buy. Another way of representing the information (*left*) is to prepare a network plan (see *above*). For further information about making choices, refer to:
SECTION THREE **Analyzing situations** (pp. 126-7)

Developing a network

A personal network is a changing collection of people to whom you can go for information and advice. A healthy personal network is also interactive; as you use your network of contacts, you might exchange information, have a discussion, or give feedback from a previous encounter.

Mobility is the essence of a network
The lines of communication that link the parts of a network are made by the person who uses it. As you move from one part of your network to another, you form the link.

You, too, are a resource on the networks of other people. For example, each member of a family of four, moving to live in a new area, will begin to acquire a network of sources of information. Each person then becomes a resource for the others.

Networks can be formal
Organizations can also be used as networks and give you access to more resources; to use such a network, you may be a client or a member.

Intelligence agents, reporters, detectives, weather forecasters, brokers and government advisors all rely upon networks; so does local gossip.

Personal networks may be combined for special projects, such as when a local community takes action in unexpected circumstances.

A network is for a purpose
Different networks may be needed for different purposes, although there may be some overlap.

Citizens Band Radio is a loosely-knit network for the different purposes of those who use it, while, in industry, a marketing-orientated company regards production and research activities as a network at the service of their sales team.

A SAMPLE NETWORK
The fictitious example shown (*below*) is the network used by Simon Tripp, the father of two children. He initiated action to prevent the imminent closure of the local school.

The information on which Simon acted
The headteacher had been informed that a proposal to close the school at the end of the current year was on the agenda of a meeting of the local education committee, to be held in two weeks' time.

Cuts in public spending were to be made by combining several smaller schools. The local school had been selected for the closure list because part of the building needed expensive repairs.

The school served not only a wide agricultural community but many children residing in the nearby university town, so good was its educational reputation.

Simon's purpose
To form an action group who would obtain a five year postponement (of the agenda to consider the closure of the local school) when the Education Committee met in two weeks' time.

A five year reprieve would be easier to achieve in the time available than a total reversal of policy, leaving the final outcome open-ended, with five years to reform policy if desired.

Simon mapped his network
Simon selected ten people from his personal network of friends, colleagues and casual acquaintances to set the wheels in motion. His first move was to influence the formation of an action program at an emergency meeting at the school, which had been called by the parents' association.

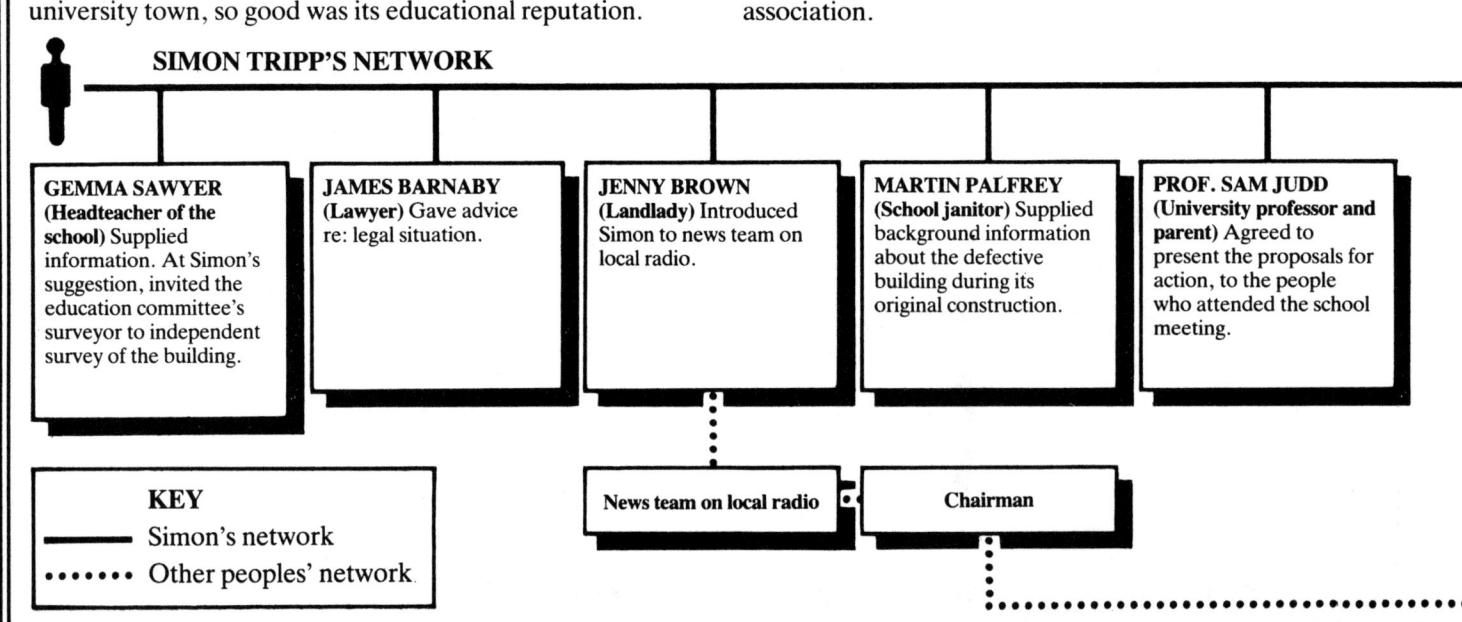

SIMON TRIPP'S NETWORK

GEMMA SAWYER (Headteacher of the school) Supplied information. At Simon's suggestion, invited the education committee's surveyor to independent survey of the building.

JAMES BARNABY (Lawyer) Gave advice re: legal situation.

JENNY BROWN (Landlady) Introduced Simon to news team on local radio.

MARTIN PALFREY (School janitor) Supplied background information about the defective building during its original construction.

PROF. SAM JUDD (University professor and parent) Agreed to present the proposals for action, to the people who attended the school meeting.

KEY
— Simon's network
······ Other peoples' network

News team on local radio · Chairman

How to develop your network

1 Get involved in activities where you are likely to make contact with people.
2 Never refuse an invitation or opportunity to meet and get to know people.
3 Contribute your own information and skills to projects being undertaken by other people.
4 Take a genuine interest in people and get to know them well; never ignore a person or area because they don't look promising on first acquaintance.
5 Join a different club, association or leisure activity each year or so.
6 Get to know local and national formal networks.
7 Ask people in your existing network to recommend others who may be able to help.
8 Develop the habit of remembering salient facts accurately.
9 Share your own information, with discrimination.
10 Show appreciation.

How to map your network

To move into action on any project, you often need the help of other people for information, advice or support. First be clear about the purpose of your project and write it down. Then map your network in the following way.
1 List all the information and support you think you will need to achieve your aim.
2 List people or agencies you know from whom, or through whom, you can get that information or support.
3 On a large piece of paper, write each person's name together with the resources they have available.
4 Plot your route round your network.
5 As you collect information, add notes to your chart and any new names to contact.
6 If your network needs developing, consider the following instructions.

Properly used networks produce results

Simon gained valuable information and support from his personal network. He shared this information with others beforehand, so that when the school meeting took place, the action program to achieve their purpose was already in operation.

The meeting itself became a powerful source of support. Pressure to defer the closure-agenda was brought to bear on individual members of the education committee, backed by well researched facts and a great deal of press coverage.

Networks can produce a bonus

A few days before the education committee meeting, which a large number of local residents planned to attend (as public observers), it was clear the decision would probably still go against the school.

What else could be done? Simon had not yet followed up the information given by his friend, Jenny Brown. So he telephoned the news desk at the local radio station. He was immediately invited to be interviewed during the midday news on the following day.

Meanwhile, the news team were making their own contacts. When Simon arrived at the studio, he found himself being interviewed with the chairman of the education committee.

The chairman was fully aware of the controversy that was raging over the proposed closure. Here was his opportunity to put the committee's case across.

For Simon, however, this situation was a bonus in the campaign. Simon diplomatically manipulated the chairman into saying (live on radio) that the committee had no intention of closing the school!

The action program finally achieved its objective when the education committee postponed the closure agenda for five years.

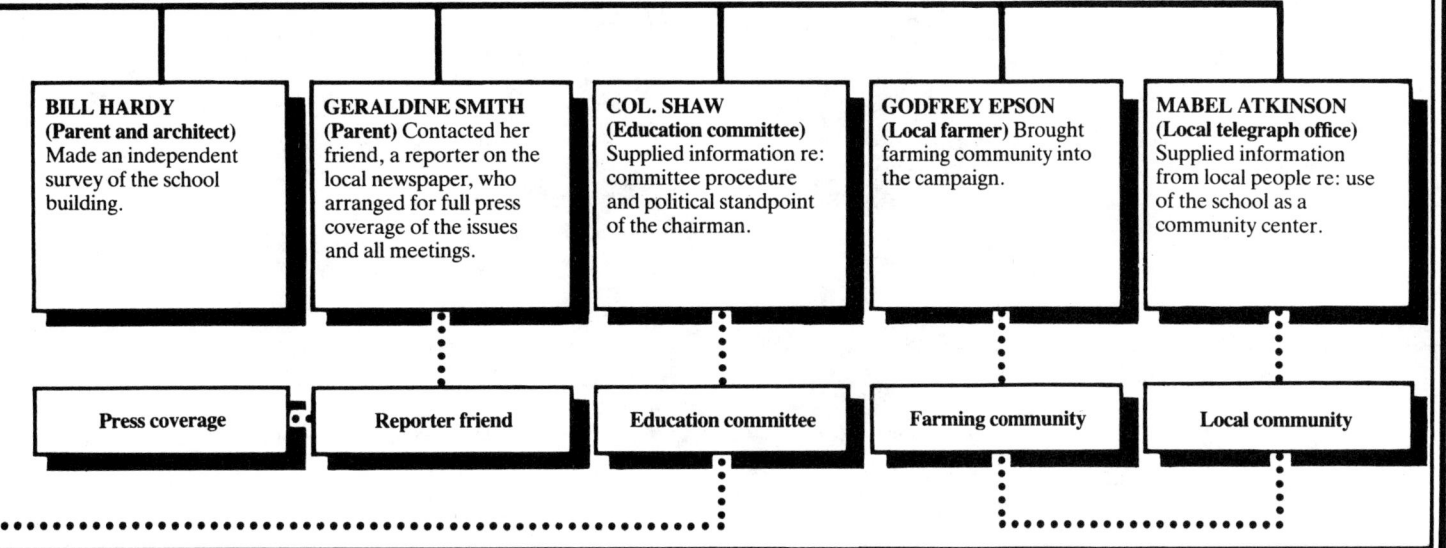

Learning and researching

Learning is something we do that brings about a relatively stable change of behavior. In childhood we learn to talk, putting sounds together to make intelligible words, thus changing our behavior. We never forget those early sounds, so learning to say a new word in adulthood is not so difficult. Early childhood experiences are the foundation for later learning.

Researching is one method of learning, which is useful when planning new ventures. Research begins with a question, which may lead to further questions, for example:

Medical research How can AIDS be cured?
Market research What kind of gadgets are in demand?
Opinion polls Which political party is popular?
Information search What is the population of India?

It is important to ask the right question in the first place. For further examples, refer to SECTION THREE **Getting yourself trained** (pp. 136-7)

Playing is a part of successful new learning
Allowing your unconscious self to give you feedback without conscious interference is the essence of play.

Playing is valuable when you have learned a great deal of knowledge and skills. It makes the difference between a technically good performance and a superb performance.

In recent years the art of inner-tennis, inner-golf, inner-riding and inner-skiing have been ways in which the value of play has been recognized and successfully applied by novices and experts. Inner-tennis consists of allowing your own hand and eye to coordinate, giving you feedback automatically, rather than you trying to apply a technique.

A DIAGRAM OF LEARNING METHODS
There are many learning methods, samples of which, with corresponding examples in brackets, are shown (*below*). On one side of the diagram are fairly passive methods. More active methods are shown on the other side.

Quite often it is necessary to utilize several methods in a successful learning process, or to begin at one end of the diagram and move toward the other, in either direction.

It should also be emphasized that all our senses, such as sight, smell, touch, hearing, spatial awareness and perceptions from inside our bodies, are important.

NOTE The higher the number on the diagram, the more knowledge, skills and experience you may need to be able to learn by using the method described, and the more likely it is that your learning will lead to a permanent change of behavior. Learning takes place, whatever the situation.

For example, a person put into prison will learn more about criminality (Method 14), just as a person can only learn to swim by getting into the water (Method 15).

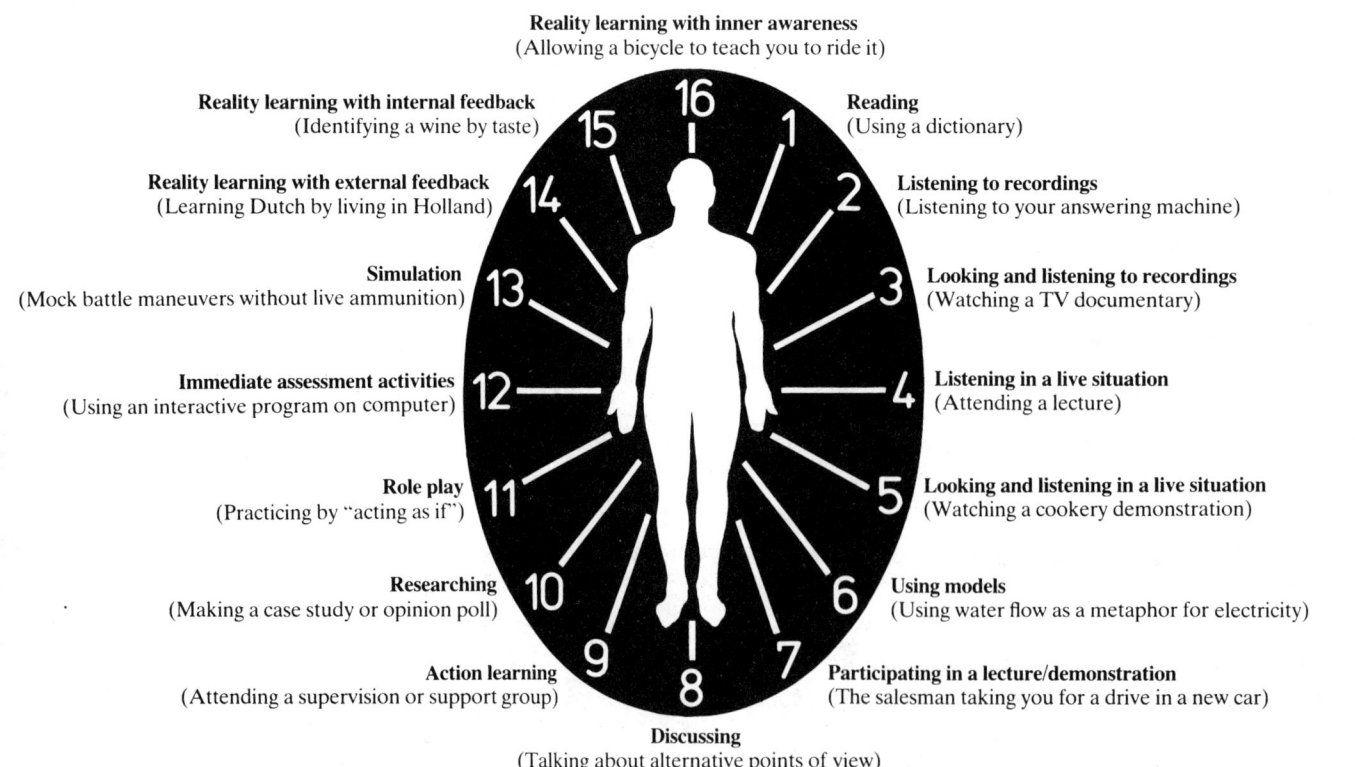

Reality learning with inner awareness
(Allowing a bicycle to teach you to ride it)

Reality learning with internal feedback
(Identifying a wine by taste)

Reading
(Using a dictionary)

Reality learning with external feedback
(Learning Dutch by living in Holland)

Listening to recordings
(Listening to your answering machine)

Simulation
(Mock battle maneuvers without live ammunition)

Looking and listening to recordings
(Watching a TV documentary)

Immediate assessment activities
(Using an interactive program on computer)

Listening in a live situation
(Attending a lecture)

Role play
(Practicing by "acting as if")

Looking and listening in a live situation
(Watching a cookery demonstration)

Researching
(Making a case study or opinion poll)

Using models
(Using water flow as a metaphor for electricity)

Action learning
(Attending a supervision or support group)

Participating in a lecture/demonstration
(The salesman taking you for a drive in a new car)

Discussing
(Talking about alternative points of view)

Playing involves enjoying discovering that you already have the skills to do something, if only you will allow them to surface. For example, bicycles wobble because the rider turns the handlebars. Push a bicycle down a slope and it won't fall over. Inner-riding consists of letting the bicycle keep its own balance and teach you how to ride it.

Ways of learning
The method you choose depends both on what you want to learn and your preferred learning style. However, it is useful to extend your learning styles, otherwise there are some things you may find impossible to learn. For example, if you prefer reading and discussing as a learning style, then you might have great difficulty learning to swim. Similarly, if you prefer to learn by trial and error, then you could be injured before you learn to parachute.

Resistance to learning
We often feel a resistance to learning something new, for example, some people "dry up" when trying to learn how to give a speech in public, and others struggle for a long time to use an unfamiliar tool.

Resistance usually occurs because either there is a lack of similar experiences in childhood, or an early experience was frightening or unpleasant.

Allowing yourself to play is helpful in overcoming both kinds of resistances.

For example, practice giving speeches on your own and then join a class or a speakers' club to gain confidence and enjoy yourself before launching into a public situation. Play around with a tool or a computer to find out what it can do; before long you will find yourself more skilled than you believed possible.

LEARNING STYLES
There are four main styles of learning; we use all of them to some extent, but if you tend to ignore one or two styles because you have a preference for the others, then your capacity for learning will be limited.

For example, you may fail to consider important angles, repeat mistakes, waste time, or fail to integrate new learning, so that when you meet a similar set of circumstances in the future, you have to begin from scratch again.

1 The Experimental Learner
This learner uses trial and error, takes chances, makes dozens of mistakes, adjusts and will try almost anything. He is often creative and favors learning in which he is totally actively involved.

2 The Reflective Learner
This learner likes to watch, listen and digest before he gets too deeply involved. He dislikes taking chances, preferring instead to make a move from passive methods into more active methods, step by step, pausing each time for further reflection.

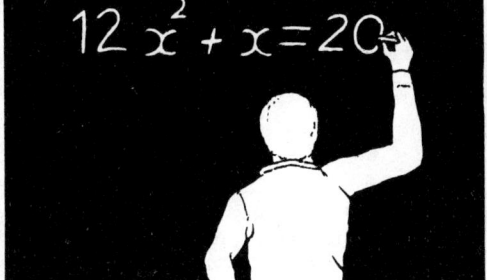

THE MOST FLEXIBLE LEARNERS USE ALL FOUR STYLES

4 The Conceptual Learner
This learner likes facts, figures and abstract ideas. He often makes generalizations and is not very keen on action unless he is absolutely sure it is going to be worth his while. He is often an intellectual.

3 The Practical Learner
This learner likes to repeat things over and over again, memorizing each word or each action until he gets it right. He watches experts and tries to emulate them. He prefers active methods, so long as he knows in advance what to do.

Getting yourself trained

The New Renaissance is a term currently being used to describe a revival in our approach to learning and the way we need to live our lives.

Renaissance means rebirth – seeking a greater breadth of knowledge, skills and understanding. Like Leonardo da Vinci (painter, sculptor, architect, musician, engineer and scientist), to survive and prosper we need many different skills.

Future careers are likely to involve retraining several times for a new occupation and spending periods of time in non-earning occupations. The opportunity to realize our potential has never been greater for those who are willing.

We can also develop our roles in family and domestic affairs to the realization of our full potential, even after retirement from full-time employment.

DISCOVERING YOUR POTENTIAL
1 Look at the world around you.
What are other people doing? Explore what is available in the world for you to do.
2 Ask for feedback on your potential.
Ask your family and friends what they see that you could develop. Try some career counseling; join a personal development workshop.
3 Try something different.
Join a club you never would previously have considered. Take a different kind of holiday than you usually take. Enrol on a course; take up a completely new sport. Talk to new people.

What kind of training?
Once you have decided which part of yourself to develop, becoming trained may be the next step. Do you need knowledge, skills and/or experience? Do you need a formal qualification? Will you need to combine training with experience? Which learning methods will be most appropriate? Refer to: SECTION THREE **Learning and researching** (pp. 134-5)

Which kind of course structure?
The organization of time and the location in which you do your training will be key factors. Training is organized in many different ways, as can be seen (*right*).

REFERENCES
SECTION ONE	**Choosing your areas of endeavor** (pp. 12-3)
SECTION TWO	**What are you good at?** (pp. 90-1)
	What advantages do you have? (pp. 94-5)
	Finding an outlet (pp. 102-3)
SECTION THREE	**Four ways to change a situation** (pp. 106-7)
	Analyzing situations (pp. 126-7)

Formal courses: usually require formal entry qualifications. Full-time or part-time. Regular attendance at a center over a stated period of weeks or years.

Open courses: no qualifications for entry. Continuing over a period of time, chosen by the student, within the limitations laid down by the training center.

Distance training: courses that involve the use of the telephone, TV, radio, computers, or correspondence.

Sandwich training: courses sandwiched between periods of practical work experience, which form part of the training requirement.

Short courses: any brief course for a specific purpose. May be residential and work or leisure related.

Action training: regular withdrawal from work to discuss current problems and to learn how to proceed.

In-service training: correctly speaking, learning by working with an expert who shows you how to do things, and is present while you do them in a work environment.

Self-directed training: teaching yourself or using training resources as a network. Any course which is designed to accommodate your style and possesses the required content.

WHERE TO GET TRAINED

You will need to do some information research to find what training resources are available.

Select resources as appropriate, from the map (*below*), and proceed as follows:

1 Be precise about what you want to find out.
For example, "I want to know what training is available in psychotherapy," or "Where can I learn to build a boat?" The questions will lead to further questions; for example, you would discover that psychotherapy has several different branches, each requiring different training. Similarly, do you want to build a wooden dinghy or a fiberglass canoe?

2 Keep control over your information.
Set yourself time limits, discard information that does not give you even a rough answer to your question, rely on expert sources and keep accurate references and telephone numbers.

3 Get precise details.
Ask when, where and for how long the training lasts. Find out what it will cost and what methods will be used. Will there be examinations and formal qualifications? What outlets are there for people undertaking this training course?

Always read brochures and prospectuses carefully and, if necessary, ask the trainer or director specific questions. Try to talk to other people who have already done the training or, if it is new, talk with people who are also considering getting involved.

4 Commit yourself fully
When you decide to embark on some training, make sure you can commit yourself fully. Do you have enough time? Can you afford the fee? Are other people in your life agreeable?

Useful organizations
Your local library will have directories containing addresses of organizations worth contacting, plus many others, including private colleges and other bodies offering training. Alternative bookshops often have a wealth of information available, as do newspapers, periodicals and journals.

TRAINING INFORMATION RESEARCH MAP

- Libraries
- Universities and colleges
- Polytechnics
- Leisure organizations
- National institutions
- Professional bodies
- Trade associations
- Chambers of commerce
- Employment agencies
- Enterprise agencies
- Career counselors
- Organizations for disablements
- Company training schemes
- Unions & cooperatives
- Religious organizations
- Computer programs
- Correspondence colleges
- Practicing experts
- Journals & newspapers
- TV and radio
- Retirement associations
- Voluntary organizations
- People on your personal network
- Close friends and/or relatives

Presenting yourself

About 30 years ago, Dr. Wayne Dennis, a psychologist, asked thousands of children from all over the world to draw a person... not a man, woman or child, but a person. No other instructions were given.

Although he, and his international co-workers, were looking at *how* children draw, they were surprised by *what* the children drew.

Over and over again, in every race and every culture, the overwhelming majority of children drew an adult; very rarely did a child draw a child.

Similarly, most children drew a male adult, although half the drawings were done by girls, and a large number of children from non-white cultures drew a male adult with white characteristics. Some children drew people they had never seen except in pictures.

It would be interesting to see if children would do the drawings differently now. However, the results indicate that we place a value on how a person looks.

As adults, we become even more conscious about the way we present ourselves... and the way other people appear to us. It is said that we judge a person by how they look within a few seconds of seeing them.

Choosing how to present yourself
The visual images you present to other people tell them something of who you are, what you can do and your general attitude towards life. Are these visual images fantasy or representations of how you really are?

Certainly you can play many parts in life and it is relatively easy to choose clothes, furniture and cars that will give the "right" impression. You can also develop your speaking voice, your movement and gestures and the way you present yourself on paper. Indeed, there are many successful businesses devoted to the art of self-presentation. Similarly, every business takes the trouble to present an image that will help to sell its products and services.

Are you selling yourself?
Self-presentation is the attempt to get a message across that the other person will understand – a message that will bring the desired response. It is said that if you want to change the way other people respond to you, you must first change your appearance.

However, appearances can be deceptive and in the final analysis we all give subtle, unconscious signals that are much more revealing, such as tone of voice, gestures and the way we listen.

REFERENCES
SECTION TWO **Appreciating yourself** (pp. 88-9)

HOW DO YOU JUDGE APPEARANCES?

Unfortunately, we often stereotype people, assuming we know a person because of the way they appear.

Look at the drawings of six people (*above*). Each person is presenting him or herself in quite a different way. Details of the gender and age, current occupation, and a self-description of each of the six people are given (*below*). Decide which details you think best match each person's appearance and, in the table (*right*), write your choices in the appropriate columns.

Gender and age
Male, aged 27   Male, aged 49   Female, aged 39
Male, aged 38   Female, aged 28   Female, aged 47

Current occupations
Singer   Occupational Therapist
Police Officer Housewife & Mother
Stockbroker   Drag Artist

Self-descriptions
1 I am reliable and experienced.
2 I am considerate and patient.
3 I am hard-working and keep myself fit.
4 I'm tough but I've a sense of humor.
5 I'm sociable and love performing.
6 I'm ambitious and enjoy variety.

Now check your results with the correct answers
How close to reality were your original first impressions? The correct answers are given below the table (*right*).

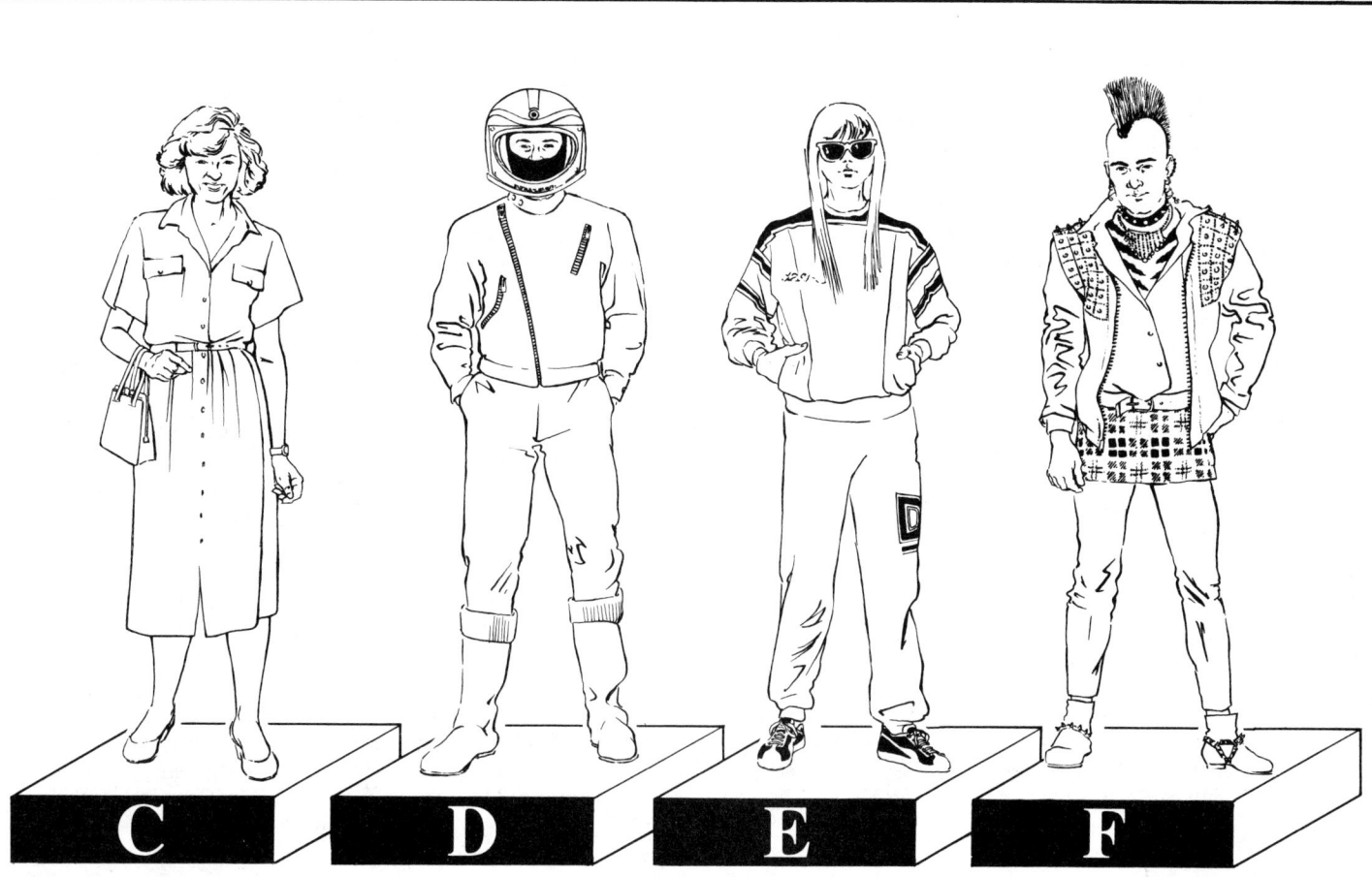

| MY IMPRESSIONS | | | | |
People	Gender	Age	Current occupation	Self-description
A				
B				
C				
D				
E				
F				

Answers **A:** Male, aged 49; stockbroker; 1. **B:** Male, aged 38; drag artist; 4. **C:** Female, aged 47; occupational therapist; 2. **D:** Female, aged 39; police officer; 6. **E:** Female, aged 28; housewife/mother; 3. **F:** Male, aged 27; singer; 5.

Knowing your environment

The environment in which you set out to achieve success in your new endeavor consists of everything and everyone around you, beginning with the space immediately outside your skin and extending ever outwards like ripples in a pool.

Many new projects fail because they are started in the wrong environment or the prevailing trends in a particular environment have not been taken into account. A plant that thrives in a shaded, north-facing position withers in hot sunlight, sunglasses sell better in summer than fur boots, and supermarkets learn where to place their goods to make the best turnover.

If you know your environment you can exploit its resources to the best advantage. To improve your status in your immediate environment, you need to know which positions are respected in your local community.

If your current environment is not suitable, you can look for another that is more compatible and move into it. For example, to take up the challenge of rock climbing, you have to go out and find a rock face to climb.

A DIAGRAM OF YOUR ENVIRONMENT
To make the diagram (*right*) into a personal reference table of environmental features relative to your endeavor, write the specific names of people, places, resources and facilities in the appropriate spaces as delineated by your chosen area/s of endeavor.

Each feature on the diagram is described in the key (*below*), and references to other parts of the book are given (in brackets) from which more information can be gained.

Key to features on the diagram
HOME is the house, apartment or room where you live, the things in it, the people who live with you and your collective beliefs and way of life. Is this the right environment for your well-being? Is it a good base from which to launch a challenging new venture? Is your's a home environment where love is shared? Do power and status figure in your home life? Is there distress or untapped potential?
SECTION THREE **A happier home life** (pp. 120-1)
TOWN/CITY is the area around your home, the town or city in which you live and all its resources, facilities and services such as information centers, museums, transport, communications, health and sport facilities, gas and electric services, police and fire services, employment agencies, businesses, clubs, associations and the general landscape, layout, climate and political leanings of your locality.
SECTION THREE **Learning and researching** (pp. 134-5)
WORKPLACE is the place or places where you do your work, the kind of work in which you are involved and all the people, businesses and resources connected with your work. If your workplace is your home, try to distinguish between your home environment and your work environment; this will give you a fresh angle on both.
SECTION THREE **Analyzing situations** (pp. 126-7)
PEOPLE are the ones with whom you make contact, and others who live in your environment whom you could contact if you wished. (It may be more useful to draw a separate diagram showing more detailed information about the people in your environment who would be helpful in your venture.)
SECTION THREE **Developing a network** (pp. 132-3)
STATE/COUNTRY refers to the wider environment beyond your town or city and the general cultural, political, moral, economic and social ethos. Included here are the major resources, natural and man-made, that may be available to you, the laws of your land, the fashions, trends and new discoveries and the common beliefs that keep you together as a nation.
SECTION TWO **What advantages do you have?** (pp. 94-7)
WEALTH: How much wealth is there in your environment? How much does it cost to live in your environment? How much debt is there? (Remember that credit is a debt.) What opportunities are there for generating wealth?
SECTION ONE **Wealth: areas of endeavor** (pp. 14-7)
POWER: What is the energy level in your environment? How powerful are the people and what kind of power do they exert? Are there opportunities for you to develop your powers or express yourself effectively?
SECTION ONE **Power: areas of endeavor** (pp. 24-7)
STATUS What is the status of your locality and of the people in it? What positions do you or your family hold? Are there opportunities for you to advance your standing or shift your position?
SECTION ONE **Status: areas of endeavor** (pp. 34-7)
CHALLENGE: What kind of challenges are present in your environment? What are the untapped potentials, the dangers or problems? Where, in your environment, can you take up the challenge?
SECTION ONE **Challenge: areas of endeavor** (pp. 44-7)
WELL-BEING: What kind of satisfactions exist in your environment? Is it a healthy, happy and good place to be? Which stresses and distresses exist? Can you improve your sense of well-being?
SECTION ONE **Well-being: areas of endeavor** (pp. 54-7)
LOVE: How loving is your environment? Is there enmity, conflict, hate, prejudice? Where is there a need for love in your environment? Where and how can you gain and give love?
SECTION ONE **Love: areas of endeavor** (pp. 64-7)

The overlap of areas of endeavor
It is important to know your environment very well, since one aspect of life, such as wealth, is invariably linked with other aspects, such as status and power.

If your endeavor is to generate wealth from home, your efforts will not only be affected by the wider environment, but other areas of endeavor may have to be taken into account, such as well-being and love.

If your endeavor involves moving outside your national environment, then use the diagram (*below*) to collect information about your new environment.

Is your environment unsuitable?
If it is, either choose a different area of endeavor or change the situation so that you can proceed with your original idea. Remember there are four ways to change a situation and only one of them would involve leaving your present environment. For more information, refer to:

SECTION ONE **Reviewing your choices** (pp. 78-9)

or SECTION THREE **Four ways to change a situation** (pp. 106-7)

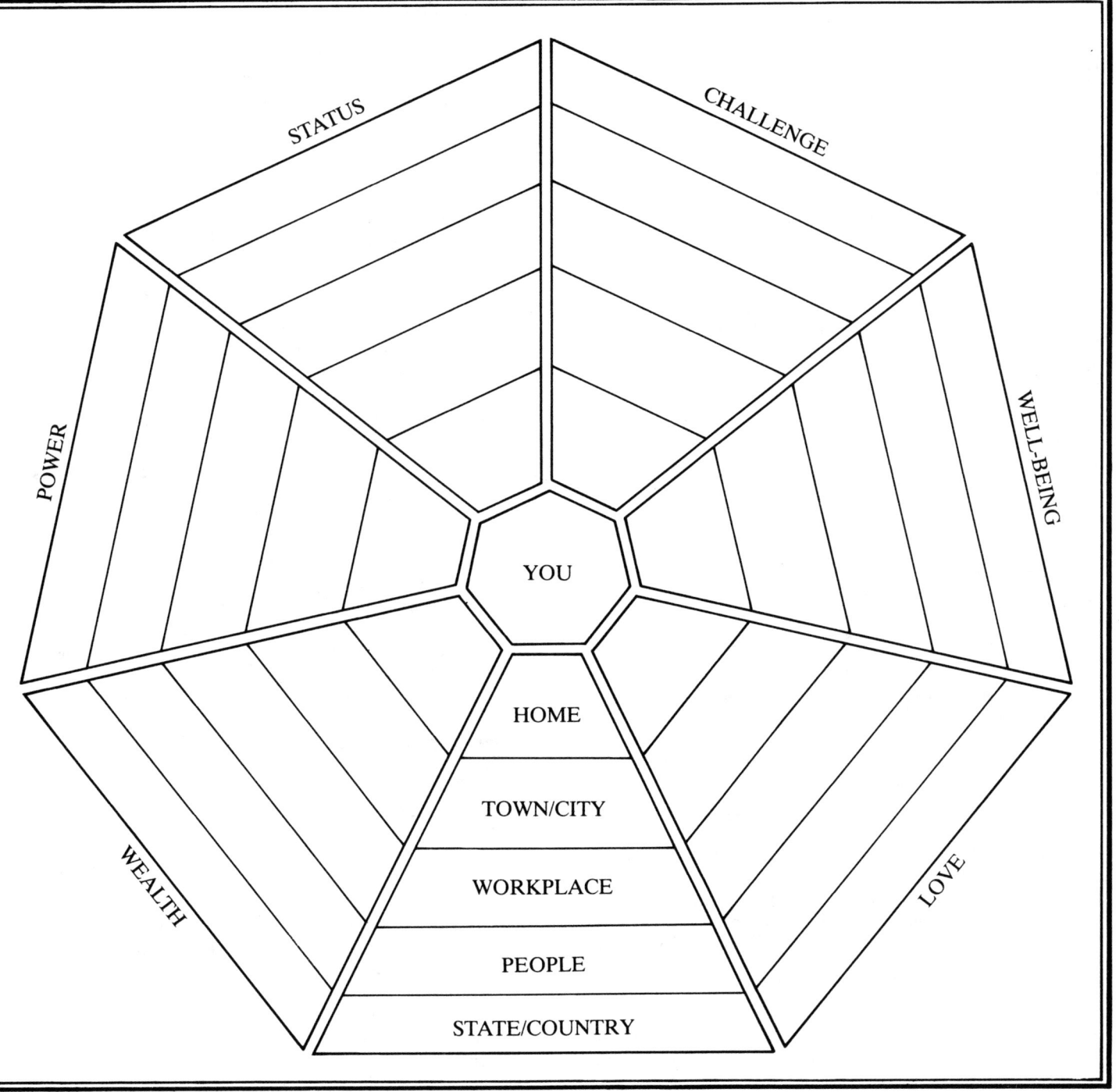

Knowing what they want

When selling or lending your time, skills, property, goods, services or your money, you need to know what your prospective employer, client, tenant or customer wants. Market research is usually associated with businesses that sell goods and services; a similar approach is advantageous to individuals applying for a job.

The most common ways in which employers expect applications in response to their advertisements for situations vacant are via letters, forms, curriculum vitae

WRITTEN APPLICATIONS
What and how should you write on your application? The short answer is:
WRITE WHAT THE READER WANTS TO SEE.
This does not mean being dishonest. Outright lies will always be found out. It means selecting what you put down and presenting it in a way that will be instantly attractive, stimulating and interesting to the reader.

To find out what the reader wants to see you should try ideally to acquire the following information before you write your application or make your telephone call.

1 Information about the organization
a What exactly is its business?
b What are its policies?
c What are the current problems, if any?
d How is the organization structured?
e Who are its major customers?
f What is its reputation among customers?
g What do current employees think about the company?
h Which unions or professional bodies are involved?
i How long is it likely to stay in business?
j How well are its shares performing?
k Is it an equal opportunities company?
l Which selection process does it use and who will be on the interviewing panel?

2 Information about the job and the people with whom you will work.
a Why is this job available?
b What exactly will you be required to do?
c Where is the job located in the hierarchy of the organizations?
d Who else is directly involved with the job?
e What are the future prospects?
f What kind of training facilities are available?
g What salary is being offered? Is it negotiable?
h What are the contractual requirements?
i Are there hidden perks or expectations?
j How much traveling would be required?
k What are the physical conditions?
l What are the distasteful aspects of the job, if there are any?
m To whom will you be accountable?
n What is his/her track-record and reputation?
o To what extent will your spouse or family become involved in your selection for the job, if at all?

By asking yourself questions about the organization and the job, you begin to find out what your prospective employer wants. Furthermore, you prepare the ground for your interview and equip yourself not only with information, but also with relevant questions that you may want to raise before or at the interview.

The interview
During an interview you will inevitably discover many other things your prospective employer wants. While you should always go into an interview well prepared, by listening with full attention, including eye contact, you will gather further information you may find useful about the organization.

An interview is a two-way process, but in the end, it is the interviewers who make the decisions. Try to establish who they are beforehand and use their names during the interview.

Unsolicited applications
If you can convince someone that you are exactly what they want, they will invite you to at least discuss working for them. To make an unsolicited approach to any kind of organization and have any hope of a positive response, you must try to discover their current requirements.

Many people who work freelance have to get their work by making unsolicited approaches. They are often ignored or turned down and learn from these experiences. Never regard a refusal as a failure but as a valuable experience in the business of finding work; you will always win some and lose some.

Using a creative approach
Whatever your reason for seeking work, it is useful to regard the process as a job in itself. An unemployed man, when asked to state his current occupation on an application form, wrote:

"I am currently self-employed in the business of selecting my future occupation."

Once you know what someone wants, even if they aren't currently looking for it, all you have to do is offer it to them in the most attractive way.

Here are the creative approaches made by ordinary, unknown people who were successfully convincing. While the examples are true, the names used are fictitious.

and the telephone. How does an employer begin to make the first selection from the applications he receives? What would you do?

Clearly first impressions count; some applications never get past the envelope stage, being thrown out unopened, but let us assume your written application has been opened and is lying on the table. Thousands of closely written words detailing every aspect of your considerable portfolio of skills and experiences will not endear you to your prospective boss.

How to try to find the information
Here is a selection of sources which may be useful.
1 The local grapevine.
2 Your personal network.
3 The media.
4 The organization's in-house publications and their description.
5 The annual accounts.
6 The local reference library.
7 The organization's sales, training or promotional literature.
8 Professional journals.
9 The telephonist on the organization's switchboard.
10 The caretaking/cleaning/security staff.
11 People who already work for the organization, including your prospective boss.

Telephoning selected people within an organization and asking specific questions can be a rich source of facts and opinion, if the people are prepared to talk to you. Such calls or subsequent meetings should be carefully timed and be in a very businesslike manner; make sure you give your name clearly and use the name of the person you are calling.

Showing an intelligent interest without wasting time is certain to get you noticed but never try to canvass. Your purpose is to gain information, not to wax lyrical about your many assets! The way that you seek information will demonstrate at least one of your skills.

When you have amassed the information, imagine you are the person who will vet your application and write it from their point of view.

What does an employer want?
1 Someone who can do the job effectively.
2 Someone who will enhance the organization and, in particular, his/her particular department.
3 Someone who can relate to people.
4 Someone who will "fit in" with the policy-structure. At the interview, personality factors will be taken into account. Your research should give you an insight into what to expect, and hopefully give you an edge over your competitors. Be ready to negotiate such things as timing, salary and job responsibilities. Never sell yourself short no matter how desperate you may be. If you make a concession, do it after some negotiation and only because you can see it will give you a long-term advantage.

It is wise to brief the people you have asked to provide references too, and to give them written information about yourself that they may not know or remember.

An unemployed sales-executive sells himself
George estimated that the time and money he would spend making applications, following up leads and persuading the headhunting fraternity to assist his search for a suitable, top-line job, would be better spent convincing prospective employers that he was an outstanding sales executive.

His aim was to have people telephone him. That way he could negotiate and choose his new job. So George invested his severance pay and a considerable slice of his savings in a professional TV advertisement. Within minutes of the advert appearing the first offer was made over the telephone, followed by several others. George successfully used the skills he had on offer to sell himself. His investment in himself paid off handsomely.

A designer plays to get the job she wants
Marjorie designed and made educational toys. She needed to expand in order to keep her small workshop going but never had enough time to spend on the sales side. She decided to get a job with a large, reputable toy manufacturer whose activities she had thoroughly researched. She was just the person they needed to join their design team... except they didn't know it. How was she to convince them?

Marjorie designed and made a range of toys compatible with those made by the firm, but took their design concepts in a new direction. She invited children to test them out and selected those that the kids really enjoyed. Meanwhile she thoroughly researched the families of the company's top executives, looking for those who had young children.

Then, with the help of several women friends and their children, she mounted a series of Saturday morning playtimes, inviting these executives and other parents and children in the locality. While the children played, she negotiated for a job; she had not invited them to steal her ideas but to buy them. Her venture paid off; she became one of their senior designers within weeks of the first Saturday playtime.

She had convinced the company that she was not only a good designer, but that her toys were in demand and enjoyed by children. She had also demonstrated her creative approach.

REFERENCES
SECTION THREE **Negotiating for what you want** (pp. 110-1)
Analyzing situations (pp. 126-7)
Learning and researching (pp. 134-5)

Displacing your hang-ups

A hang-up is the remembered effect of a real or imagined unpleasant previous experience that holds us back, blocks progress or interferes with the free flow of energy, ambition, interest, action and ideas.

We unconsciously refer back to earlier experiences and information whenever we come across a new situation. Even in the most unusual of new adult situations we automatically receive some feedback from the past. Without it we would be lost, but feedback that turns into a hang-up can be a nuisance at best. At its worst, a hang-up can cause us to behave in a way contrary to the way in which we would normally behave.

For example, Bill is a kindhearted man who sometimes feels angry but has a hang-up about expressing anger to those close to him. Recently his children have been cluttering the kitchen with their toys so that at breakfast nobody can move without tripping up over them. It makes Bill angry that they are so inconsiderate. He is also irritated because he thinks that his wife, Jean, ought to do something about it.

Diagram A shows the consequences of Bill's hang-up and how a simple change of attitude on his part could displace his hang-up, and break the cycle into which he becomes trapped.

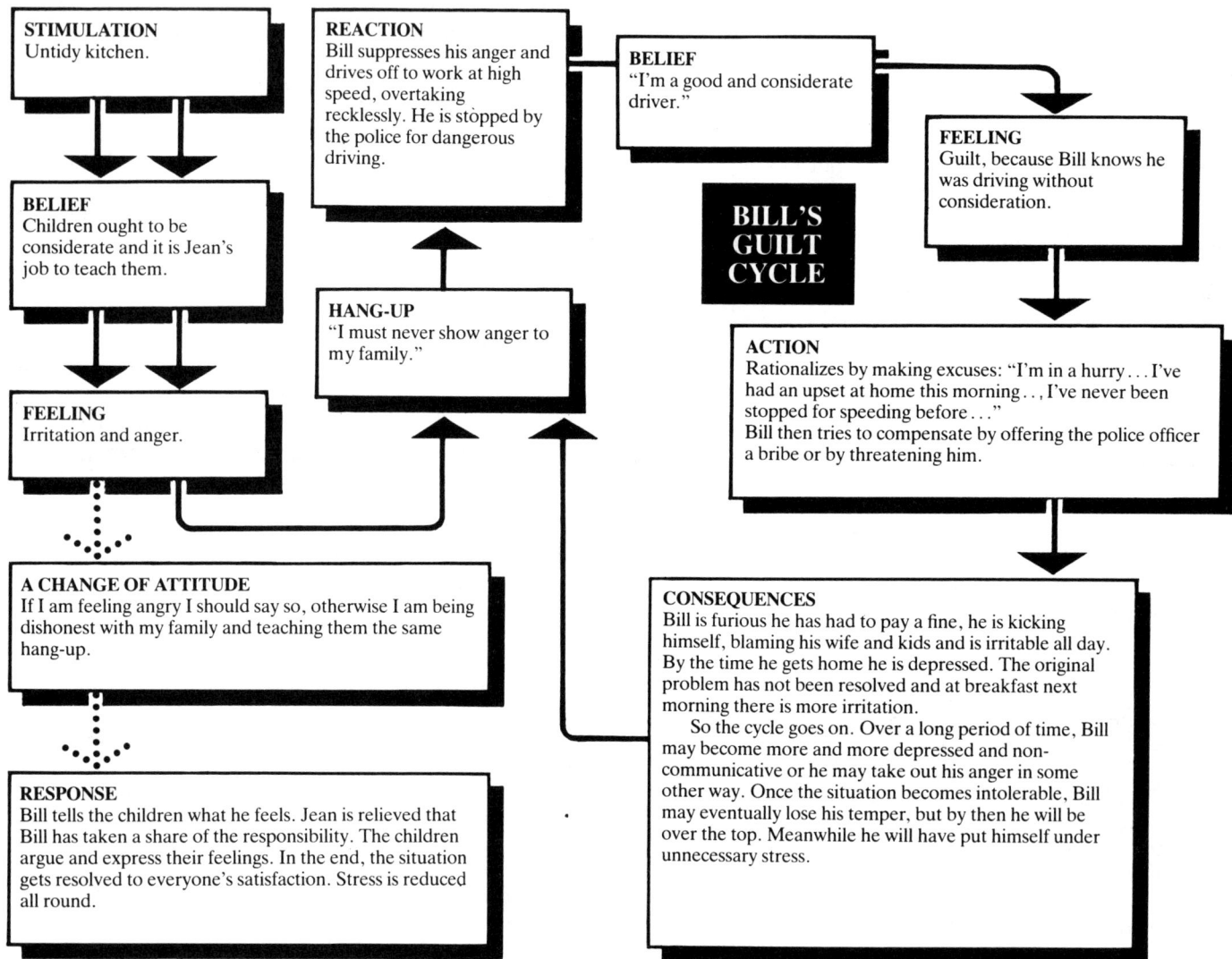

DIAGRAM A
A hang-up leads Bill into a guilt cycle

STIMULATION
Untidy kitchen.

BELIEF
Children ought to be considerate and it is Jean's job to teach them.

FEELING
Irritation and anger.

REACTION
Bill suppresses his anger and drives off to work at high speed, overtaking recklessly. He is stopped by the police for dangerous driving.

HANG-UP
"I must never show anger to my family."

BELIEF
"I'm a good and considerate driver."

BILL'S GUILT CYCLE

FEELING
Guilt, because Bill knows he was driving without consideration.

ACTION
Rationalizes by making excuses: "I'm in a hurry...I've had an upset at home this morning..., I've never been stopped for speeding before..."
Bill then tries to compensate by offering the police officer a bribe or by threatening him.

CONSEQUENCES
Bill is furious he has had to pay a fine, he is kicking himself, blaming his wife and kids and is irritable all day. By the time he gets home he is depressed. The original problem has not been resolved and at breakfast next morning there is more irritation.
So the cycle goes on. Over a long period of time, Bill may become more and more depressed and non-communicative or he may take out his anger in some other way. Once the situation becomes intolerable, Bill may eventually lose his temper, but by then he will be over the top. Meanwhile he will have put himself under unnecessary stress.

A CHANGE OF ATTITUDE
If I am feeling angry I should say so, otherwise I am being dishonest with my family and teaching them the same hang-up.

RESPONSE
Bill tells the children what he feels. Jean is relieved that Bill has taken a share of the responsibility. The children argue and express their feelings. In the end, the situation gets resolved to everyone's satisfaction. Stress is reduced all round.

Hang-ups cause stress
Even if we have to go ahead regardless, a hang-up will prevent our full flow of awareness and make us tense, so we make mistakes, get tied up into all kinds of knots and acquire physical aches and pains.

For example, Jo has a hang-up about speaking in public, but she has to give a presentation outlining her company's policies at an important meeting. In **Diagram B** (*above right*) you can compare what happens to Jo with the performance of her colleague Tom, who enjoys public speaking.

DIAGRAM B

Jo prepares and makes her speech
1 Jo has a hang-up about public speaking and rewrites her speech several times, even staying up late the night before to practice it. She can't decide what to wear and wastes time fussing over small details.

2 Jo arrives at the meeting tired and tense. She hardly listens to what previous speakers are saying, so misses an important point she could have included in her own speech.

3 Jo gets a cold sweat and drops her papers on the way to the rostrum. She mumbles her introduction and barely looks at the audience as she reads her speech too quickly and with little expression. Nobody is impressed and some people have gone to sleep.

Tom prepares and makes his speech
1 Tom enjoys public speaking and is enthusiastic about the new products he is going to present. He concentrates totally on the content and techniques he will use. The night before he checks that all is ready before going out for the evening to play squash as usual.

2 Tom arrives at the meeting bright and relaxed. He manages to talk to several people beforehand and picks up some useful information. He listens carefully to the previous speakers and adjusts his brief speech headings accordingly.

3 As he walks to the rostrum, Tom feels the familiar knot of anticipation in his stomach which dissolves as he smiles, takes a deep breath and launches into his speech, pausing to look at everyone from time to time and responding to the mood of enthusiasm he has stimulated in his audience.

How could Jo displace her hang-up?
Her best move would be to join a class or a speakers' club and practice gaining confidence by speaking on a variety of topics. She could also examine the belief that lies behind her hang-up and change her attitude.

Often a fear of being ridiculed or making a fool of oneself is the source of a public speaking hang-up. The best way out is to concentrate on what you think will interest your audience and laugh with them if you make a mistake. Learning to pause and breathe deeply does wonders for butterflies in the stomach, which is how anxiety usually shows itself.

How to displace hang-ups
Hang-ups may be physical, mental, emotional or all three. The first thing to do is accept that you will have quite a lot of them and learn to love them. They have probably been with you for a long time and were once quite useful. Hang-ups are leftovers from childhood survival tactics.

They can be modified or displaced with practice and a sense of humor. Eventually they will go away of their own accord.

Methods to use
1 Find which belief lies behind a hang-up and replace it with a change of attitude. Then act upon the new attitude. Inevitably you will have to tolerate some anxiety or fear in the process. Try out new attitudes for fun rather than with a serious purpose.

2 Get involved with the reality of a situation, discover new points of view and facts you didn't know. This is especially important when you have hang-ups about situations where intellectually you know you are wrong but emotionally you are convinced you are right. For example, phobias and prejudices.
3 Never make unbreakable resolutions; think things over, take your time and observe what happens. You will make mistakes but these aren't failures; they are the means by which we learn a new approach. You could suggest alternative possibilities to yourself or ask a friend for another point of view.
4 Set your own goals realistically. You can always raise your standards whenever you have reached one goal, but it is debilitating never to reach a goal because you have set your sights too high in the first place.
5 Join a personal growth class or group and learn more about your own mental, emotional and physical patterning. If a hang-up causes you a lot of distress, seriously consider taking some personal therapy or getting medical help.
6 Listen to other people. Often they will suggest some hang-ups you didn't know you had because there is a part of ourselves to which we are all blind. Others can also see some of your positives that you don't see for yourself, so ask for feedback and take it into consideration. Quite often we accuse others of things we aren't aware we do or think ourselves. These projections we put onto others are useful when checking out our hang-ups.

Managing others

Executive, foreman, teacher, boss, mother, conductor, captain, director... there are many titles given to those who take the lead and manage others. So what does a leader do and what makes a good leader?

According to the Chinese philosopher, Lao-Tzu, leadership is for the benefit of the followers, not the leader: "When the best leader's work is done the people say 'We did it ourselves'."

Basic assumptions about people
Your success as a manager will depend on your attitude toward the people you lead, more specifically your assumptions about what makes us tick. In 1960 Douglas McGregor outlined two theories, summarizing opposite attitudes, which he called Theory X and Theory Y.

THEORY X assumes that:
1 We hate work and would prefer to do nothing.
2 We have to be controlled and driven, threatened, cajoled or manipulated to work.
3 We dislike responsibility, preferring the security of being looked after; we like being told what to do and need an "authority-figure" to make all the tough decisions for us and to blame when things go wrong.

THEORY Y assumes that:
1 We enjoy work and need something to do.
2 We motivate ourselves and work much harder of our own accord when we have the right environment.
3 We enjoy taking responsibility for common objectives when we see they are also satisfying our personal needs, such as the need for a decent living, the need to belong socially, the need for a little applause and the need for personal development and choice.

Theory X has its roots in distant historical times when, on average, people were uneducated, dependent, and at the mercy of those who wielded the authority of money and power. The message was "Obey orders and we will take care of you; disobey and you will die."

ARE YOU A THEORY Y MANAGER? Give yourself a rating of 1 to 5 for each item listed **1-12** (*below*) by placing a check in the appropriate column.	5	4	3	2	1
1 I am available to my team members if they have a problem they can't solve, but I encourage them to suggest solutions.					
2 I delegate interesting jobs and real responsibilities and hold people to their promises.					
3 I communicate useful information and put my team in touch with contacts who might be helpful.					
4 I give appreciation when fair and appropriate.					
5 I have a sense of humor, including occasions when the joke is on me.					
6 I make mistakes, admit them and learn from them and encourage my team to do so as well.					
7 Formal meetings are infrequent, short and used to ratify and communicate decisions already discussed and researched.					
8 My team and our objectives have priority over my time. I discourage interruptions for non-essentials.					
9 I take an interest in the aspirations and ambitions of my team.					
10 I actively regard supporting workers, such as telephonists, secretaries, caretakers and cleaners, as important members of my team.					
11 I spend more time with my team than in an office on my own.					
12 I neither accept nor give perks and gifts.					
Totals					
Total score					

ARE YOU A THEORY Y MANAGER? (*left*)
Results: if your score is below 30 you are a theory X manager; if above 45 you are a Theory Y type. If your score is between 30 and 45 you ought to decide which way you are going before total confusion sets in.

IS YOUR BOSS A THEORY Y MANAGER? (*right*)
Results: A score of under 15 indicates that you have a Theory X boss. The lower the score, the more traditional he is, and the less responsible you are. A score of over 25 and your boss is definitely working on Theory Y assumptions. 15 to 25 and you should look a little more closely at the situation. Either his attitude is ambiguous or yours is. The higher the score, the more you are both working toward a Theory Y situation.

McGregor maintains that many organizations, including some governments and churches, still operate on Theory X assumptions.

Managers who have a Theory X attitude fail, sooner or later, to fulfill the objectives of the organization because they have not provided a climate in which people can fulfill their personal needs and enjoy the satisfaction of achievement.

Theory Y has its roots in reality. Observe successful modern organizations and reflect upon your own experiences if you have been fortunate enough to be a member of a team managed by a Theory Y leader.

Do you have the characteristics of a Theory Y manager? Are you a leader in community affairs or of a team at work? Do you have to manage others who work for your business? Are you a member of a team and which kind of assumptions do you make? Are you still in the Dark Ages, behaving according to Theory X or have you grown up to be a fully fledged Y type?

X or Y behavior?
Use the tests (*below left* and *below*) to rate yourself and then ask people in your team to rate you. If you are a Theory Y leader, you will welcome and use the information you can gain from these tests. You can then use the second test to rate your own boss and discover if you are a Theory X or Theory Y team member.

REFERENCES
You may like to distinguish managing from persuading, asserting or negotiating; if so refer to:
SECTION THREE **Negotiating for what you want**
(pp. 110-1)
On being assertive (pp. 112-3)
Persuading others (pp. 114-5)

IS YOUR BOSS A THEORY Y MANAGER?
Score one point for every statement which you agree is true on the whole. If your boss is a woman, replace "he" with "she".

1 My boss is available to discuss problems.	
2 He encourages me to present and implement solutions.	
3 He delegates real and interesting responsibilities.	
4 He does not allow me to make excuses or pass the buck when I have taken responsibility for something.	
5 He is fair-minded.	
6 He gives praise when I have done well and encourages me to do the same for others.	
7 He shares information and gives me good contacts and opportunity for stimulation.	
8 He is genuinely interested in me, my work, my colleagues and the development of our careers.	
9 He does many of the boring jobs himself and works with us when appropriate.	
10 He has a sense of humor.	
11 I do not always agree with him but I respect him.	
12 He is very clear about our objectives and keeps them before us.	
13 The meetings he calls are never a waste of time.	
14 He helps me to learn from my mistakes and admits his own.	
15 He is first to arrive and last to leave.	
16 He respects everyone's contribution to the job.	
17 I never get perks, gifts or favors from him.	
18 I am learning a lot under his management.	
19 I thoroughly enjoy my work.	
20 He is patient but does not suffer fools.	
21 When he is away, he always delegates full responsibility to one of us and backs our decisions.	
22 When things go wrong he does not waste time on recriminations but encourages solutions.	
23 He does not mix business and social life.	
24 He judges people on merit and does not discriminate on the grounds of gender, age, race, etc.	
25 I can speak to him in confidence.	
26 I enjoy and respect the work of my colleagues.	
27 The work I do is valuable.	
28 He enables me to keep up-to-date with new technology, developments and skills.	
29 Our organization is successful and I am proud to belong to it.	
30 I thoroughly enjoy my leisure time and do not take work problems home.	

Total score

Resolving conflicts

To resolve any problem, we have to make a change. Conflict arises because some forces are working toward the change and other forces are working against the change. Hence the opposing forces in a conflict keep things as they are.

Kurt Lewin, a psychologist, developed a method for resolving conflicts which he called force-field analysis. By listing the opposing forces on either side of a central line, labeled the status quo, it can be seen that, to change the situation, forces working for change need to be increased and those opposing change need to be reduced.

AN EXAMPLE OF HOW CONFLICT ARISES
Tarzan (*above*) is trying to find a permanent route along a ravine in the jungle. He comes across a rock that is blocking his chosen route. He tries to push it out of the way. The rock is heavy and resists. There is a conflict between Tarzan, who wants to change the situation, and the rock, which is working against change.

1 Defining the problem
Many conflicts never get solved because nobody takes the trouble to confront the underlying problem. In fact, some people seem to thrive on conflict and prefer to put more effort into finding good reasons for perpetuating the conflict than for resolving it.

For example, Tarzan could spend all day trying to push the rock out of his way, perhaps because he can't bear the thought of failure. He would probably end up frustrated, having wasted his energy. Alternatively, Tarzan could stop and define his problem.

TARZAN'S PROBLEM: To find a permanent route along the ravine. The problem is *not* how to remove the rock. The removal of the rock is only one of the ways to proceed. It is very important to clearly define the problem, otherwise the conflict may never be solved.

2 What is keeping the status quo?
The weight of the rock is blocking the route Tarzan wants to take. Tarzan is using all his strength to push the rock, which tips slightly, but always rolls back into its original position, due to its great weight.

At present Tarzan and the rock are locked in a futile battle because these two opposing forces are equal and the situation is static. The force-field analysis of the situation (*above right*) also reveals two less obvious forces at work. The strength of the opposing forces is indicated by the thickness of the arrows.

A FAMILY PROBLEM
The fictitious Thornton family took a 90% mortgage on an expensive new house when Tom got a very well paid job in the developing off shore oil industry. Tom, his wife, Ann, and their two young children, Adam and Jane, settled down happily to life in New Town.

Eight years later, the fortunes of New Town crashed as some oil companies went out of business. Tom was fired but was fortunate to obtain work on a slightly higher salary in a city 600 miles (966 km) away. The Thorntons put their house up for sale, intending to move to the city within three months. Meanwhile, Tom found lodgings in the city during the week, returning home for the weekends.

18 months later the house remained unsold. There was high unemployment in New Town and many houses for sale. The Thornton's financial resources were strained and their family life disrupted. They defined their objective as to move to the city near Tom's work. Then they made a force-field analysis of their situation (*far right*). Again, the strength of the opposing forces is indicated by the thickness of the arrows.

The Thornton's strategy for change
They realized that their biggest obstacle to changing the situation was their fundamental assumption about house selling and home ownership.

They sold the house at a loss, taking a bank loan to cover repayment of the existing mortgage, and looked to the future. They negotiated for a small house to rent and moved in, taking advantage of all the city had to offer.

The family car was no longer necessary, so they sold it. Within a year, all the family were fully employed, had no debts and were actually saving money.

REFERENCES
SECTION TWO — **What advantages do you have?** (pp. 94-5)
SECTION THREE — **Four ways to change a situation** (pp. 106-7)
Negotiating for what you want (pp. 110-1)
Making decisions (pp. 124-5)
Analyzing situations (pp. 126-7)

How to resolve a conflict
1 DEFINE THE PROBLEM
2 LIST WHAT IS INVOLVED IN KEEPING THE STATUS QUO:
- the forces working toward change.
- the forces working against change.
- the importance of the various forces.

3 PLAN STRATEGIES FOR CHANGE
4 SELECT AND CARRY OUT THE MOST USEFUL STRATEGY

Tarzan's force-field analysis   THE STATUS QUO

FORCES PUSHING FOR CHANGE   FORCES RESTRAINING CHANGE

Tarzan's strength. (i) ➡️ ⬅️ (i) The weight of the rock.

Tarzan's creative mind. (ii) ➡️ ⬅️ (ii) Tarzan's current attitude of mind.

3 Tarzan's strategies for change
Change can be achieved by altering the importance of the four opposing forces; i.e. by increasing the forces for change and decreasing the forces working against change. The questions Tarzan would need to ask himself are listed (*below*).

TO REDUCE THE FORCES OPPOSING CHANGE:
(i) The weight of the rock: Can I reduce the effect of the weight of the rock? For example, by climbing over it.
(ii) My current attitude of mind: Can I look at this situation from a different angle? For example, by considering taking an entirely different route along the ravine.

TO INCREASE FORCES WORKING FOR CHANGE:
(i) My strength: Can I use my strength to better advantage? For example, by using leverage.
(ii) My creative mind: Can I think up some alternatives: For example, cutting steps in the rock.

4 Selecting the most useful strategy
Tarzan's objective is to find a permanent route along the ravine. With this aim in mind, he considers how the strategies he has discovered will alter the balance of forces and overcome the impasse.

He decides to look at the situation from several different viewpoints. (Reducing the opposing effect of his present attitude of mind.)

He uses a few creative ideas to explore the surrounding area, sees that the rock is tilted slightly and successfully applies leverage to roll the rock out of his way.

Taking a completely different, but much longer, route would have been his final resort.

Complex conflicts of interest
Many situations involve complicated issues between several people. The same method can be used to resolve them, by dealing with one objective at a time.

The Thornton's force-field analysis   THE STATUS QUO

FORCES PUSHING FOR CHANGE   FORCES RESTRAINING CHANGE

Cost of Tom's accommodation in the city. (i) ➡️

Tom's traveling expenses. (ii) ➡️

⬅️ (i) Lack of buyer for house at price needed to repay mortgage.

Time spent traveling by Tom. (iii) ➡️

⬅️ (ii) Attachment to friends in New Town.

Ann's fear that their marriage may deteriorate. (iv) ➡️

Better job prospects in the city for Adam and Jane. (v) ➡️

⬅️ (iii) Ann's part-time job in New Town.

Rapidly rising prices of houses in the city. (vi) ➡️

Adam leaving school soon. (vii) ➡️

Retraining available for Ann. (viii) ➡️

Checking your progress

Method one
Here are some comments that might be made by people who have recently made some positive progress in their lives. Check any which you recognize as being similar to your own situation. You may like to add others in the spaces given. If you refer to the beginning of SECTION ONE **What do you want out of life?** (pp. 10-1), you will see that these comments are a progression from the starting thoughts, printed in the same order. If you checked any of those in SECTION ONE, find the matching comments (*below*) and see if you would agree that you, too, have progressed.

Method two
There is an old proverb that says: "If you aren't getting better you must be getting worse." Perhaps there is some truth in it. Human life is like a river, changing slowly as we move onwards, even though we may not notice most of those changes until we look back. Life never stands still, so consider the question: Are you feeling better or worse than say, six months ago? Be realistic; if unexpected events have produced new problems, ask yourself if you are now in a better position to handle the situation. A positive answer means you have made great progress.

HAVE YOU FOUND NEW IDEAS AND DIRECTION?

☐ **1** While finding six things I could do for which there are good prospects, I have begun to discover who I am.

☐ **2** Since the future is uncertain, I have made a choice of career that will allow me to be flexible.

☐ **3** I now have more satisfaction over a broader spectrum of my life and my work hasn't suffered at all.

☐ **4** Losing my job was a blessing. I have found a new occupation with fresh purpose and made new friends.

☐ **5** After the first year of bereavement, I came to regard life as an exciting new challenge.

☐ **6** My physical limitations obliged me to look in directions I had never even considered before.

☐ **7** I resolved my conflicts by organizing my life so I could enjoy both activities to the fullest extent.

☐ **8** We hadn't recognized that we both have separate needs as well as common ones. Now we are happier.

....
....
....
....
....
....

HAVE YOU RESOLVED ANY RESERVATIONS YOU HAD?

☐ **1** I couldn't afford not to make the change, so we sat down and resolved the financial problems together.

☐ **2** I was the only person doubting myself, so I took a management course and I'm now in charge.

☐ **3** Careful analysis proved the advantages outweighed the disadvantages of spending five years in training.

☐ **4** I now enjoy my failures because I learn so much more from them, and my project is progressing well.

☐ **5** Once we began to discuss things as a family, we found ways in which we all could benefit from a move.

☐ **6** I stopped worrying about recognition and put all my enthusiasm into the project. Now I feel appreciated.

☐ **7** I've learnt how to make an organized plan and take successful, active decisions on the basis of that plan.

☐ **8** I selected a training program that matched my learning style. Now I'm eager to learn more.

....
....
....
....
....
....

Method three
You will find a chart on the pages overleaf to help you to rate your present position with regard to different aspects of your life. By giving careful consideration to each separate aspect, you can see where any minor improvements need to be made. If you have already used this chart to mark your starting positions, you will be able to check your progress in each aspect. The progress chart is a way of counting your blessings. Never put yourself down just because you have a weak point. Similarly, brilliance in one aspect doesn't mean you can't benefit from improvement in another.

Method four
It is not always easy to see your own progress. Things may even seem worse temporarily because changes need a readjustment. An excellent way to assess progress is to ask other people to give you feedback. Refer to SECTION THREE **Getting feedback** (pp. 116-7) to find out how to set about doing this. You can also get silent feedback from the way other people respond to you. There are also formal ways of assessing your progress – for example, weighing yourself if you are on a diet or asking for an assessment of your driving by an instructor or by examination.

HAVE YOU ACQUIRED NEW STRATEGIES AND SKILLS?

☐ **1** I talked to people on my network and discovered some exciting opportunities for self-development.

☐ **2** Once I had analyzed my financial situation I made plans to redirect my spending and increase my income.

☐ **3** I began to change the situations in which I failed to assert myself; this renewed my confidence.

☐ **4** I analyzed the market changes and selected three new skills which I am developing over the next two years.

☐ **5** I have made a basic plan to follow so that in the next five years I shall have several new options.

☐ **6** I put my energies into improving my performance instead of my obsession and soon became a winner.

☐ **7** I have learnt how to make a realistic time-scale and now I achieve more than before, and with less strain.

☐ **8** I started to improve my lifestyle by analyzing my present situation and changing one thing at a time.

....
....
....
....
....
....

HAVE YOU GOT OUT OF YOUR TRAP AND MADE A CHANGE?

☐ **1** I examined the different ways I could set about changing my situation and began with my own attitude.

☐ **2** My spouse and I agreed to enlist some professional help. Now we are both much clearer about our marriage.

☐ **3** My own attitude was limiting my enjoyment of life. I am now enjoying membership of a self-awareness group.

☐ **4** Assertiveness training helped me to stop being subservient to my spouse, who also likes the changes in me.

☐ **5** I decided to stop drifting and now I have found several ways in which to change my situation.

☐ **6** I think I thrived on conflicts! Now I have my priorities sorted out and enjoy positive challenges.

☐ **7** My attitude was always so negative it is no surprise I was always getting passed over for promotion.

☐ **8** I checked out my assumptions by asking for feedback. Now I realize I can make a move sooner than I thought.

....
....
....
....
....
....

Rating your progress

HOW TO USE THE PROGRESS CHART
Rate how you are currently feeling in general about each part of your life by selecting from the scale of feelings numbered **1** to **7** (*below*) the one which is most appropriate to you. Then place a pencil dot in the column headed by the number of your choice. The meaning of the scale is listed (*below*): **1** is feeling low, **4** is middling and **7** is feeling high.
Some spaces have been left for you to add any very personal items that you may find helpful to rate. You may, for example, want to chart how you feel about your progress in a specific activity or how you feel about a particular person, animal or place.

The scale of feelings
If an item is not applicable to you, place a cross in the column headed **N/A**.
1 Dreadful, terrible, awful, feeling very low.
2 Unhappy, somewhat depressed, blank or sad.
3 Fairly dissatisfied on the whole.
4 Mixed feelings – sometimes up, sometimes down.
5 Fairly satisfied on the whole.
6 Very satisfied, pleased and positive.
7 Absolutely delighted, happy, and full of life.
* Place a star in the star column if the point on the scale that you have chosen is the highest you have ever reached so far in that area of your life.

When you are sure you have placed the pencil dots at the correct points on the progress chart, choose a color, mark each dot with that color, and join up the dots. Then fill in the key (*below*) with the color you have chosen and the date.

KEY Color	Date

The next time you fill in this progress chart, choose a different color, so that you can see your progress.
IT IS BEST TO LEAVE THE CHART FOR THREE MONTHS BEFORE DOING THE RATINGS AGAIN.

Using the chart in the future
Follow the instructions as you did on the first occasion. If you join the dots vertically on the first and subsequent occasions and use a different colored pen, you will be able to analyze the peaks and troughs in various parts of your life.
When you have used the chart four or five times, you will be able to see clearly your general trends and take appropriate action by giving some special attention to those areas about which you tend to feel low. The strategies and skills in Section Three will be of help, especially **Displacing your hang-ups** (pp. 144-5).

On judging your general situation
If you are a hardened perfectionist, you will never progress! Others who may find it difficult to progress are those who always think of themselves as bad.
Finally, it is perfectly normal to have ups and downs. It is impossible to live on a "high" in every area of your life all the time. You only know you are high because sometimes you feel at a lower ebb. Like the tide, everything happens in cycles.
Knowing your own cycles, which you can discover from this chart, will help you to choose in which direction to move next and which areas of your life need a little more attention.

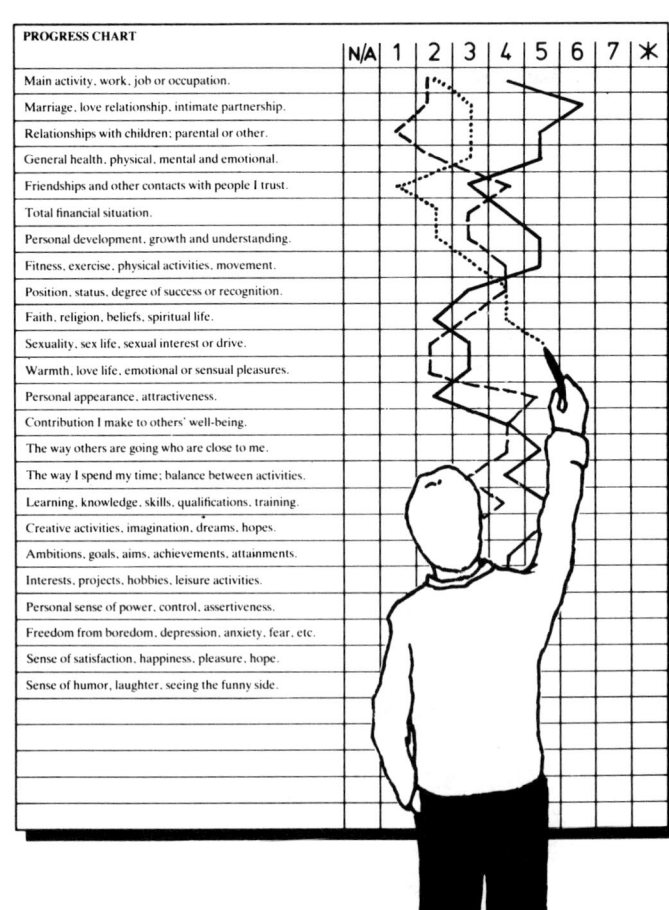

152

PROGRESS CHART	N/A	1	2	3	4	5	6	7	∗
Main activity, work, job or occupation.									
Marriage, love relationship, intimate partnership.									
Relationships with children; parental or other.									
General health, physical, mental and emotional.									
Friendships and other contacts with people I trust.									
Total financial situation.									
Personal development, growth and understanding.									
Fitness, exercise, physical activities, movement.									
Position, status, degree of success or recognition.									
Faith, religion, beliefs, spiritual life.									
Sexuality, sex life, sexual interest or drive.									
Warmth, love life, emotional or sensual pleasures.									
Personal appearance, attractiveness.									
Contribution I make to others' well-being.									
The way others are going who are close to me.									
The way I spend my time; balance between activities.									
Learning, knowledge, skills, qualifications, training.									
Creative activities, imagination, dreams, hopes.									
Ambitions, goals, aims, achievements, attainments.									
Interests, projects, hobbies, leisure activities.									
Personal sense of power, control, assertiveness.									
Freedom from boredom, depression, anxiety, fear, etc.									
Sense of satisfaction, happiness, pleasure, hope.									
Sense of humor, laughter, seeing the funny side.									

A little applause

Everyone not only wants to feel important but *needs* to feel important. Self worth does not appear from a vacuum. Babies of any species, including we humans, can survive alone under the most appalling conditions for a few days immediately after birth but our future well-being does not depend only upon food, water and protection from cold and predators.

Our sense of self and of self worth, and our eventual recognition of others as beings worthy of respect, grow from contact with other people... people who demonstrate they genuinely care and who recognize and appreciate our differences and separateness. In adulthood, the simplest way to gain a little essential applause is to give it.

What's in a name?
It is true that most endeavors depend for a large part of their success on good relationships between people. One of the most effective ways to establish a good relationship with someone is to remember and use that person's name. A good relationship does not depend on liking but on respecting and recognizing.

There is a story about Andrew Carnegie, the American steel tycoon of the 1930s, that illustrates this point. It is said that when he was a child in his native Scotland he kept rabbits. Needing some help in other childhood ventures, he promised to name the newborn rabbits after his friends. The result was magical, he had recognized each of them. After that, Andrew was never short of help, since he had demonstrated everyone's importance. Is it not true that many parents name their children after someone?: James the son of James, Diana like a Princess or Adam the first born.

While some people long to see their names associated with public buildings, in lights outside the theater, among the TV credits or immortalized on the cover of a book, others covet engraved cups won in sports competitions or eagerly trace the ancestry of their family name. Even in death, a name is added to the roll of honor or the tombstone.

**"What's in a name? that which we call a rose
By any other name would smell as sweet."** said William Shakespeare and it is true that your name does not define who you are, no matter how famous or infamous your parents. However, the use of your name by others does demonstrate that they recognize you... and the reverse applies. The sharing of names is one of the most effective ways of making good contact and building a genuine sense of self worth for all of us.

Guide to terms

A brief summary of definitions, checklists and concepts used in the book are given here with page numbers for quick reference.

ACTION TREE .... Pages 124-125
A method for making decisions using seven steps: defining aim; collecting information; anticipating implications; following options; adding alternatives; reviewing aims; defining success.

ASSERTION .... Page 112
Self-expressive power that stems from personal conviction. To become more assertive, review your perceptions.

BONDING .... Page 68
Attachment to, or deep love of, a person.

CHALLENGE .... Pages 44-53
A drive to do something totally involving. A challenge has five characteristics: change; process; involvement; flexibility; originality.

CHANGE .... Page 106
Doing, thinking or feeling in a new or unfamiliar way. Four ways to manage change: change situation; change self; live with it creatively; leave situation.

CONGRUENCY .... Pages 27 and 29
Our condition when there is no discrepancy between what we think, feel, say and do.

DEPENDENCY STATES .... Pages 42-43
Three ways of relating to mutual benefit: through a hierarchy (order-dependent); in a network (interdependent); by differences (independent).

DISAPPOINTMENT .... Pages 118-119
A state of mind when events do not come up to expectations. Disappointment can be handled by releasing negative feelings, talking to others or yourself, reviewing your beliefs, reducing stress and taking advantage of the situation.

ENDEAVORS .... Pages 12-13
Six areas into which to channel your efforts: wealth, power, status, challenge, well-being and love.

ENVIRONMENT .... Pages 140-141
Everything outside yourself.

FAILURE .... Pages 108-109
Situations that have not turned out as you wished. Failure is courted by doing things in a different manner than is usual and can be a valuable aid to learning.

FEEDBACK .... Page 116
Information about the effect of an action used to adjust the action. Feedback can be internal, external, positive, negative, anticipatory or conditioned.

FORCE-FIELD ANALYSIS .... Pages 148-149
A method of resolving conflicts by defining the opposing forces that are keeping the status quo, planning strategies to change the strength of each force and carrying out the most useful strategy.

HANG-UP .... Pages 144-145
The effect on the present of real or imagined unpleasant previous experiences.

GUILT-CYCLE .... Page 144
A repetitive cycle of behavior caused by a hang-up.

HELP & SUPPORT .... Pages 100-101
Temporary structures enlisted to enable you to take another step forward which would otherwise be difficult or impossible.

HOME .... Pages 120-121
A concept that embraces you, your family or others you live with and the place in which you live.

IDEAS .... Pages 84-85
Alternative perceptions generated by various methods such as brainstorming, borrowing, making new connections, synectics and asking why.

INJUNCTIONS .... Pages 30-31
A transactional analysis term for five beliefs learnt by rote in childhood, namely: be strong, be perfect, try hard, be good and hurry up.

INTUITION .... Pages 52-53
A store of normally unconscious information which can be valuable or neurotic.

LEARNING STYLES .... Page 135
Four ways in which learning takes place: by experiment; by reflection; by practice; by concept.

LIFESTAGES .... Pages 74-77
Fifteen periods of life, each of roughly seven years.

LOVE .... Pages 64-73
The expression of a powerful feeling which can heal, support, endure adversities and rejuvenate.

MARKET .... Pages 102-103
An outlet for an endeavor that brings a return.

NEEDS .... Page 58
Conditions necessary to human life which can be described as having, being and doing.

NEGOTIATION .... Pages 110-111
A transaction between two parties to their mutual satisfaction. The seven rules for negotiating are: never undersell yourself; create an impact; assume everything is negotiable; never be generous; encourage the other party to negotiate; never accept the first offer; leave yourself room to negotiate.

NETWORK .... Pages 132-133
A changing collection of people whom you can contact for information or advice.

PLANNING .... Pages 86-87
Making decisions and acting upon them by stating intention, method, resources, feedback and adjustment.

PERSUASION .... Page 114
Inducing a belief in others so they act accordingly.

PPC SYNDROME .... Pages 82-83
The qualities of passion, persistence and commonsense which are demonstrated by successful people.

PROGRESS .... Pages 78-79, 150-153
Evidence of achievement.

POWER .... Pages 24-33
An urge to express yourself effectively; an energy source that has quantity, quality and an effect.

RELATIONSHIP GAMES .... Pages 122-123
Roles that prevent intimacy, such as Peter Pan & Wendy.

RESOURCES .... Pages 94-95
Whatever you can use to advantage such as your own beliefs, your ability to learn new skills, other people's knowledge, your natural personality and environmental factors.

R.R.TUCH CONCEPT .... Page 120
A checklist for healthy relationships: respect; responsibility; trust; understanding; concern; honesty.

SKILLS .... Pages 90-91 and 124-151
Practical methods for short-term accomplishment, such as: manipulating objects, organizing information, creating ideas and relating with people.

STANDARDS .... Pages 98-99
The degree of excellence determined by statutory, environmental, market or personal requirements.

STATUS .... Pages 34-43
A clearly recognized position in society.

STREET OF LIFE .... Pages 108-109
A metaphor to describe four kinds of behavior. The neutralizer avoids life, the rejector controls life, the acceptor pays for life, while the responder enjoys life.

SUCCESS .... Pages 10-11
Achievement accompanied by a glow of satisfaction.

SYNECTICS .... Page 84.
A method for generating ideas using direct analogy, personal analogy, symbolism or fantasy.

THEORY X & THEORY Y .... Pages 146-147
Management theories. Theory X states that people hate work, have to be driven and will not take responsibility. Theory Y states that people enjoy work, motivate themselves and take responsibility.

TOP DOG & UNDER DOG .... Page 115
The two sides of humanity. Top Dog is the creative, active side that enjoys negotiation. Under Dog is the compliant, submissive side that enjoys persuasion.

USP .... Pages 98-99
Your unique selling proposition, i.e. what you have on offer that will make others want your product more than the product of your competitors.

WALL OF LIMITATIONS .... Pages 92-93
Whatever prevents you from making progress such as your own beliefs, lack of skills, other people, inherited factors or world events.

WEALTH .... Pages 14-23
Riches beyond your wildest dreams.

WELL-BEING .... Pages 54-63
Whatever is most satisfying to you.

Acknowledgements
Some of the concepts and techniques described in this book were originated and developed by Maya Pilkington in her work as a management trainer and group facilitator for personal growth. Their application in this book has been modified.

The author wishes to acknowledge the influence on her work of Kim Chernin, Anton Ehrenszweig, George Groddeck, Stanley Keleman, Melanie Klein, Sybil Marshall, Margaret Mead, A. S. Neill, Rajneesh, Wilhelm Reich, Lilian Rubin and Dale Spender, and the concepts and techniques, originated by others, that have been adapted to enrich this book, including:

John Adair – Learning Styles.

Eric Berne – The Street of Life.

Colette Dowling – The Cinderella Complex.

Erich Fromm – The R.R.Tuch Concept.

Dan Kiley – The Peter Pan Syndrome.

Mavis Klein – Five Injunctions.

Kurt Lewin – Force-Field Analysis.

Douglas McGregor – Management Theories.

Fritz Perls – Top Dog and Under Dog.

Gail Sheehy – Passages of Life.

Index

A
Abrahams, Harold 36
Action 104-154
   skills 124-149
   strategies 106-123
   tree of 124-125
Advantage, gaining 119
Advantages, what do you have 94-95
Age, does age make any difference 74-75
Allen, Woody 82
Amundsen, Roald 34
Analyzing situations 126-127
Andersen, Hans Christian 27
Appearances, judging 138-139
Applications, written 142-143
Appreciating yourself 88-89
Aptitude 90-91
Assertive, being 112-113

B
Bears, The Three 55
Beatles, The 77
Beliefs
   and power 30-31
   reviewing 119
Birō, Lāzlo 14
Blondin, Charles 82
Bonaparte, Napoleon 24
Bonding 68
Boredom 50
Borgia, Lucrezia 34
Borrowing ideas 84
Brainstorming 84
Brown, Helen Gurly 82

C
Carnegie, Andrew 16 154
Cartland, Barbara 65
Casanova 64
Cassidy, Butch 67
Cavell, Edith 57
Challenge
   advantages and pitfalls 48-49
   areas of endeavor 44-47
   do you seek 50-51
   which kind do you want 52-53
Change, do you welcome 50
Changing a situation 106-107
Changing your status 42
Chaplin, Charlie 14
Checking your progress 150-151
Chicago, Judy 56
Children 85
Choices, reviewing your 78-79
Choosing
   challenge 13
   love 13
   power 12
   status 12
   wealth 12
   well-being 13
Choosing what you want from life 10-11
Choosing your areas of endeavor 12-13
Churchill, Sir Winston 56
Columbus, Christopher 44
Commonsense 82
Conflicts, resolving 148-149
Connections 84
Conrad, Joseph 45
Corrigan, Mairead 36
Courting failure 108-109
Curie, Marie 56

D
Daimler, Gottlieb 77
de Gaulle, Charles 76
Deciding what you want from life 10-11
Decisions, making 124-125
Dennis, Dr Wayne 138
Dependencies, table of 43
Developing a network 132-133
Diana, Princess 76
Different, enjoying being 50
Disappointment, how to handle 118
Displacing your hang-ups 144-145
Domingo, Placido 27
Dowling, Colette 122
Duckling, The Ugly 67

E
Eiffel, Alexandre-Gustave 44
Einstein, Albert 24
Elizabeth II, Queen 77
Elvis Presley 55
Employers 142-143
Endeavor
   challenge 44-47
   choosing your areas of 12-13
   and love 64-67
   outlets for 102-103
   and power 24-27
   reviewing your choices 78-79
   and status 34-37
   and wealth 14-15
   and well-being 54-57
Enlisting help 100-101
Environment
   diagram of your 140-141
   knowing your 140-141
Epp, Martin 55
Evans, John 76

F
Failure, courting it 108-109
Family
   finance 128-129
   and home life 120
   reasons for starting 85

Feedback 116-117
Finance 128-129
Finding an outlet 102-103
Force-field analysis 149
Fossey, Dian 57
Francis of Assisi, St 66

G
Galileo Galilei 46
Geldof, Bob 65
Generating ideas 84-85
Genghis Khan 77
Guide to terms 155-156
Guilt cycles 144
Gulbenkian, Calouste Sarkis 17

H
Habeler, Peter 47
Hammarskjold, Dag 35
Hang-ups, displacing your 144-145
Héloise and Abélard 66
Helen of Troy 54
Help, enlisting 100-101
Hillman, Sidney 27
Hilton, Conrad 17
Home life, a happier 120-121
Hulme, Keri 25

I
Interviews 142
Intimate relationships 122-123
Intuition, and challenges 52-53

J
Joan of Arc, St 37
Job table 130-131
Joyce, James 76

K
Keller, Helen 45
Kelly, Grace 15
Kennedy family 14
Kiley, Dan 122
King, Martin Luther 26
Kissinger, Henry 25
Knowing what they want 142-143
Knowing your environment 140-141

L
Ladders, of social status 40-41
Lao-Tzu 146
Lawrence of Arabia 37
Learning methods 134
Learning and researching 134-135
Learning styles 135
Life-situations, analyzing 126-127
Lifestage achievements 76-77
Lifestages, table of 75
Limitations, what are your 92-93
Love
  advantages and pitfalls 68-69
  areas of endeavor 64-67
  how loving are you 70-71
  key list of loves 73
  what is it 70
  which kind do you want 72-73

M
MacDonald, Flora 64
McGregor, Douglas 146
MacLean, Duncan 76
Madame de Pompadour 26
Maharishi Mahesh Yogi 36
Making decisions 124-125
Man from Mars approach 60-61
Management of situations 106-107
Managing other people 146-147
Marriage 122-123
  balance of power in 33
Marx, Jenny 67
Mead, Dr Margaret 77
Messner, Reinhold 47
Methuselah 77
Miller, Lee 34
Monroe, Marilyn 35
Montessori, Maria 64
Mozart 76
Mumtaz Mahal 65
Murdoch, Rupert 25

N
Napoleon 24
Nascimento, Edison Arantes Do 17
Needs, the three basic 58
Negotiating for what you want 110-111
Negotiation and persuasion 114-115
Network
  developing a 132-133
  plan 131
  sample 132-133
New Renaissance 136
Newman, Paul 115

O
O'Keeffe, Georgia 57
Outlet, finding an 102-103

P
Pan, Peter 54
Pankhurst, Emmeline 47
Passion 82
Pelé 17
Perception and assertion 112-113
Persistence 82
Persuading others 114-115
Peter Pan 54
Planning 80-103
  basic 86-87
Poisson, Jeanne Antoinette 26
Pompadour, Madame de 26

Pope, The 16
Pope John XXIII 77
Positive attitude, acquiring a 118-119
Power
   advantages and pitfalls 28-29
   areas of endeavor 24-27
   balance in marriage 33
   do you want more 30-31
   table of powers 32
   which kind do you want 32-33
PPC syndrome 82
Presley, Elvis 55
Progress
   checking your 150-151
   rating your 152-153
Progress chart 153

Q
Queen Elizabeth II 77
Queen Mother 76

R
Rating your progress 152-153
Relationships, intimate 122-123
Renaissance, The New 136
Researching and learning 134-135
Resolving conflicts 148-149
Reviewing your choices 78-79
Rockefeller, John Davidson 15
Rubenstein, Helena 35

S
St Francis of Assisi 66
St Joan of Arc 37
Seagull, Jonathan Livingstone 37
Selection 8-79
Self-image 88-89
Self-worth 88
Setting standards 98-99

Shah Jahan 65
Shaw
   George Bernard 77
   Percy 46
Smart, Elizabeth 66
Social climber, are you a 40-41
Standards, setting 98-99
Standards reference table 99
Stanley, Sir Henry Morton 46
Status
   advantages and pitfalls 38-39
   are you a social climber 40-41
   areas of endeavor 34-37
   which do you want 42-43
Street of life 108-109
Stress, how to reduce 119
Success, what does it take to succeed 82-83
Sugar, Alan 15
Sullivan, Anne Mansfield 45
Synectics 85

T
Table of dependencies 43
Table of fifteen life stages 75
Table of powers 32
Table of standards 99
Talking to someone 118
Talking to yourself 118
Terms, guide to 155-156
Thatcher, Margaret 26
Theory X and Theory Y 146-147
Thompson, Daley 24
Time on your side 130-131
Time-scale, making a 96-97
Top Dog 115
Training 136-137
Tree of action 124-125
Turgenev, Ivan Sergevitch 16
Twain, Mark 47

U
Ugly Duckling, The 67
Under Dog 115
Understanding finance 128-129

V
Van Gogh, Vincent 45
Victoria, Queen 54

W
Walls of beliefs 93
Walls of limitation 92
Watson, T.J. 116
Wealth
   advantages and pitfalls 18-19
   areas of endeavor 14-17
   what is your potential 20-21
   which kind do you want 22-23
Weekly time-scale 96-97
Well-being
   advantages and pitfalls 58-59
   are you well 60-61
   areas of endeavor 54-57
   the twelve kinds 62
   which kind do you want 62-63
Williams, Betty 36
Wright
   Frank Lloyd 77
   Wilbur and Orville 77
Written applications 142-143

Y
Young, Brigham 44